Russians today are the world's heaviest drinkers. The consumption of alcohol permeates family life, shapes the economy, and plays an occasional but striking role in presidential politics. And it was in Russia in the 1980s that the most sustained attempt of its kind was made to eliminate alcohol abuse, even drinking itself. Drawing upon a wide range of original sources, including interviews, surveys and the local press, Stephen White provides the first full-length study of this extraordinary campaign. He traces the profound influence of alcohol through Russian history, and charts the campaign from its initiation under Mikhail Gorbachev to its disappointing aftermath in the post-communist 1990s. Attractively written and fully illustrated, *Russia goes dry* is an entertaining as well as instructive guide to a changing society and a classic case study of the limitations of politically directed social reform.

Russia goes dry

Russia goes dry

Alcohol, state and society

STEPHEN WHITE

Department of Politics
University of Glasgow

Published by the Press Syndicate of the University of Cambridge
The Pitt Building, Trumpington Street, Cambridge CB2 1RP
40 West 20th Street, New York, NY 10011–4211, USA
10 Stamford Road, Oakleigh, Melbourne 3166, Australia

First published 1996

Printed in Great Britain at the University Press, Cambridge

A catalogue record for this book is available from the British Library

Library of Congress cataloguing in publication data
White, Stephen, 1945–
Russia goes dry: Alcohol, state and society/
Stephen White.
          p.   cm.
Includes bibliographical references (p.   )
ISBN 0 521 55211 7. – ISBN 0 521 55849 2 (pbk.)
1. Alcoholism – Russia (Federation) – History. 2. Alcoholism –
Soviet Union – History. 3. Temperance – Russia (Federation) –
History. 4. Temperance – Soviet Union – History. I. Title.
HV5515.15.W48 1996
362.29'2'0947 – dc20   95–13221 CIP

ISBN 0 521 55211 7 hardback
ISBN 0 521 55849 2 paperback

Contents

Illustrations

Preface

No way, Alec Nove used to remark, has yet been found to stop a German from working. No way, he might have added, has yet been found to stop a Russian from drinking. Russians, the records suggested, had embraced Christianity rather than Islam as it allowed them to drink. Russians, it was said, had continued to drink as a response to the powerlessness that had been imposed upon them by communist rule. But it was under postcommunist rule, in 1993, that Russians overtook France and became (taking all forms of consumption together) the world's hardest-drinking nation. There was certainly no shortage of evidence, in the early 1990s, that alcohol was as prominent a feature of the Russian scene as it had ever been. An inebriated Muscovite was found on one of the domes of St Basil's cathedral in the Red Square (he got five years for 'hooliganism'). There was a Zhirinovsky vodka, a Gorbachev vodka (reputed to make those who tried it 'talk uncontrollably about *perestroika*'), even a 'Terminator vodka'. A man was reported to have bitten an Alsatian dog that sprang at him, attracted by the smell of alcohol. Meanwhile, in politics, a Beerlovers' Party had been founded, the former Communist Party first secretary in Minsk was arrested as he tried to arrange the sale of 500,000 bottles of vodka on the black market, and the Russian president, Boris Yeltsin, missed an appointment with the Irish prime minister at Shannon airport in circumstances that were widely attributed to in-flight refreshment (the former vice-president, Alexander Rutskoi, later accused him of being in a 'permanent state of visiting Ireland').

There had, in fact, been several attempts to reduce the level of alcohol consumption in Russia and the Soviet Union, through temperance societies in the late nineteenth century and then through a formally constituted sobriety society in the late 1920s. There was a ban on alcohol sales after the start of the First World War, which was effectively extended by the Bolsheviks once they had come to power. And then, in 1985, the Gorbachev leadership launched the campaign to reduce or even eliminate alcohol abuse which is the subject of this study. The campaign was one of the most determined that has ever been seen, comparable with Prohibition in the USA and Finland in the 1920s; it was promoted by a government that had an unusually wide range of powers, with little to fear from the press, or the courts, or the ballot box; and it was promoted with more consistency than had been usual for Soviet campaigns. In what follows I have sought to examine the campaign from its origins, considering the social issues that it sought to address, the manner in which it was devised, the success it appeared initially to enjoy, and the disappointment and recrimination that accompanied its demise in the late 1980s. A final chapter considers the legacy of the campaign, and goes on to relate it to a wider literature on Soviet campaigns and to 'implementation studies' and the policy process more generally.

This study has been some years in the making, and many people and institutions have helped to make it possible. I am indebted in the first instance to the Alcohol Education and Research Council, based in London, for their willingness to support this inquiry and to make it possible to employ Walter Joyce, himself an authority on the subject, for two fruitful years. The Council's support also made it possible to visit Moscow and other parts of the Soviet Union, for interviews and library work. In Moscow we were received by Dr A. A. Glazov, Chief Specialist on Alcohol and Drug Dependence at the USSR Ministry of Health, and by Dr Vadim Pelipas and his colleagues at the All-Union Narcological Centre. Later it was possible to interview I. G. Astaf'ev of the sobriety society, based then as now at 18 Chekhov Street. Some use was made of the newly opened party archives, held for this period at the Centre for the Preservation of Contemporary Documentation in Moscow, and of unpublished survey material; I was also able to use the interviews conducted by Angus Roxburgh and others for the BBC series of programmes on the 'Second Russian Revolution', and for the Soviet Elites Project at the University of Glasgow. For the most part, however, the study is based upon a wide range of printed sources: the temperance press particularly, but also the medical and more general press, and a mass of pamphlet literature of all kinds and from all parts of the former Soviet Union.

Apart from those already mentioned, I am indebted to many more scholars and institutions for their advice, information and support. Martin Dewhirst fed me press cuttings, and Gerry Smith helped me document the Brezhnev period. Christopher Williams showed me his own work in typescript. Michael Ryan passed me a series of his articles on health matters; Bill Maley alerted me to some sources on alcoholism in the armed forces; and David Wedgwood Benn kindly lent me his own notes on the alcohol problem as it was reported in the 1970s and early 1980s. I owe a great deal to the advice I received from colleagues at the University of Strathclyde, particularly David Marsh, Gerry Stoker, Brian Hogwood and Tom Mackie, for orienting me in the literature on policy studies, as did Christopher Hood at the LSE. Several seminar or conference audiences gave me a useful lead, particularly Archie Brown and Judith Pallot at St Antony's College, Oxford; and I have been greatly helped by earlier writings on Russian and Soviet alcoholism including those by David Christian, David Powell, Boris Segal and Vladimir Treml in the West and Boris Levin and Grigorii Zaigraev in Russia itself. I am grateful for more specific references to Ian Thatcher, Richard Sakwa, Zhores Medvedev, Martin Eve, Terry Cox, Brian Pearce, Sarah Meiklejohn Terry, John Greenaway, Jane McDermid and Annie Feltham; among libraries, I should particularly like to thank the Wellcome Institute for the History of Medicine in London and Tania Konn and colleagues of the Russian studies collection at the University of Glasgow.

I would like to dedicate this study to the memory of Alec Nove, teacher, colleague, friend and neighbour, who died shortly before it had been completed. He followed the progress of the campaign with no great sympathy and it is a great and very personal sadness that he will not be able to read for himself this account of its defeat by a combination of native cunning and bureaucratic ineptitude.

1.1 M. Dmitriev, 'A quarrel at the dosshouse, 1900' (Society for Cooperation in Russian and Soviet Studies)

1

Russia, alcohol and politics

'Drinking is the joy of the Russes', Grand Prince Vladimir is supposed to have remarked in the tenth century; 'we cannot do without it'.[1] Centuries later it is difficult to dispute the accuracy of his observation. For the Grand Prince himself the fact that Christianity rather than Islam allowed the consumption of alcohol was sufficient reason for the whole country to embrace that faith in AD 988. For ordinary citizens, ever since, drinking has been a central part of virtually all aspects of their daily life. The first references to spirits as an alcoholic drink appeared in the written chronicles as early as the twelfth century.[2] By the nineteenth century, vodka was the 'single most important item in the peasantry's festive diet'; it was a 'basic ingredient of all celebrations' and a 'sort of seal on ceremonials'. 'Without it', explained a contemporary, 'friendship is no longer friendship, happiness is no longer happiness'; as for the local people, it 'warms them in the cold, cools them in the summer heat, protects them from the damp, consoles them in grief, and cheers them when times are good'.[3] Writers took up a position, from Pushkin's 'Bacchic Song' of 1825 to the sternly abstentionist Tolstoy, to Mayakovsky in the 1920s who believed it was 'better to die of vodka than of boredom', and on to Venedikt Erofeev in the 1960s and his 'zonked-out traveler from Moscow to Petushki – or rather from nowhere to nowhere'.[4] Drinking entered the folklore: 'nothing beats water – provided it's distilled from grain', the lexicographer Vladimir Dahl was told in the 1850s. In another nineteenth-century tale St Peter tried to turn away a village drunkard, but was told 'I drank and praised God with every swallow, but you denied God three times, and you are in heaven!'[5] Other peoples drank, of course, but Russians seemed to drink more than anyone else. Despairingly, it was thought, drinking had become – by the early twentieth century – part of the 'national character of the Russian people'.[6]

The Russian state, over the centuries, has taken an equally close interest in a commodity which – as in other societies – has played an important part in the generation of wealth, employment and budgetary income.[7] One aspect of this concern was public health. The army needed sober recruits, especially at times of national emergency; a far-reaching reform of the drink trade followed Russia's humiliating defeat in the Crimea, and a 'dry law' was introduced during the First World War. Industry needed punctual, conscientious operatives, and the state needed revenue to cover its own expenses, particularly on military purposes. The process of production and consumption required a network of inspectors to monitor the quality of the output and the honesty with which each successive transaction was reported to the authorities. Attempts to evade the law, particularly during brief periods of prohibition, nourished a growing subculture of corruption and organised crime and a corresponding mechanism of law enforcement. During the nineteenth century alcohol duties were the most important single source of government revenue, accounting for up to 40 per cent of income from all sources; alcohol consumption accounted for about 20 per cent of internal trade, and the industry was responsible for 7 or 8 per cent of national income.[8] Neither the tsarist government, nor the Soviet government that followed it, could be indifferent to such a central means of sustaining and satisfying the refreshment and recreational needs of the society over which they ruled.

For the communist authorities, after 1917, drinking presented a more particular challenge. Brewers were often the most generous supporters of conservative and nationalist political parties, at least in other countries. Alcohol, in turn, was seen as one of the ways in which working people were impoverished, degraded and deprived of a clear vision of their class interests. Soviet sources regularly quoted Friedrich Engels on the *Condition of the Working Class in England*, first published in 1845:

The working man comes home tired and exhausted. His dwelling is comfortless, damp, repulsive and dirty. He must have some recreation, he *must* have something to make the work worth his trouble, to make the prospect of the next day endurable . . . His enfeebled frame, weakened by bad air and bad food, demands some external stimulus . . . Apart from the physical influences that drive the working man into drunkenness, there is the example of his colleagues, the neglected education, the impossibility of protecting the young from temptation, in many cases the direct influence of intemperate parents, who give their own children liquor, the chance to forget the wretchedness of life for an hour or two in an alcoholic stupor . . . Drunkenness, in these circumstances, has ceased to be a vice for which the vicious can be held responsible; it has become the inevitable effect of particular conditions upon an object possessed of no volition, at least, in conditions of this kind. Those who have degraded the working man to a mere object must be the ones who bear the responsibility.[9]

A socialist society, by contrast, would have no reason to debase the working class for whose emancipation it had come into existence; rather, the problem of alcoholism would recede into the past, together with religion, nationalism and other 'survivals' of the class-divided past. Successive Soviet governments committed themselves to the 'struggle for sobriety' on this basis, and at particular periods, such as the late 1980s, it became the object of a comprehensive and centrally directed campaign.

Drinking before the revolution

Foreign visitors were certainly in no doubt that Russians were formidable topers. The Venetian ambassador Contarini, in Moscow in the 1470s, observed that Russians were 'great drunkards and take a great pride in this, despising abstainers . . . Their life takes the following form: they spend all morning in the bazaars until about midday, when they set off to the taverns to eat and drink; it is impossible to get them to do anything afterwards'.[10] The poet George Turberville, a visitor in the 1560s, concluded that 'Drink is their whole desire, the pot is all their pride; the sobrest head doth once a day stand needfull of a guide.'[11] Giles Fletcher, a visitor of the late sixteenth century whose account of pre-Petrine Russia is the fullest and most authoritative of its kind, noted that

in every great town of his realm [the Tsar] hath a *kabak* or drinking house where is sold *aqua-vitae* (which they call Russe wine), mead, beer etc. . . . Wherein, besides the base and dishonourable means to increase his treasury, many foul faults are committed. The poor labouring man and artificer many times spendeth all from his wife and children. Some use to lay in twenty, thirty, forty rubles or more into the cabak and vow themselves to the pot till all that be spent. And this (as he will say) for the honour of *gospodar'*, or the Emperor. You shall have many there that have drunk all away to the very skin and so walked naked . . . To drink drunk is an ordinary matter with them every day in the week.[12]

Adam Olearius, a member of the Holstein embassy to Moscow in the seventeenth century, found that prominent Russian noblemen and even royal ambassadors charged with defending the honour of their rulers in foreign lands knew no limits when it came to alcohol. 'If something they rather like is put before them, they pour it out like water, until they begin to behave like people robbed of reason, and finally must be picked up as though they were dead'.[13] The Grand Ambassador sent to the King of Sweden in 1608, indeed, drank so much of a particularly fiery vodka that the very day he was to have been given an audience he was found dead in his bed.[14] Olearius concluded that Russians were 'more addicted to drunkenness than any nation in the world'. As he explained:

> The vice of drunkenness is prevalent among this people in all classes, both secular and ecclesiastical, high and low, men and women, young and old. To see them lying here and there in the streets, wallowing in filth, is so common that no notice is taken of it. If a coachman comes across any such drunken swine whom he knows, he throws them aboard his wagon and takes them home, where he is paid for the trip. None of them anywhere, anytime, or under any circumstances lets pass an opportunity to have a draught or a drinking bout.[15]

The avidity of Russians for their 'fiery poison' was 'astounding', wrote another German visitor, J. G. Kohl. The phrase 'A glass of vodka!' should, he thought, 'occur at least ten times on every page of a Russian dictionary that pretends to convey a proper idea of the frequent use of a word and its importance.'[16]

The *kabaks*, Olearius found, accepted money as well as every conceivable item as payment for drink. As he explained,

> While we were there, taverns and pothouses were everywhere, and anyone who cared to could go in and sit and drink his fill. The common people would bring all their earnings into the tavern and sit there until, having emptied their purses, they gave away their clothing, and even their nightshirts, to the keeper, and then went home as naked as they had come into the world. When, in 1643, I stopped at the Luebeck house in Novgorod, I saw such besotted and naked brethren come out of the nearby tavern, some bareheaded, some barefooted, and others only in their nightshirts. One of them had drunk away his cloak and emerged from the tavern in his nightshirt; when he met a friend who was on his way to the same tavern, he went in again. Several hours later he came out without his nightshirt, wearing only a pair of underpants. I had him called to ask what had become of his nightshirt, who had stolen it? He answered, with the customary 'F . . . your mother', that it was the tavernkeeper, and that the pants might as well go where the cloak and nightshirt had gone. With that, he returned to the tavern, and later came out entirely naked. Taking a handful of dog fennel that grew near the tavern, he held it over his private parts, and went home singing gaily.[17]

An earlier traveller, Anthony Jenkinson, heard of men and women that had drunk away their goods and even their children at debauches of this kind.[18]

Drinking was not confined to men, or the laity, or even to Russians. Women, as Olearius observed, 'did not consider it disgraceful to themselves to get intoxicated and collapse along with the men'. In Narva he witnessed an

amusing spectacle. Several women came with their husbands to a carouse, sat with them, and drank amply. When the men had got drunk, they wanted to go home. The women demurred, and though their ears were boxed, nevertheless, they declined to get up. When at last the men fell to the ground and went to sleep, the women sat astride them and continued toasting one another with vodka until they, too, became dead drunk.[19]

It was not unusual, apparently, for men and women who were drinking together to engage in sexual intercourse in full view of laughing onlookers without any sense of shame.[20] Not only women of the 'meaner sort', John Perry reported in 1716, but 'even women of Distinction and Fashion' would 'make no Scruple to own, that they have been very drunk'.[21] In the taverns men and women would 'lie about on the dirty floor with no thought for their dress or the exposure of parts of their body'; at village weddings, even girls of nine or ten would be 'made to drink so that they would dance for everyone's entertainment'.[22] According to the evidence that was collected between 1903 and 1908 in Moscow, men were six times as likely as women to be admitted for treatment; alcoholism, however, was especially marked among divorced and single women workers, and among prostitutes and the down and out, and Russian levels of alcoholism among women were unusually high in comparative terms.[23]

Even priests and monks were known for their alcoholic inclinations. The English traveller Richard Chancellor, in the mid-sixteenth century, found the holy fathers were 'notable toss-pots'.[24] The common people, Jacques Margeret reported in the early seventeenth century, were 'given to drunkenness more than to anything else', and priests 'as much or more than the others'.[25] Monastic life was often very strict, but the monks made up for it outside the monastery walls; the rites for the dead were particularly liable to abuse. Olearius remarked that 'One is as apt to meet a drunken priest or monk as a layman or peasant.' Within the monasteries themselves they drank no wine, vodka or mead; but when they were the guests of outsiders 'they not only feel that they cannot refuse a good draught, but even demand it; and they drink greedily, taking such delight in it that they may be distinguished from lay drunkards by nothing but their clothing'.[26] Passing through Novgorod, Olearius

saw a priest in a robe or underwear (he had undoubtedly pawned his cloak in a tavern) staggering along the streets. When he came opposite my inn, he wanted to bestow the customary blessing upon the *strel'tsy* [musketeers] who were standing guard. When he extended his hand while endeavouring to bend over somewhat, his head proved too heavy, and he pitched over into the mud. After the *strel'tsy* picked him up, he blessed them anyway with his besmeared fingers. Since such spectacles may be seen daily, none of the Russians are astonished by them.[27]

Excesses of this kind were particularly common after the major feastdays, John Perry reported some years later; it was 'very ordinary to see the Priests, as well as other Men, lie drunk about the Streets, and if any one comes to speak to them and help them up when they are down, they say . . . What you will, Father, it is [a] Holiday, and I am drunk.'[28]

Alcoholism extended less widely among traditionally Islamic groups, but by the early twentieth century it had reached most of the Empire's minority nationalities. A linguist and ethnographer, Kastren, travelling in northeastern Russia in 1838–44, described how he tried to find someone who could teach him the language of the nomadic Nenets. This was very difficult since almost all of the Nentsy were chronically drunk:

I chose the soberest of all, but even he turned out to be drunk. I tried to invite a woman, but she soon succumbed. Having called all the Nentsy out of the tavern, I explained the nature of my mission and asked them to find the soberest man who could act as my teacher. They brought him to me, but he was so incoherent that I lost patience and threw him out the door. Soon I saw him lying on the snow beside the tavern, dead drunk.

Another time Kastren witnessed a similar scene at a wedding:

When we arrived everyone had already regaled themselves well. Many lay unconscious in the street, with uncovered heads, buried in snowdrifts and the wind was covering them with snow . . . In another place, I saw them put a senseless drunk on a sledge, tie him to it, harness his reindeer to the sledge and drive off. In the *chum* [dwelling] the bridegroom himself was lying among the completely drunken guests. Even the bride, a child of 13, was already drunk.

Kastren spent some time in Siberia, where he found similar customs. In the village of Molchanovo, for instance, he was quartered on the top floor of a *kabak*: 'Here, for the whole riotous week, I had no rest, neither night nor day, from noisy drunks.'[29]

Did Russians and the other inhabitants of the Empire really drink more than anyone else, or did it just seem that they did? Expenditure on alcohol per head of population, in fact, was not particularly high in prerevolutionary Russia. In the early twentieth century, according to official sources, spending on alcohol per head of population was 6.8 rubles a year, 'significantly lower than in the Western countries'. The same was true of expenditure on alcohol compared with public spending on defence, education and health; in these terms, again, Russian expenditure was not particularly high.[30] The same was also true when expenditure was expressed in terms of average income. The average family in early twentieth-century Russia spent about 3 per cent of its income on alcohol; the proportion of family income that was expended in this way at the same time was 10.5 per cent in Britain, 12.8 per cent in Germany and 13.5 per cent in France.[31] Comparisons of total alcohol consumption per head of population reached similar conclusions. Dmitriev, for instance, compared average consumption levels between 1885 and 1905 and found Russia below all of the other countries except Norway in total consumption, and below Denmark, Austria-Hungary,

1.2   A. P. Ryabushkin, 'The tavern'
(painting, 1891)

France, Belgium, Germany and Sweden for consumption of spirits alone.[32] By the early twentieth century levels of consumption, though higher, were still very modest as compared with the position elsewhere in Europe or North America (see Table 1.1).

It would be equally wrong, however, to suggest that Russia was a home of cultured and moderate drinking during the prerevolutionary years. For a start, levels of consumption of distilled spirits, such as vodka, were much higher than the European average. Russia ranked twelfth for all forms of alcohol consumption in the early twentieth century, but fifth when the comparison was limited to hard liquor, and nearly 90 per cent of all drink was consumed in the form of vodka.[33] Russians, secondly, had a predisposition towards periodic bouts of heavy drinking, rather than a steady level of more moderate consumption. In Italy and France, as Alexander Herzen remarked, there was plenty of wine but no drunks; in the whole of Europe there was 'simply no other people that emptied a tumbler at a gulp'.[34] Drinking, for 'climatic reasons', was mostly indoors, not outside in the fresh air.[35] And finally, official calculations were based upon the whole population of the Russian Empire at the time. This included Jews, who tended to drink moderately, and the much larger population of Old Believers and other schismatics, who also drank very sparingly. The same was true of the substantial Muslim population.[36] Per capita consumption of alcohol on the part of the Orthodox Great Russian population was accordingly much greater than official statistics suggested.

Levels of alcohol-related morbidity and mortality were in fact rather higher than in comparable Western countries at this time. In 1911 there were 55 alcohol-related deaths for every million population; in France, where alcohol consumption was much greater, the figure was 11.5, and in Prussia it was 12. In St Petersburg, similarly, there were up to 20 alcohol-related deaths for every 100,000 members of the population, compared with 3 in Berlin and 6 in Paris (patterns of mortality were in other respects very similar).[37] Premature deaths were related particularly closely to alcohol: 1 in 4 were associated with excessive consumption, but in Prussia (for instance) only 1 in 20.[38] Virtually all forms of alcohol abuse, indeed, were worse in Russia. In pre-war Vienna, for instance, 1 drunk was detained for every 1,220 population, but in St Petersburg there was 1 for every 25.[39] And there were 15 times as many arrests for public drunkenness in St Petersburg as in Berlin and 700 times as many as in Paris, although alcohol consumption was much greater in the French capital.[40] About half the inmates of Russian prisons, in the early

Table 1.1. *Alcohol consumption in selected countries, 1891–1895 (column 1) and 1901–1910 (column 2); litres per head per annum)*

	France		USA		UK		Russia	
	(1)	(2)	(1)	(2)	(1)	(2)	(1)	(2)
Spirits	8.5	8.8	5.3	5.5	5.2	4.2	4.3	6.1
Wine	91.0	44.0	1.4	2.4	1.7	1.2	3.3	0.9
Beer	25.0	37.2	58.9	76.3	135.0	123.1	4.6	6.5
Total absolute alcohol	17.4	22.9	5.8	6.9	10.9	9.7	2.3	3.4

Source: Derived from *Bol'shaya meditsinskaya entsiklopediya*, 2nd edn, vol. 1 (Moscow: Gosudarstvennoe izdatel'stvo meditsinskoi literatury, 1956), cols. 729–30; the figures quoted refer to European Russia.

twentieth century, had been incarcerated for crimes committed in a state of drunkenness.[41] There were relatively few suicides, compared with other European countries, but more of them were connected with alcohol, and a higher proportion of divorces took place on these grounds.[42] There was a particularly close association between alcohol and the pogroms that swept through many Russian and Ukrainian cities in the late nineteenth and early twentieth centuries, in some cases with the connivance of the imperial authorities.[43]

Drink and the state in prerevolutionary Russia

Public activity on this scale could scarcely remain a matter of indifference to the authorities, and from about the sixteenth century its production and consumption began to come under government control. Two main processes were involved: first of all, control and sometimes a monopoly over production, and then taxation of the various stages of consumption, particularly of the stronger liquors. Vodka, it appears, first entered Russian life at some point in the early sixteenth century.[44] It began to constitute a source of budgetary revenue from the mid-eighteenth century; its value and share of government revenue rose steadily thereafter, reaching about a third of all government income by the early twentieth century and as much as 46 per cent in certain years.[45] This was a sum large enough to cover most of the expenses of the peacetime army, and there were periods when the revenue from alcohol consumption substantially exceeded defence expenditures. Vodka also accounted for a large share of the country's internal trade. In the 1850s the total turnover was at least 200 million rubles, which represented over 20 per cent of the value of all internal trade and a substantial proportion of national income as a whole. Meanwhile, the entrepreneurial revenues generated through the vodka trade were large enough to account for a significant share of the capital invested in economic development in the late nineteenth century.[46]

The governing authorities had initially shown little interest in the new trade. But in the late 1540s Ivan IV, impressed by the Tatar kabaks he had seen during the siege of Kazan, began to establish special government taverns-cum-distilleries of his own. Kabaks soon appeared in most major towns, and their profits went straight into the royal treasury. In order to protect the revenues earned by the kabaks, the government adopted the simple but effective device of forbidding potential rivals to distil or trade in vodka. The privately owned *korchmy* or ale-houses were soon outlawed; a few great secular and ecclesiastical lords were allowed to establish their own kabaks, but by the end of the sixteenth century the vast majority were owned by the state and most legal revenues from the vodka trade entered the royal treasury.[47] The claim to a government monopoly was asserted clearly in the law code, or *Ulozhenie*, of 1649; this made it illegal to buy or sell vodka except through kabaks, prescribed savage punishments for offenders including beating and indefinite imprisonment, and made it clear that all revenues from the sale of alcoholic drinks were considered a royal prerogative.[48] By the early seventeenth century kabaks could be found in most towns and even, occasionally, in villages; they were run to begin with by appointed officials, but the government also rented them out in return for fixed payments. Those who rented the taverns were allowed to make profits, and were given certain immunities; generally only individual taverns were rented out in this way, for a period of up to five years. In the seventeenth century many different taxes were farmed out, including customs dues, salt taxes and liquor taxes; but by the nineteenth century tax farming was confined to the vodka trade.[49]

Tax farming still coexisted with the state administration of kabaks, and the government 'wavered between the two systems for the next two and a half centuries'.[50] Tax farming was finally abolished in 1861, a reform that was one of the great series of changes – including the

1.3 Ivan Bilibin, advertisement for 'New Bavaria' beer (1903)

abolition of serfdom – that were introduced by Alexander II. Drinkers had already been plundering taverns, outraged by the poor quality of the diluted vodka that was being sold in them (more than 260 distilleries were sacked in 15 different *gubernii*, and several hundred were exiled to Siberia for their participation);[51] there had been an increase in levels of public drunkenness, and an increasing number of deaths from alcoholic poisoning.[52] Tax farming was replaced by an excise-based system that lasted for about thirty years, at which point – between 1894 and 1902 – it was again replaced by a state monopoly (the aim, Witte explained to Alexander III, was to 'free the local Christian population from Jewish dependence'). The monopoly was gradually extended over nearly all the Russian Empire, and in 1914 it had reached all but a few outlying areas.[53] The reversion to a government monopoly was in part a response to a rising incidence of adulteration and fraud; the liquor sold in kabaks, visitors reported, was 'horribly adulterated', with 'up to 50 per cent water but, to make it intoxicating, narcotic herbs, tobacco, belladonna, etc., are added'.[54] The reintroduction of a state monopoly helped to eliminate these abuses, and some of the richer tax farmers went out of business; consumption continued to increase, and state tax revenues nearly trebled.[55]

Bolshevik and later Soviet commentators insisted that the tsarist authorities had a direct interest in the drink trade such that they could never take effective steps to end its worst abuses. Trotsky, for instance, argued that the government and propertied classes were directly responsible for a culture that could 'not exist without the constant lubricant of alcohol'.[56] Many within the temperance movement argued similarly that the elimination of alcoholism would be achieved only when other social reforms had been accomplished, including a shorter working day and better housing.[57] For her part, Catherine II is supposed to have remarked that a drunken people was easier to rule; and the noted Russian conservative, K. N. Leont'ev, went so far as to argue that 'schools [were] more harmful than taverns'.[58] One constant of the late tsarist period was certainly an increasingly close control over the alcohol industry, which provided a growing share of state income; nonetheless, there was also an attempt to minimise the consequences that almost inevitably followed. Temperance societies had originally been suppressed, but in the late nineteenth and early twentieth centuries they were set up in increasing numbers by government itself.[59] The result was a deeply ambiguous one. The societies, for a start, promoted moderation rather than abstinence; and they reported to the Ministry of Finance, which refused some applications for a local dry law and offered no support to a number of the more energetic associations. Public pressure led, at the same time, to a number of further restrictions upon the alcohol trade during the late tsarist period; concerns of this kind could be expressed through the State Duma, the limited parliamentary body that was established in 1905, and through the medical profession, which established its own commission on alcoholism in 1898 and convened two all-Russian congresses on the subject in 1909–10 and 1912, and also through a developing temperance press.[60]

At least one other feature of the prerevolutionary drinking culture survived into the Soviet period: its close connection with corruption and organised crime. The bribing of local officials was a common practice; indeed in Moscow, an illicit alcohol trade flourished right beside the imperial palace.[61] Tax farmers often defaulted on their loans, and many of them watered down their vodka and tried to drive beer distillers out of business. The inspectors who were sent to impose official policies sometimes commandeered the alcohol for themselves and sold it clandestinely. Bribes were often necessary to obtain permission to open a tavern; prices were inflated; the drink itself was adulterated; and the police were paid off in order to avoid prosecution.[62] The government had in practice to collude in this network of criminality, given the extent to which (until the 1860s) it depended upon the income that tax farmers were able to generate. Apart from the abuses that were connected with the official sale of alcohol there was a substantial illicit trade, estimated at about 30 per cent of the value of the trade that was officially recorded.[63] As well as private distilling, smuggling was a factor of some importance, particularly along the borders with Austria and Prussia. In the Russian part of Poland it was estimated that only a fifth of the vodka consumed had made its proper contribution to public revenues; nor could the authorities readily intervene, as guards with binoculars kept watch from observation towers on the distilleries and the inspectors had in any case been bribed.[64]

The Bolsheviks and alcohol

Having attained power in 1917, the Bolsheviks wanted to put an end to the social ills of the capitalist system as well as the forms of ownership with which (in their view) such problems were necessarily associated. As in other European countries, the Russian socialist movement had a strong temperance tradition: particularly so as the drink trade was in the hands of government itself. In 1905 the very first Soviet, at Ivanovo-Voznesensk, had decided to close the wine shops in the town, and there were workers' temperance societies in many parts of the country.[65] In line with this, the new Soviet government extended the dry law on its accession and brought the liquor industry and existing stocks of alcoholic beverages into state ownership.[66] The Party Programme of 1919, adopted shortly afterwards, committed the new regime to an urgent struggle with 'social diseases' like tuberculosis, syphilis and alcoholism.[67] Unlike capitalist countries, Lenin explained in 1921, in which spirits and 'narcotics of the same kind' were allowed to circulate freely, a socialist government would not contemplate a trade that would lead Russia 'back to capitalism and not forward to communism'.[68] Lenin himself, according to the testimony of the time, was a firmly committed abstentionist. Klara Zetkin, who met the Soviet leader in late 1920 to discuss a number of other issues, recalled Lenin's own words. The proletariat, Lenin explained, had 'no need of intoxication'; it derived its 'strongest stimulant to struggle from its class position and from the communist ideal'; and what it needed was 'clarity, clarity, and once again – clarity'.[69] Speaking to the 11th Party Congress two years later, Lenin was just as emphatic that there could be no 'trade in rotgut'.[70]

For the American journalist John Reed, the revolution itself had been a sober and peaceful affair: 'not a single hold-up occurred, not a single robbery'. Just three days after the Bolshevik government had been installed he was able to report that there had been 'not even a drunken fight'.[71] There were 700 storehouses in the Russian capital at this time with a stock valued at millions of rubles, and there were further stocks in the cellars of the Winter Palace to the value (Reed reported) of $5 million; the accumulations were particularly large because of the ban that had been imposed on alcohol trading during the war. Lists of these storehouses were circulated and workers – encouraged, apparently, by *agents provocateurs* – were urged to 'liberate' them. Initially it had been proposed to keep the wine and spirits and sell them abroad, but there was a 'storm of protest' and a real danger that they would be seized and distributed in the streets. An armed guard around the Winter Palace had already been breached, and dozens had literally been drowned in the flood of liquor. The Military Revolutionary Committee had already ordered local soviets to place alcohol stores under close guard; in these circumstances it was felt safest to destroy the entire stock. The task was entrusted to selected groups of Red Guards, who attacked the bottles and barrels with iron bars and hammers; spirits and wines were pumped into the gutters of the capital with the aid of fire hoses. The comrade responsible for the destruction, Trotsky told an American journalist, 'used to be a drinker himself before he became a Communist, and it hurt him to see that good wine destroyed. But it was necessary to preserve order in Petrograd'.[72]

On 28 November 1917 it was decided to go still further and to close all wine and spirits factories, and to forbid the production and sale of alcoholic beverages. Any offenders, and any who were apprehended in a state of intoxication, were to be brought before military-revolutionary tribunals. In December of the same year the post of 'commissar for the struggle against alcoholism and gambling' was established, with representation in local areas as well as the major cities.[73] The death penalty was introduced into the Red Army at the same time, for abuses that included alcoholism ('When the Communist gets drunk, the Menshevik can celebrate', explained the chairman of the Military Revolutionary Council, S. I. Gusev).[74] In May 1918 the new Russian parliament approved a decree making the illicit manufacture of alcohol a criminal offence liable to a penalty of not less than ten years' imprisonment together with confiscation of property and compulsory labour.[75] In December 1919 the Soviet government passed the still more far-reaching decree 'On the prohibition on the territory of the RSFSR of the making and selling of spirits, strong drinks and other alcoholic substances'. The penalty for infringing this decree was imprisonment for a period of not less than five years, together with confiscation of property; the same penalty applied to the 'distillation, filtration, [or] enriching . . . of denatured spirits, lacquer, varnish, and other . . . mixtures not meant for human consumption with the purpose of extracting alcohol or weakening their taste or colour for selling, and the carrying or conveying of such mixtures'.[76]

Visitors were certainly impressed by the results. The German doctor Alfons Goldschmidt, in Russia in the summer of 1920, recorded in his diary that he had found many 'intoxicated . . . with the Soviet idea', but 'not a single drunk'.[77] The British socialist Sylvia Pankhurst, a visitor at the same time, was convinced Russian workers had 'mostly forgotten the very existence of alcohol'.[78] 'We shall never go back to vodka', the commissar for health, Nikolai Semashko, assured American journalist Anna Louise Strong. Wine would be forbidden as soon as possible; and after that there would be 'total prohibition on the American plan'.[79]

Russia, another American visitor concluded, was already the 'soberest nation in Europe'.[80] 'Occasionally a man is seen on the street who has had more than is good for him', a more representative workers' delegation reported a few years later, 'but to those who knew Russia before the Revolution there is certainly very much less drunkenness in the streets and public places than formerly'.[81] For Leon Trotsky, writing in 1923, the ban on the sale of vodka was one of the 'two big facts' that had set a 'new stamp on working-class life after the revolution' (the other was the introduction of an eight-hour working day). The tsarist regime had certainly prohibited the sale of drink during the war; but it was 'only with the conquest of power by the working class, which became the conscious creator of a new economic order, that the public struggle against alcoholism, by education and prohibition, was able to receive its due historic significance'. The abolition of the system by which the state systematically intoxicated its people was, he declared, 'one of the iron achievements of the revolution'.[82]

The revolution was not, in fact, quite as sober as these accounts suggested. There were pitched battles between drinkers and anti-alcohol brigades: one such incident at a vodka factory in Petrograd in December 1917 left three Red Guards and eight soldiers dead. In Odessa a crowd of about 1,000 attacked a liquor store and had to be dispersed by machine-guns; in Samara a group of rioters had got drunk on printer's ink and stormed the local shops.[83] In Petrograd a restaurant held out for some time, guarded by 'twenty or so hefty chaps provided with rifles, machine guns and grenades', before it too succumbed.[84] As another account made clear, the operation at the Winter Palace had in fact been much more problematic than John Reed suggested. The Preobrazhensky regiment, assigned to guard duty, 'got completely drunk'. The Pavlovsky regiment 'did not withstand temptation either'. Guards from different detachments were sent but also became intoxicated. Other guards from the regimental committees were assigned; 'they too succumbed'. Men from the armoured brigades were ordered to disperse the crowds; 'they paraded a little to and fro, and then began to sway suspiciously on their feet'. An attempt was made to flood the cellars, but 'the fire brigade sent to do this themselves got drunk'. Finally the Finnish regiment, 'led by men with anarcho-syndicalist leanings, declared a state of siege . . . and announced that they would blow up the wine cellars and shoot plunderers on sight'. Only then did the 'alcoholic lunacy' subside.[85]

Levels of alcohol consumption fell during the civil war years, but for reasons that were connected with the Allied blockade and a lack of grain.[86] The return of more settled economic conditions led to a resumption of earlier levels of consumption, particularly in the form of illicit distilling; indeed, the low prices that were paid for agricultural produce meant that it was more profitable for peasants to convert their grain into illicit alcohol than to sell it on the market. At least a third of rural households were estimated to be distilling on this basis in the 1920s; there were villages not 150 miles from Moscow, complained *Pravda*, where 'everyone was occupied in this "craft"'; in the city itself it could be obtained by 'asking for "lemonade" and winking at the salesman meaningfully'.[87] And there was widespread use of surrogates, such as eau de cologne – 'a drink for intellectuals', as it was known in Rostov on Don.[88] From the end of 1922 the treatment of illicit distilling became more severe: the courts were ordered to increase the fines that they imposed on such activities, and there were special two-week and month-long campaigns against illicit distilling, timed to coincide with the Christmas and Easter holidays. After dark, wrote an observer, the police 'spent almost all their time rounding up drunks'; in 1922, in the Russian republic alone, there were half a million prosecutions.[89] Nonetheless, even these efforts had only a limited effect. The peasants needed the income that homebrewing provided, the police were unreliable, the courts began to collapse under the strain, and the government itself was somewhat inconsistent: the strength of alcoholic beverages that could legitimately be sold was steadily increased, and then in 1925 all remaining restrictions were removed. The production and sale of alcohol at the same time became a state monopoly, the production of homebrew with intent to sell was made a criminal offence, and by the late 1920s the sale of drink was once again making a substantial contribution to government revenues.[90]

By the later 1920s there was in fact a considerable body of evidence to suggest that older traditions had fully reasserted themselves. A 'wave of alcoholism engulfed the whole country', wrote the neuropathologist V. M. Bekhterev. Everybody drank: 'the well and the sick, men and women, adults and children'; they drank at 'celebrations, at weddings, at parties, on name-days, for appetite, for warmth [and] to refresh themselves'.[91] The statistics certainly bore him out. Levels of consumption, including homebrew, had already overtaken the pre-war figures.[92] Alcohol-related deaths increased sharply: in Leningrad, there was a sixfold increase in just four years; in Moscow, a rise of nearly fifteen times between 1923 and 1928.[93] There were more arrests: in Leningrad, again, there had been 2,000 arrests for drunkenness in 1923 but by 1927 the

1.4   The tsarist liquor monopoly
(from 'A short history of the "benign" rule of Nicholas II', *Sovetskii kalendar'
na 1919 god* (Moscow: VTsIK, 1918))

figure was 113,000, almost one adult in every four.[94] The number of arrests for public drunkenness in all Russian cities, in the late 1920s, was running at 2 million a year.[95] The average urban family spent up to 14 per cent of its income on alcohol at this time;[96] the income that the state received from the sale of alcohol was hardly much less, at 12 per cent of all revenues.[97] Studies of the life of ordinary workers in Moscow and Berlin in 1929 found that they had relatively similar real incomes; but the Moscow workers spent five times as much as their German counterparts on alcohol.[98] The Communist Party was itself affected, with about a third of all the disciplinary cases involving its members in the late 1920s associated with alcohol, and another third associated indirectly; in some local areas, according to contemporary accounts, party conferences were 'just one big drinking party'.[99] The output of illicit alcohol, meanwhile, was barely affected, with up to half a million litres being consumed on average by the late 1920s; this, in turn, accounted for as much as 80 per cent of all the alcoholic beverages that were consumed in any form.[100]

A different approach to the alcohol problem began to take shape from the mid-1920s, prompted by an increasingly open acknowledgement that the repressive measures of earlier post-Soviet years had failed to achieve their purposes and indeed that they had simply deprived the state of much-needed revenue.[101] There were people, Stalin told the 14th Party Congress in December 1925, who thought socialism could be constructed with 'kid gloves'. This was a 'very crude mistake'; if there were no other sources of capital, where else could it be found?[102] Which was better, he asked in 1927, to accept the terms of foreign capital as a condition of their assistance or to resume the sale of vodka, which Lenin himself had been prepared to sanction in such circumstances?[103] As Stalin explained to a group of foreign workers at this time, the reintroduction of a state monopoly was in any case a temporary measure; as soon as new sources of revenue had been found the sale of vodka would be reduced to the level that was required for 'technical purposes', and then eliminated entirely.[104] He spoke in similar terms to the 15th Party Congress in December 1927, calling for the gradual reduction of vodka sales and the development, in its place, of 'such sources of income as radio and television'.[105] Nikolai Bukharin, speaking to the Komsomol the following year, pointed out that if the sale of vodka was eliminated, all they would do was create a '*samogon* ocean'; it was this 'curse' that was the source of their difficulties.[106]

The resumption of the vodka monopoly was at the same time accompanied by a liberalisation of the criminal law (the preparation of *samogon* 'for one's own use' was no longer a crime after 1926),[107] and there was a greater emphasis upon educational and other measures designed to reduce the incidence of alcohol abuse. As early as 1924 in a number of regions of the country informal groups had been formed 'for the struggle against narcotics', which were then transformed into 'commissions for healthy work and living'.[108] An Institute of Social Hygiene had been established in 1923, with responsibilities that included the study of alcoholism as well as other public concerns; it operated under the auspices of the Commissariat of Health and took the view that alcoholism was the product of social circumstances rather than of individual predisposition.[109] In September 1926 the Soviet government took matters further by providing for the compulsory treatment of alcoholics as well as a programme of school lectures and a wide range of anti-alcohol activities in reading rooms, clubs and the mass media.[110] In October 1926 the first sobering-up stations were opened in Leningrad, where deaths and alcohol psychoses had increased sharply with the relaxation in official policy.[111] Commissions on alcoholism were set up the following year in local soviets, charged with the 'coordination of the struggle against the consumption of alcohol' as well as the search for effective methods of treatment.[112] In 1929 a government decree went still further, allowing local soviets to close down liquor stores on public demand or for 'sociocultural' reasons, forbidding the opening of new stores in industrial areas, and banning the sale of drink on weekends or public holidays.[113]

A much more important step was taken in February 1928 when a 'Society for the Struggle against Alcoholism' was formed as a popular focus for the temperance movement.[114] Among its patrons were military leaders like Nikolai Podvoisky and Marshal Budenny as well as writers like Dem'yan Bedny, Vsevolod Ivanov and Vladimir Mayakovsky, together with a large detachment of doctors and health workers. In April 1928 the Society issued a public appeal, explaining (in Bukharin's words) that its purpose was 'to assist Soviet power in the rapid elimination of alcoholism: (i) by the development of the culture of daily life and of healthy recreation, allowing state incomes to be found from less harmful sources; (ii) by inculcating a consciousness of the personal and social harmfulness of alcoholism and weaning working people off alcoholism in their daily lives'.[115] By January 1929 more than 200 branches of the Society had been formed with a membership of a quarter of a million, and an All-Union Council of Anti-Alcohol Societies had been set up to coordinate their efforts. From August 1928 to January 1929 there were organised demonstrations against alcoholism in more than a hundred towns, in a further fifty there were 'workers' conferences on the struggle against alcoholism', and in many cases local authorities were persuaded to restrict the times and places at which alcoholic drink could be sold.[116] The Society began to publish a monthly journal, *Trezvost' i kul'tura* (Sobriety and Culture), from July 1928; its first issue announced that through

broad agitation and propaganda, personal example, the unmasking . . . of the wreckers of socialist construction who are active on the alcoholic front, [and through] the development of cultured entertainments . . . merciless struggle with homebrewers and tavernkeepers, the replacement of bars and other places for the sale of spirits by Soviet teahouses and other cultural institutions, the upbringing of the new generation and similar measures – we can defeat alcoholism'.[117]

The campaign began to widen in scope. At least 20,000 workers had already abandoned drink, the Society was told in 1929.[118] Already, it was claimed, they had the 'soberest army in the world'.[119] There were demonstrations led by children against the drunkenness of their parents: in Vologda, Perm' and other towns 'thousands' took to the streets with slogans such as 'We demand sober parents!', 'Down with drunk fathers!', 'Papa, don't beat mama', 'Papa, don't go to the *monopol'ka* [state alcohol retail outlet], take the money home to the family!', 'Down with vodka!', and even 'Shoot drunks!' In Irkutsk, 15,000 children took part in one such demonstration; there were gatherings at factory gates on payday, and even 'excesses' in which the windows of wine shops were broken.[120] In April 1929 the Council of Anti-Alcohol Societies sent a special anti-alcohol 'cinema expedition' to the Donbass with speakers, a mobile screen, films and mobile exhibitions; it visited mines, screened films to mass audiences, gave talks and lectures, and organised anti-alcohol cells anywhere it could.[121] The practice developed of calling anti-alcohol conferences of 'drinking girls' (the first were in the Vyborg district of Leningrad), or 'drinking youth'. Family members were encouraged to make use of the press to urge their relatives to give up the habit. A worker and a peasant in a Volga village went so far as to conclude a 'socialist contract of sobriety', by which if either of them succumbed he had to buy a banner for the local Young Pioneer detachment. Worker anti-alcohol brigades went from the towns into the countryside, and the first anti-alcohol theatre opened in the Ukraine; it toured the Donbass, and presented public lectures as well as plays that dwelt on the dangers of alcohol abuse.[122] And there were individual success stories like comrade Pankratov, who regularly drank all his pay, but who was then persuaded to join the Communist Party and receive treatment; for three years already he had not touched a drop. 'The Party saved me!', a grateful Pankratov told the sobriety journal.[123]

This innovative campaign, in the end, was a relatively brief one. At the beginning of the 1930s official policies changed again, and instructions were given to switch from 'narrow anti-alcohol work' to an 'all-out struggle for improvements in the conditions of everyday life'. It was socialism and the socialist way of life, it was explained, that would 'destroy drunkenness'.[124] The struggle against alcoholism had become, in practice, a 'struggle for the fulfilment of the programme of the 5 Year Plan in four years',[125] and it was also a struggle against the 'seedbeds of alcoholism' such as church festivals, weddings and funerals.[126] In April 1930, in these new and different circumstances, the Anti-Alcohol Society was abolished and its functions transferred to the Moscow organisation; the Society's journal *Sobriety and Culture* meanwhile became *Culture and Daily Life*, with the rather different objective of assisting the 'struggle to fulfil the plans of the third, decisive year of the Five Year Plan'.[127] Then in April 1932 all of the Societies for the Struggle against Alcoholism were merged with the 'Union of the Godless' and the 'Down with Illiteracy Society' and the new hybrid became known as the 'Healthy Life Society'. The medical interpretation of alcoholism as an illness changed at the same time: the broader approach of the social hygienists was replaced by a narrower focus on individual psychology, the institute was renamed and given a much more limited responsibility for the organisation of health care, and alcohol itself was recognised as a form of treatment. The theme of alcoholism disappeared from the press, and no more statistics on the production and sale of alcohol were published.[128]

The leading anti-alcohol campaigner, Yuri Larin, who was vulnerable as a former Menshevik, had lost his position by this time and died in 1932. Larin had called for the 'complete elimination of alcohol', and with a steady reduction in output he thought the final victory of the campaign 'predetermined'.[129] A Central Committee resolution of May 1930 took issue with these views, and with the 'entirely unfounded, semifantastic, and therefore extremely harmful attempts of some comrades [including Larin] "with one leap" to jump over all the obstacles on the way to a socialist reconstruction of daily life'.[130] The 16th Party Conference, in April 1929, had originally approved a programme for the 'dealcoholisation of the economy', but the chairman of Gosplan, Gleb Krzhizhanovsky,

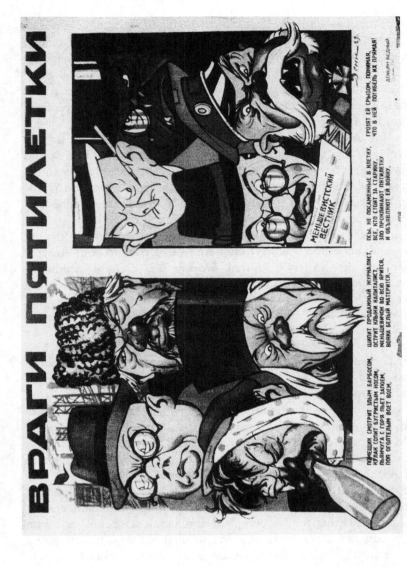

1.5 Viktor Deni, 'Enemies of the Five Year Plan' (poster, 1929)

lost his position a few months later and a plenary meeting of the Central Committee in November effectively reversed the earlier decision. By September 1930 Stalin was directing Molotov to 'increase . . . the production of vodka' and to 'aim openly and directly for the maximum increase in output'.[131] And as the increases were being introduced by state bodies that were 'organs of proletarian dictatorship', any criticism of their decisions was to be regarded as a 'crude political mistake'.[132] The spirits industry was reorganised and placed under central government control, new factories were built, and by 1940 there were more shops selling drink than meat, fruit and vegetables put together; the output of alcohol rose sharply as a result, although it fell again during the war and levels of consumption of the immediate post-war period were, in fact, no higher than they had been in the late tsarist years.[133]

2.1   Untitled, 1970s
(from Vladimir Sichov, *Les russes*)

2
_____

A drunken society

Secrecy is a long-standing Russian tradition. In tsarist times not only military but also quite harmless social information was withheld from the population at large, and especially from foreigners.[1] The Bolsheviks briefly abolished secret diplomacy and other restrictions when they came to power, and indeed there was consternation in Allied capitals when they published the annexationist secret treaties on which the conduct of the war had been based. Older practices, however, soon reasserted themselves, and for many Western students of Soviet affairs control over the flow of information came to represent a basic element in the communist system of power (it was, for instance, one of the issues about which Soviet leaders were most concerned during their negotiations with Czech reformists in 1968).[2] Secrecy extended even to relatively straightforward matters, such as population numbers. The first census of what was then the Russian Empire took place in 1897, and there were further exercises under Soviet auspices in 1920 and 1926. The next census was originally planned to take place in 1930 or 1935. When it was finally carried out, in 1937, the results were suppressed because they would have given a clear indication of the impact of collectivisation and the purges and were lower than the figure Stalin had publicly predicted. The organisers were described as 'enemies of the people' and 'Trotskyist–Bukharinist spies'; the head of the census bureau was shot; many others were dismissed from their posts; and the results finally appeared in 1990. A further exercise, under the direction of Vyacheslav Molotov, was carried out in 1939; it 'found' nearly 3 million extra citizens and thus confirmed Stalin's proud boast at the 18th Party Congress that the Soviet population had already reached 170 million.[3]

The quality of public information deteriorated once more during the Brezhnev period, as problem after problem was 'resolved' by simply discontinuing the publication of any information about it. The first post-war census, for instance, was carried out in 1959 and published in sixteen volumes between 1962 and 1963. The next, in 1970, appeared in seven parts between 1972 and 1974. The following census, conducted in 1979, produced only a single summary volume, published five years later.[4] The annual statistical handbook, published since 1956, became notably slimmer as the 1970s progressed; by the early 1980s it was down to a positively anorexic 500 pages or so, compared with 800 or more in the early 1970s. Figures on life expectancy, which was evidently declining, were not updated: the latest available, in the early 1980s, were those for ten years earlier. The publication of figures on infant mortality, which were embarrassingly high, was simply discontinued; nor were there figures of any kind, after the 1920s, for crime, suicide, abortion, income distribution, and balance of payments and much more.[5] With an information base of this kind, it was difficult to dispute official claims that the USSR had entered the qualitatively new phase of 'developed socialism' in the late 1960s and that any remaining problems would be eliminated as it completed the transition to a fully communist society.

The production and consumption of alcohol was a part of this unhelpful picture. The annual statistical handbook, *Narodnoe khozyaistvo SSSR*, discontinued its reporting of vodka output in 1963, although various republican handbooks continued to provide figures up to the late 1970s.[6] Similarly, until 1962 official handbooks published figures for the sale of alcoholic and non-alcoholic beverages within the totals that were reported for state retail trade. Starting with the 1963 volume, however, sales of beverages were concealed by adding them to the figures for ice cream, coffee, cocoa, mushrooms and various spices, and labelling this new category 'other foodstuffs' (it immediately became the largest single item in the retail sales statistics, accounting for about a third of the total). A separate vodka price index was discontinued in 1969; figures on retail trade inventories ceased to appear in 1976.[7] Statistics on *samogon* or homebrew, accounting for as much as 50 per cent of the reported figure for total consumption, were almost entirely ignored in official sources.[8] In the 'last forty years', it was noted in 1977, there had been no published study in the USSR on the economics of alcohol, as compared with a whole series of serious works on the subject during the late prerevolutionary period;[9] from the 1930s to the 1960s, similarly, there was virtually no serious study of the legal or social issues to which alcoholism gave rise, such as the rising incidence of juvenile drinking.[10] Writing in a *samizdat* source in the late 1970s, a Soviet author complained that the subject of alcohol had 'completely vanished from the press' and that it was 'steadily fading even from statistics'.[11]

The production and consumption of alcohol

Until the late 1980s, when official statistics improved markedly, the production and consumption of alcohol had to be inferred from a series of indirect measures. Alcohol, for instance, bore a relatively constant relationship to the figure for total food sales, allowing an approximate figure to be extrapolated. Inferences could be drawn from the sale of sugar, an important raw material for the production of home brew. National figures could, with some ingenuity, be reconstructed from the figures reported by individual republics. A number of officials emigrated during the 1970s, and then made themselves available for interview. Much larger numbers of ordinary citizens left the USSR, often for Israel, where they provided an opportunity for survey-based research into consumer behaviour, economic activity outside the state sector and family budgets; a high proportion, however, were Jews, whose alcohol consumption (about 2 per cent of family income) was considerably below the levels of the society they had left.[12] Western agencies, including the CIA, published sets of data based on closed as well as open sources of information. None of this was entirely satisfactory; and yet concealment was difficult to achieve because (as a Western scholar has put it) the needle was much too large for the haystack in which it had been hidden.[13]

At least two systematic attempts were made to construct a set of data on Soviet drinking in the absence of official statistics; of these, Vladimir Treml's, published in 1982, is by far the more rigorous.[14] Treml found that consumption of alcohol from state and illegal sources rose steadily from the 1950s: in 1955 it was 7.3 litres per head of population, in 1960 8.5, in 1965 10.2, in 1970 12.9, in 1975 14.6 and in 1979 (when his series concluded) 15.2.[15] Of the 1979 total of 15.2, 9 litres represented strong drink, and 3.3 litres *samogon* or its local equivalents. These totals did not include other homemade beverages such as grape, fruit and berry wine and beer, which accounted for an estimated 1 litre of absolute alcohol per head in the 1970s.[16] Nor did the statistics include the theft of alcohol, which was frequently significant. In the early 1970s, for instance, about 7 million litres of pure alcohol was reported to have been stolen from the railway system in the Russian Republic alone.[17] Theft of alcohol from places of work was also commonplace, and stolen alcohol of this kind was estimated to add a further litre to the real level of consumption.[18]

Including *samogon* but excluding these further sources, levels of alcohol consumption placed the USSR in seventh or eighth position in the 1970s among a group of thirty Western nations; without *samogon* (a quarter or more of total consumption) the USSR ranked only thirteenth or fourteenth in the same statistics.[19] The share of strong drink within the total was however unusually high in the USSR: about 65 per cent, including *samogon*, compared with about 31 per cent for other countries for which statistics were available. The USSR thus ranked fourth in the consumption of strong drink and eighth in the consumption of alcohol per person aged fifteen years or older.[20] Another striking feature of these reconstructed Soviet data was the rapid rate of increase in alcohol consumption. The rate of growth was relatively constant over the entire post-war period, averaging 7.2 per cent a year for consumption of state-produced beverages and 4.4 per cent if *samogon* was included. The rate of increase in more than twenty comparable countries over the same period, however, was just 2.7 per cent.[21] There was a particularly rapid rise in the incidence of alcoholism in rural areas (although levels were still lower than in the towns), and in the consumption of low-grade fruit and berry wines.[22] These, moreover, were USSR-wide totals; there was, as before, considerable evidence that consumption differed by age, gender, ethnicity and location, with the traditionally Muslim Central Asian nations, for instance, consuming between a third and a quarter of the quantities consumed by their Slavic counterparts,[23] and with Russians in those areas drinking much less than Russians in the Slavic republics.[24] On other estimates differences between the republics could be still greater, with alcohol consumption in Latvia (for instance) running at seven times the total of traditionally wine-drinking Armenia, and with levels of alcoholism itself up to fourteen times higher.[25] Even within a single republic there were significant variations, with the traditionally Muslim areas of the Russian Federation averaging about a quarter of the vodka sales of traditionally hard-drinking Karelia, Kamchatka and Sakhalin.[26]

It was clear, because of high levels of consumption and relatively high retail prices, that Soviet consumers spent an 'extraordinarily large share of their budgets on alcohol'.[27] Soviet studies of family budgets published before the 1980s suggested a number of improbably low figures in this connection. An investigation into workers' family budgets in Siberia in the 1946–57 period, for instance, found that alcoholic beverages accounted for no more than 3.4 per cent of all expenditure.[28] A study carried out in the late 1970s of Siberian families of mixed social background suggested an average alcohol expenditure of 6.6 per cent;[29] and a study in the Gorky region suggested a figure of 6.7 per cent.[30] These figures were difficult to reconcile with the information that was available about the sale of alcoholic beverages and average incomes during the same period: indeed expenditure on alcohol, as reported by surveys, was consistently below the actual levels of expenditure that were included in the retail trade statistics. The explanation appeared to be that official condemnation of alcohol abuse, together with some reluctance on the part of drinkers to acknowledge the real scale of their expenditure, had led – as in many other countries, but still more so – to a substantial degree of underreporting.[31]

Alternative calculations, based largely upon surveys of *émigré* families, suggested much higher totals (indeed the USSR, according to a different set of calculations, was almost certainly the country with the largest number of alcoholics in the world).[32] Between 8 and 9 per cent of all urban families, according to these *émigré*-based calculations, spent 40 per cent or more of their family budgets on state-produced alcohol, and between 10 and 11 per cent of collective farmers spent 40 per cent or more of their budget on state-produced alcohol and *samogon*.[33] More generally, it could be estimated that expenditure on alcohol accounted for between 15 and 20 per cent of average disposable incomes, a figure that was 'exceptionally high by international standards'.[34] The combined effect of high alcohol consumption and relatively high prices for alcoholic products, in Treml's view, made a considerable contribution to poverty and social tensions in the USSR.[35] More than half of the families with unusually high levels of alcohol expenditure were already below the poverty line, and more than 3 million urban families with incomes above the minimum were pushed below it by their disproportionate consumption.[36] The rapid increase in alcohol consumption was also apparent from Treml's figures for state retail trade, which showed sales of alcoholic beverages nearly quadrupling in value between 1960 and 1979.[37] Other *émigré*-based studies found that nearly a third of those who had left the USSR and settled in the United States in the late 1970s thought that alcoholism or absenteeism was 'often' or 'nearly all the time' a problem in the workplace; this was particularly the case in transport, construction and manufacturing, much less so among the white-collar professions.[38]

A rather different attempt to calculate the unpublished was made by A. Krasikov (real name Mikhail Baitalsky, 1903–78), the pseudonym of a Soviet-based journalist and dissident.[39] By 1956, Krasikov found, the Soviet Union had surpassed the level of alcohol consumption of late tsarist times; by 1970 levels of consumption were nearly twice as high, at 6.4 litres of pure alcohol per head of population.[40] But, he pointed out, information of this kind was not presented straightforwardly in official statistics: it had to be inferred from other sources. The annual statistical handbook, for instance, had given a breakdown of the structure of state retail trade, including a figure for 'alcoholic and nonalcoholic beverages'. In 1963, as we have seen, the figure suddenly vanished. 'Could it be', asked Krasikov, 'that "drinking" had ceased to be our "national joy"? Or had we gone over to *kvass*? But if so, what would be the point of concealing such remarkable progress?' The truth emerged, as it had done for Treml, from another figure, that for 'other foodstuffs'. Formerly a relatively minor item of expenditure and less (for instance) than spending on butter, in 1964 it made an 'incredible jump', increasing more than ten times. Up to 1963 the yearbook had itself explained that 'other foodstuffs' included 'coffee, spices, vitamins, mushrooms [and] soyabean products'. After 1964 such details had to be omitted as either beverages would have had to be added, or mushrooms, laurel leaves and coffee would have had to be sold on a scale that could scarcely be imagined.[41] There was separate reference to butchers' meat and poultry, cheese and eggs, salt and tea; even fruits, berries, water-melons and melons had their own subheadings. Everything was identified, it appeared, except that nearly a third of total expenditure on foodstuffs was not accounted for, and tea was the only beverage to be mentioned directly.[42]

Until 1963 sales of 'other foodstuffs' had accounted for about 3.2 per cent of all food purchases. Deducting the same proportion from the declared total for 1970, Krasikov estimated that about 2.8 billion rubles had been spent on mushrooms, spices and related goods in that year, and that a much more substantial 24.2 billion rubles had been spent on alcoholic and non-alcoholic beverages.[43] What proportion of this recalculated total was accounted for by lemonade, mineral water and so forth? Looking back at the figures for the output of both vodka and soft drinks between 1950 and 1963, which in fact were relatively similar in their proportions of the total, and making conservative assumptions about price, Krasikov concluded that expenditure soft drinks was just under 4 per cent of the total for alcoholic and non-alcoholic beverages.

In 1970, it appeared, about 1 billion rubles had been spent on soft drinks, but 23.2 billion on alcohol.[44] This was about 15 per cent of the total value of all retail trade, or more than a quarter of the value of the sale of all foodstuffs. The figures, moreover, had been increasing rapidly. If consumption in 1940 was taken at 100, in 1950 it was 75 (attributable to post-war conditions), in 1960 it was 200, in 1965 283, and then in 1970, 439.[45] So important had alcohol become in the structure of consumer purchases that Krasikov named it 'Commodity Number One'.[46]

Alcohol led the field, moreover, not simply in the amount purchased and the rate of increase, but also in its profitability, which exceeded that of every other branch of trade. The prices of all foodstuffs, excluding alcohol, had risen to 133 per cent of their 1940 level by 1970. The prices of alcoholic beverages, however, had risen by 262 per cent, or twice as much.[47] Neither the price, nor the increase, bore any direct relationship to the costs of production (which had probably fallen). 'In the USSR', the *Great Soviet Encyclopedia* had explained in 1951, vodka prices were 'fixed by the state at a level which facilitates the struggle against alcoholism and stimulates the consumption of the most beneficial and nutritious foodstuffs. In the USSR the production of vodka is not governed by fiscal considerations and the income obtained from selling it accounts for an insignificant proportion of state revenues'.[48] In late tsarist Russia, according to Krasikov's calculations, about 78 per cent of the selling price of vodka went back to the government in the form of duties. Little was published about the Soviet vodka industry and its costs, but such information that was available suggested that the state in fact received no less than 92 per cent of the purchase price of every bottle of vodka.[49] The income that the state received from the sale of vodka, and of other drinks, in turn accounted for about 12 per cent of total budgetary revenue.[50] In the 1960s and 1970s, according to another calculation, a highly regressive alcohol tax provided more than a third of all government revenues, and about a ninth of the entire state budget; taxes on alcohol matched the declared defence budget and even exceeded it in the early 1970s.[51]

The obscurity that had surrounded the drink trade, and many other aspects of Soviet life, began to be dissipated in the later 1980s under the Gorbachev leadership. The central statistical administration was elevated to the rank of a state committee, retitled and given a new head, appointed in 1987.[52] The Politburo, meeting in April of that year, emphasised the need to 'increase the accuracy and openness of statistical information, improving reports and ensuring their absolute reliability'.[53]

In one of the most notable developments, the annual statistical handbook reversed the diminishing trend of the 1970s and became larger and more detailed. The first 'Gorbachev' issue, published in 1986, was almost thirty pages larger than its predecessor; more important, it contained a wealth of information that had not been available for some time. Figures for infant mortality, for instance, were again reported: at 26 per 1,000 live births they compared poorly with those for the developed capitalist nations. Life expectancy figures returned, at 64 for men and 73 for women; themselves an improvement on the figures belatedly provided for the 1970s, they were still up to ten years less than those for other industrial nations. Later issues continued this improvement in the quality and quantity of data provided; the 1987 yearbook recognised the 'second economy' for the first time, and in 1988 standard gross national produce measures began to be employed. The annual handbooks were followed from late 1988 by a series of sectoral volumes dealing with population, labour, industry and so forth; and there were new figures for crime, abortions, suicides, executions and many other forms of social behaviour that had last been reported in the 1920s.[54]

The first figures for many years on alcohol production were included in the 1985 statistical yearbook, released in August 1986. There were also figures for the sale of alcoholic drink, although it continued to appear among 'other foodstuffs' in the figures for retail trade as a whole.[55] The 'jubilee' statistical yearbook that was released in August 1987 improved still further, reporting the share of family budgets that was accounted for by alcohol consumption (a modest 2.2 per cent); the 1988 yearbook, published in 1989, went further still and reported alcoholic drink within the figures for retail trade, where it accounted for about a quarter of the total.[56] The figures made it clear, for the first time so far as official statistics were concerned, that the output of vodka and other hard liquors had more than trebled between 1940 and 1980; wine, beer and other beverages had increased still more rapidly (see Table 2.1). The consumption of all forms of alcoholic drink had meanwhile increased nearly eight times between 1940 and 1984, although vodka and other liquors had fallen as a proportion of the total;[57] consumption of absolute alcohol per head of population, a useful summary measure, had trebled by 1970 and quadrupled by the early 1980s.[58] All of this made it difficult to sustain the claim of the Soviet health minister, in 1980, that unlike the capitalist countries, alcohol consumption in the USSR had 'decreased dramatically';[59] the rates of increase in fact exceeded the estimates that had been suggested by Treml, Krasikov and

2.2 'Where's the money – but what about the family?'
(poster, c. 1930)

other independent scholars. On other calculations up to 15 per cent of the population could be classified as alcoholic by this time, with 99.4 per cent of all men and 97.9 per cent of all women at least occasional drinkers.[60]

These large and highly aggregated trends concealed a number of more specific and often more alarming developments. It was clear, first of all, that increasing levels of consumption of other drinks had not depressed the demand for spirits: wine and beer consumption had been increasing rapidly, but so had the consumption of vodka and other liquors.[61] Drinkers, moreover, were younger than they had ever been: in the early 1960s men began to drink systematically at the age of twenty-four, but by the 1980s the average age was nineteen.[62] Among industrial workers there had been a comparable increase, and there were cities, in the late 1970s, where the average consumption among working adults was as much as a bottle a day.[63] There was an increasing level of alcoholism among women more particularly: in 1940 they had accounted for 4 per cent of all heavy drinkers, but by 1960 they accounted for 8 per cent and by the early 1980s they were up to 15 per cent of the total;[64] women also made up an increasing proportion of those who had to be detained overnight in sobering-up stations.[65] There were further increases, even more so than among men, by the early 1980s, by which time almost 90 per cent of women drank regularly.[66] This 'alcoholic emancipation' was particularly rapid among women of childbearing age, with a consequent increase in the number of children born with mental and physical defects; divorced and unmarried women drank more than married women with children, but childless married women drank most of all.[67]

School children, at the same time, were drinking more, and drinking at an earlier age. Juvenile alcoholism was 'almost unknown' before the Second World War and it accounted for no more than 1.5 per cent of the total in the 1950s and 1960s, but it was up to 5 per cent of a much larger total by the early 1980s.[68] Among senior school pupils in 1965, 49 per cent had at least experimented with alcohol; by the early 1980s the figure was 80 per cent.[69] School-age girls had begun turning up at parks with bottles in their hands, and told teachers they had 'spent the whole time drinking';[70] university students, according to reports that reached the KGB, 'drank every day . . . before lectures, after lectures, and now in the breaks as well'.[71] There were repeated calls, in these circumstances, for a 'dry law' for juveniles; other warned of the dangers of 'infantile alcoholism' as children of a still younger age were poisoned by their

Table 2.1. *Production of alcoholic beverages, 1944–1985 (official data, million decalitres)*

	1940	1960	1970	1980	1985
Beer	121.3	249.8	419	613	657
Grape wine	19.7	77.7	268	323	265
Fruit and berry wine	n.a.	20.6	49.1	149	70
Cognac	n.a.	1.5	5.4	9.4	7.0
Champagne (m. bottles)	8.0	37.4	86.7	178	248
Vodka and liquor	92.5	138.1	243	295	238
Absolute alcohol (litres)	2.2	3.9	6.8	8.7	7.2

Sources: Adapted from *Promyshlennost' SSSR* (Moscow: Statistika, 1964), pp. 454–5, and *Narodnoe khozyaistvo SSSR*, various years.

alcoholic mothers.[72] Paternal alcoholism had an influence upon older age-groups as well: in particular, there was a direct relationship between parental drinking and a child's success at school, or even his attendance,[73] and there was also a close relationship between parental drinking and 'problem families' (in Leningrad, researchers found that as many as 88 of every 100 families of this kind were ones in which either or both of the parents were habitual drinkers).[74]

Drinking and social life

For Krasikov, writing in the 1970s, alcohol was not simply 'Commodity number 1' but also 'Calamity number 1'.[75] Its impact on family life, in particular, was documented in a series of studies of an academic and more popular character. One of the clearest consequences of alcoholism was upon the stability of family life, and specifically divorce. The incidence of divorce was falling in the Soviet Union in the 1980s, after more than thirty years of rapid growth, and levels were in any case below those of some Western countries, notably the United States (there were 3.5 divorces per 1,000 population in the early 1980s, compared with 2.9 in the United Kingdom and 5.3 in the USA).[76] The figures concealed a very large regional variation: if the average was 2.8 divorces per 1,000 population for the USSR as a whole in the 1970s, it was 1.1 in the Central Asian and Transcaucasian republics, 2.9 in the Ukraine, 4.5 in the Baltic, 5.1 in Moscow and 5.6 in Leningrad.[77] Whatever its incidence, alcohol was identified in virtually every study as the single most important cause of marital breakdown and of its damaging effects on other aspects of family life.

In a study of over 3,000 divorce proceedings in the Ukraine, for instance, Chuiko found that motives were varied, interconnected, and not always to be taken at face value. The drunkenness of the husband was however the factor that was most often cited in such circumstances.[78] In 47 per cent of the cases that were brought by wives, the drunkenness of the husband was the main justification that was advanced; psychological factors were cited much less often, in 21 per cent of cases, and other factors still less frequently.[79] The longer the marriage the more likely it was that drunkenness would be cited as a ground for divorce, though age was not itself a significant influence (in about half of these cases the husbands insisted they drank only 'occasionally'). The drunkenness of the husband as a basis for divorce was more commonly encountered among industrial workers than among other social groups; for office staff it was the second most important cause to be identified, after psychological circumstances.[80] The same was true in Muslim republics, like Uzbekistan: husbands were likely to cite their wives' 'lack of respect' for their own parents, but nearly half (44.2 per cent) of all divorcing wives gave their husbands' drinking and abusive behaviour as their grounds for a petition.[81]

Attempts to reconcile partners when drink was the apparent cause of their problems were 'rarely' successful, Chuiko found in Kiev. Only in 8 cases for every 100 of this kind was there a reconciliation, and only 6 did not proceed to a court action. Wives apparently hoped, in these cases, that their husbands would 'turn over a new leaf' and stop drinking. But in not a single case had their hopes been realised.[82] Drunkenness and alcoholism were sometimes the only motive for divorce. More often they were accompanied by charges of cruelty, assault, lack of material support and 'major scandals' of other kinds.[83] Men themselves were much more likely to identify psychological or related factors as grounds for divorce: 44 per cent of all men in the Kiev districts that were surveyed gave psychological grounds for their action, and a further 16 per cent quoted marital infidelity. Only 4 per cent of the men concerned identified drunkenness as the main reason for their wish to bring proceedings. Of all the divorces considered, only 6–7 per cent ended in reconciliation, with a further 2–4 per cent who did not take their action as far as the courts after the decision to initiate proceedings.[84]

Other studies reached similar conclusions. A survey of 500 divorce proceedings in Leningrad, for instance, again found that 'amoral behaviour' or 'drunkenness' was the reason most frequently given for divorce, accounting for more than a third (38.1 per cent) of all cases. A 'lack of common views and interests' came second, with 33.9 per cent, and then a variety of psychological and other causes.[85] A study conducted in the Lithuanian and Belorussian republics found a slightly different picture: drunkenness was given as the reason for divorce in 14 per cent of the cases considered, after 'the existence of another family' (21 per cent) and 'betrayal' (17 per cent) but before 'personality differences' (13 per cent) and other circumstances.[86] A study in Latvia found that personality and related differences were much the most important cause of divorce, accounting for 64 per cent of all the cases that were considered: drunkenness came second, with 16 per cent, followed by marital infidelity (13 per cent) and other reasons.[87] A further study of young families in Moscow, Novosibirsk, Odessa and Grodno, however, found that alcoholism was again placed first among the reasons for divorce;[88] the overwhelming majority of wives in fact stayed with their drunken husbands, although only one husband in ten was willing to accept a drunken wife.[89] Whatever their detailed findings, there was very general agreement in these and other studies that alcoholism was a major and usually the most important cause of divorce and family breakdown, with up to 80 per cent of all cases attributable to its influence.[90]

The increasing consumption of alcohol could equally be blamed for a fall in life expectation, and for other kinds of morbidity and mortality. The average life expectation in the USSR had been steadily increasing, from 32 in the 1896–7 census of the Russian Empire up to 46.9 just before the war and then 67 in the mid-1950s. There was a further, less rapid increase in life expectancy up to the early 1970s, when the figure stood at 69.5 (64.5 for men and 73.6 for women); by this time the average life expectation was only two years less for men and six months less for women than the average in the world's most advanced capitalist countries.[91] These impressive results had been regularly recorded in the annual statistical yearbook, published since the late 1950s. In the late 1970s, however, life expectancies began to fall, a development without precedent in the industrial world in peacetime (there were comparable falls in some East European countries such as Czechoslovakia). The response of the authorities was to discontinue the publication of new figures. The life expectation that was reported, up to the early 1980s, was that for the early 1970s (the figures for tsarist Russia were included so that there appeared to have been an overall improvement); later editions of the yearbook, up to 1986, took the still more radical step of publishing no figures at all, leaving only the table that reported a 'natural increase of population' over the period.[92]

The reasons for the fall in life expectancy are still unclear, and alcohol consumption was only one of them.[93] The facts, however, were certainly remarkable. As the 1985 statistical yearbook made apparent, life expectancy for men had fallen to 62.5 years at the end of the 1970s, and for women to 72.6; this was the lowest life expectancy for men of any European country,[94] and the size of the difference between male and female expectancies was in itself without a parallel in the industrial world. The figures were even worse for the Russian republic, with an average expectation for men in the late 1970s of just 61.5.[95] The lowest point of all was reached in the early 1980s, just before the start of the campaign against alcohol abuse, with an average expectancy for men of 61.4 and for men and women in rural Russia of just 59.3.[96] By the time this information became available, in 1986, there had been a considerable improvement, up to 64.8 for men and 74.4 for women; the average expectation of life in the USSR was still at a lower level than in any of the major capitalist countries.[97] The main contributors to the death of the population of working age, by the late 1980s, were diseases of the circulatory system, accidents, poisonings and traumas, neoplasms and diseases of the respiratory organs;[98] alcohol made a contribution to several of these and was itself directly responsible for 20,000 deaths every year.[99] Altogether, it was estimated, there had been a total population loss between 1960 and 1987 of between 30 and 35 million as a result of alcohol and its abuse.[100]

The effects of alcohol on public health were apparent in a number of other ways. One of them was traffic accidents: alcohol was associated with about a third of all accidents that were the responsibility of the driver, and with nearly half of the cases in which the driver had exceeded the speed limit or violated other rules of the road, and with over 80 per cent of road deaths[101] (there were ten times as many cases of this kind, relative to population, as in the USA).[102] Alcohol abuse was the most important single cause of suicide; and the higher the level of alcohol consumption, the greater was their number.[103] Alcohol, similarly, was associated with about a third of all the accidents that took place in the countryside, and it was the most important single cause of accidental drowning.[104] As in other countries, the excessive use of alcohol made a contribution to health disorders, including cirrhosis of the liver and duodenal ulcers.[105] There was a further connection between alcohol abuse and venereal disease, gynaecological complications during pregnancy, and disorders of the central nervous system. Up to 90 per cent of all cases of syphilis and 95 per cent of all cases of gonorrhoea, for instance, were associated with alcohol abuse.[106] Alcoholic mothers were much more likely to have underweight babies, their levels of infant mortality were two or three times higher than the average, they were much more likely to have abortions, premature births and retarded children, and they were likely to become infertile at a younger age.[107] Alcohol also had effects that were specific to men: they were more likely to suffer from impotence, up to 30 per cent suffered from a reduced sex drive, and habitual drinkers could become infertile as early as their mid-forties.[108]

Many of these cases, including some tragic individual instances, reached the columns of newspapers and magazines. There was the case of Ira, a fourth-year school pupil from Leningrad, who wrote in to *Pravda* for a cure for her mother, who drank all they earned, and for her sister,

2.3   Boris Efimov, 'I had an accident at work . . . '
(cartoon, 1972)

who smoked and drank. 'That's all, I'll write no more, mama has come in', she concluded hastily.[109] A letter from Vitya of Krivoi Rog, rather earlier, led to an extended correspondence. Only twelve years old and perhaps 'still too young to be writing to the newspaper', she told *Izvestiya* that she and her mother had to leave the family home and stay with friends until their father had spent all his earnings. Her sister had been boarded out for her own protection, and her mother had been beaten to unconsciousness; she herself was 'forced to sing and dance' when her father came in at three o'clock in the morning. How could she cope with schoolwork and what was she to do?[110] Lidia, from the Kurgan region, had lost her 18-year-old son as a result of alcoholic overindulgence. On the way to a neighbouring village in a stupor he had lost his direction, collapsed and died of exposure. Her husband had initially encouraged him to drink and was guilty, in Lidia's view, of the death of his own child.[111] Another distressing case involved a young boy, Igor, who had stabbed his father to death in a desperate attempt to free himself and his mother from parental alcoholism; the family arguments could be heard through the walls of their apartment, and children and mother often had to seek refuge elsewhere until their father had come to his senses.[112]

The effects of alcohol abuse were not limited to the physical health, including the longevity and reproductive capacity, of the Soviet people. They also influenced patterns of behaviour, particularly crime. And of all crime, alcohol was particularly closely associated with serious and violent crime. About 74 per cent of all murders in the Russian republic, for instance, were committed – according to court statistics – under the influence of alcohol, and about the same proportion of rapes; alcohol was associated with 90 per cent of all cases of hooliganism, 84 per cent of all robberies, and 60 per cent of all cases of theft.[113] There were even cases, as in the Gorky region during the 1960s, when every single case of murder in a particular year was associated with alcohol.[114] About 30 per cent of all crime involving juveniles was associated, similarly, with alcohol, and up to 90 per cent of the cases of murder and hooliganism in which juveniles were implicated.[115] And the more the parents drank, the more likely that the juveniles concerned would have a criminal record.[116] As a rule, the more serious the crime the greater the likelihood that alcohol was involved, and the greater the degree of injury to the victim: 28.5 per cent of cases of accidental homicide involved alcohol, but 48.5 per cent of cases of murder, and 73.1 per cent of cases of murder under aggravating circumstances.[117] Alcohol was also associated with group crime, and with crimes of a sexually perverted nature;[118] but there was a close association with all forms of crime, about half of which (on the basis of court statistics) were committed in a state of intoxication.[119]

Alcohol was also associated with recidivism (or repeated crime). A study of those sentenced for a second or subsequent term of imprisonment found that the proportion that had committed their crime in a state of intoxication was 63.5 per cent. Among those that received a second or subsequent sentence for grievous bodily harm or hooliganism the proportion that had committed their crime under the influence of alcohol was 20 to 30 per cent higher than among those sentenced for the same offences for the first time. Court evidence from Kazakhstan suggested that 85–90 per cent of those that had been released from prison committed a further crime in an alcoholic state or in order to obtain a drink, and about three-quarters of them were chronic alcoholics. Some 80 per cent of recidivists, as a rule, systematically abused alcohol, and (at least in Kazakhstan) over 90 per cent of the rapes and murders for which they were responsible were committed in a state of intoxication.[120] Crime, as in other countries, had 'peaks' and 'troughs'. There were three or four times as many admissions to sobering-up stations on payday as on other days of the week; and in general Saturdays were the worst for alcohol-related crime, followed by Fridays and then Sundays.[121] There were variations during the working day as well: about 4 per cent of those who were detained in sobering-up stations had begun before 10 in the morning, a further 11 per cent were apprehended before lunch, and nearly two-thirds had sought refreshment before the end of the working day.[122]

Alcohol had a still wider range of criminal consequences. It was connected, for instance, with unusual or bizarre crimes. One of these was the latter-day 'phantom', a former milling machine operative, who had begun to make 'unusual expeditions to women's dormitories at night', climbing up a drainpipe and then threatening the inmates with a knife.[123] In another incident, three college students, after a drinking bout, broke into Moscow zoo and killed three wallabies.[124] Drink, if the newspapers were to be believed, had led a Russian dancer, Yuri Stepanov, to defect to the United States. Concerned about his 'unrecognised talent' during a tour of Italy, Stepanov 'had a few cocktails' in his hotel room and formed the impression that foreign theatres were 'yearning for [his] presence'. In a 'strange, almost dreamlike state' he made his way to the American embassy in Rome and sought political asylum, later returning, sadly disillusioned, to his homeland.[125] Alcohol could encourage the most inventive overtures to women, such as the rapist who had invited a girl to come with him to read the eighteenth-century philosopher Helvetius.[126] And alcohol was connected with fires, often involving loss of life as well as property: by the early 1980s two-thirds of them, and 'alcohol plus adult' had replaced 'children plus matches' as the most important single cause of these conflagrations.[127] Violations of the legislation relating to alcohol had meanwhile almost doubled between 1973 and 1985; by this time more than 10 per cent of all Soviet males were involved every year in a criminal offence of this kind.[128] Overall, as one Soviet study of these matters concluded, 'if there was no drunkenness and alcoholism, there would be no more of the crimes that make up most of the elements of criminal statistics, above all violent, domestic and mercenary crime'.[129]

Alcohol, economy and military security

It was not only personal and community affairs that were affected by Soviet alcoholism: it was also the sinews of the state itself, the economy and the armed forces. There was certainly no shortage of anecdotal evidence of the place occupied by alcohol in the Soviet workplace. According to the then USSR deputy procurator general, Sergei Shishkov:

One of the chief reasons for absenteeism is people coming in to work in a state of intoxication, or not coming at all for the same reason. Unfortunately, one can quote many examples of alcohol consumption even in factories. Pitenko, a punch operator at the Frunze heavy electrical engineering works, got so drunk at work that he fell into a pit in the carpentry shop . . . There are many cases where drunkenness leads not only to a drop in labour productivity and plan targets not being met, but to outrageous violations of safety regulations and even to serious accidents.[130]

The economist Abel Aganbegyan wrote despairingly in 1981:

Drunks are to be found on the shop floor more and more frequently. At some enterprises, special brigades have been formed to 'grab' those who have drunk too much and stop them getting to their machines, in order to prevent accidents. They drink during working hours, they drink after work . . . This is the ultimate in lack of respect for work, the ultimate negative attitude towards it.[131]

And *Pravda* wrote in December 1982 that, as a result of alcohol abuse, 'machinery stands idle, building sites come to life on Tuesdays instead of

Mondays and close down again by Friday; while on payday the women wait for their husbands at the factory gates to prevent them from drinking their paypackets away'.[132] In a typical enterprise in the chemical industry, investigated in the early 1980s, 3.5 per cent of the workforce were confirmed alcoholics, 2.2 per cent showed its early characteristics, 18.8 per cent 'abused' alcohol and 79.4 per cent drank 'moderately'; only 1.4 per cent were complete abstainers.[133]

Any calculation of the losses that the Soviet economy suffered from the abuse of alcohol must necessarily be provisional. It was clear, however, that those losses were very considerable. There was, first of all, the cost of absences from work, up to 75 per cent (in some investigations, as high as 90 per cent) of which were connected with alcohol.[134] At any time, it was estimated, about 1 per cent of the labour force was absent for reasons that were associated with alcohol, although the real reasons were often obscured by explanations in terms of 'conditions at home', 'seeing off friends' and so forth.[135] As levels of investment rose, the loss of output that was involved increased from 1.3 million rubles a year in the mid-1960s up to 4 million or more in the early 1980s.[136] The productivity of those who reported for work was also affected, although drinkers themselves took a very different view of the matter.[137] Moderate consumption of spirits, it was found, reduced output the following day by 4–5 per cent; heavy consumption reduced it by up to 30 per cent.[138] Factory output fell by up to a third after weekend excesses of this kind, and some sections did not operate at all.[139] There were similar problems on payday and after the weekend, when productivity was up to 30 per cent lower.[140] *Pravda* estimated that 'morning after' losses on a Monday were about 3 billion rubles annually.[141] In the countryside, collective farm chairmen were able to find sober workers only in the first half of the day; by the afternoon they were too drunk to function.[142]

There were many further costs that resulted from alcohol and its abuse. Violations of labour discipline, for instance, were nearly always associated with alcohol.[143] At least half of all industrial accidents arose in the same way;[144] according to some estimates the proportion could be over 60 per cent.[145] There was the cost of the substandard production with which alcoholism was associated,[146] and the overtime that had to be paid because of alcohol-related absences.[147] There was the cost of illness – which was substantially higher among alcoholics[148] – and the direct and indirect costs of early death (up to 60 per cent of alcoholics died before they were fifty years old).[149] Drinkers were much more likely to change their place of work,[150] leading to higher retraining costs, and they were more likely to steal or damage state property.[151] There were also the costs associated with the maternity of alcoholic mothers, including the higher incidence of abortions,[152] premature births and the subsequent illhealth of mother and child.[153] And there was the cost of importing alcoholic products, which was mounting rapidly in the 1970s.[154] In a 1985 letter to the Central Committee on the subject, a group of Novosibirsk scientists suggested that losses of these various kinds were as much as 180 billion rubles annually, four times the income that was derived from the sale of drink.[155] The impact of alcohol on labour productivity has been described by other scholars as 'astonishing' and 'far greater than the profit from alcohol sales'.[156] As the Novosibirsk scholars concluded, alcohol abuse was one of the main causes of the failure of the five-year plans of the early 1980s and of the economic crisis that succeeded it; indeed it had been the 'most appalling tragedy in Russia's entire thousand-year history'.[157]

In an attempt to calculate the losses that the economy had suffered as a result of alcohol abuse, the *émigré* scholar Boris Segal included, first of all, working days lost through absenteeism and decreased productivity. Just over 30 per cent of the Soviet labour force, Segal calculated, were alcohol abusers.[158] A Soviet survey, reported in the government newspaper *Izvestiya* in 1985, found that about 27 million employees could be considered alcohol abusers and absentees, a lower but still comparable figure.[159] An average alcohol abuser, according to Soviet investigations, lost about forty working days annually. The total loss of working days as a result of alcohol abuse was accordingly enormous – at least 1.4 billion, a figure close to the total that arose from illness and maternity leave.[160] Soviet research also suggested that the efficiency of an alcoholic worker was 36 per cent lower than that of his non-drinking counterpart, the equivalent of 93 lost workdays every year.[161] The average drinking worker, accordingly, lost about twice as many days a year as a result of sickness or absenteeism and reduced efficiency as the workforce as a whole, or about 16 per cent of all working time in Soviet industry.[162] Alcohol abusers, similarly, consumed a disproportionate share of Soviet health expenditure, and placed a disproportionate burden upon the welfare services. There were the costs of sobering-up stations, the costs of crime committed while under the influence of alcohol, and the cost of police investigations and legal proceedings. There was the cost of fires and vandalism, and of the programmes that were undertaken at public expense to reduce the incidence of alcohol abuse.[163]

2.4   An unsteady worker, 1970s
(Endeavour Group)

Authoritative estimates in the 1970s suggested an economic loss from alcoholism of at least 10 per cent of national income. The economists Strumilin and Sonin, for instance, argued in 1974 that abstinence would increase Soviet productivity by 10 per cent.[164] *Izvestiya* also reported that sobering up the labour force would raise productivity by 10 per cent.[165] Other Soviet estimates in the 1980s were much higher: Korobkina, for instance, estimated the overall loss of productivity at between 15 and 17 per cent,[166] and Zagoruiko put losses at up to 20 per cent.[167] It was also clear that the direct costs of alcohol abuse were at least as great as the revenues that arose from the taxation of sales. It was estimated, for instance, that the budgetary costs of alcohol consumption in the 1980s were up to three times greater than the income that the state derived from excise duties.[168] Even in a traditionally wine-drinking republic with low levels of alcoholism like Georgia, the costs were up to half as much again as government revenues.[169] According to the fullest available study of these matters, the direct cost of alcohol abuse in the USSR amounted to more than a third (36.9 per cent) of the Soviet national income in the mid-1980s; these costs, in turn, were about five or six times the income that accrued from taxes on the sale of alcohol, and very much greater in relative terms than the losses that were incurred in other developed economies.[170]

There was an equally rich body of evidence about the abuse of alcohol in the Soviet armed services. The use of alcohol by conscripts was, in fact, forbidden. It was not allowed in the barracks, and restrictive arrangements for leave in many units severely limited opportunities to acquire alcohol off-post.[171] Ordinary servicemen were poorly paid, in part, it appeared, so that they would have no spare cash for such purposes. Despite these restrictions, drinking was a common problem in many units. Alcoholic beverages were frequently smuggled in by soldiers returning from leave, by civilians working on the base, or by support staff (who were not ordinarily confined to barracks in their offduty hours). Alcohol was sent through the post, mixed with pots of jam or concealed in toothpaste tubes or hot water bottles.[172] Conscripts whose assignments took them outside direct military supervision often capitalised on the opportunity by buying alcohol for themselves and their friends. Free time on pass was often used for getting drunk, and obtaining alcohol was a common motive for going off post without a pass. Drink, and the struggle to obtain it, was described as an 'obsession' by soldiers themselves.[173]

Alcohol consumption in the Soviet armed forces certainly led to some remarkable scenes. A case reported in the Western press, for instance, concerned a Soviet tank that got lost on manoeuvres in Czechoslovakia as night was falling. The tank was driven into a village where the only pub was still open and then sold to the pub owner for two cases of vodka with some pickles and herring thrown in 'as a gesture of goodwill'. The crew was found sleeping it off some days later; the tank, however, could not be located. It later emerged that the owner had sold it to a metal recycling plant.[174] The absence of a regular source of supply led, as in civilian life, to a ceaseless search for alternatives. Antifreeze, brake fluid, eau de cologne or even shoe polish were consumed in its place. The MIG-25 fighter-bomber, which needed 14 tons of jet fuel and half a ton of alcohol for its braking systems, was for this reasons known in the Soviet air force as the 'flying restaurant'.[175] Indeed in some reports 'practically every' crime or disciplinary incident in the armed forces could be related to alcohol. There were cases of the attempted rape of fellow conscripts' mothers; in another 'routine occurrence' a sergeant had consumed a bottle of beer and a bottle of spirits presented by some grateful parents, after which he 'tumbled out' of a third-storey window and was taken to hospital in a critical condition.[176] The highest rates of alcohol abuse were probably among officers and NCOs, who had a greater amount of time on their hands and more rubles at their disposal;[177] there was some evidence that this problem was greatest among the artillery and strategic rocket forces, lower among the armoured divisions, and lower still among infantry regiments.[178]

Newspaper reports and interviews with former servicemen conveyed the same impression. An analysis of articles in the press, for instance, suggested that 'Russian soldiers at all ranks have at least the same high rates of alcoholism and alcohol-related pathologies as the society at large – in some cases probably considerably higher'.[179] The level of chronic alcoholism was estimated at about 20 per cent of the armed forces as a whole, with an additional 30–35 per cent that might be regarded as 'heavy drinkers'.[180] Interviews with soldiers themselves suggested that hard drinking was 'part of Soviet military life'. Articles in Soviet military journals complained of the Soviet soldier's eagerness to spend most, if not all, of his meagre monthly pay on vodka. Moreover, his tendency to steal equipment in order to barter with the local population for vodka was also well documented. A common practice was to sell articles of clothing that farmers could use; Soviet soldiers in forward areas also traded their insignia for alcohol. Military periodicals suggested that heavy drinking and alcohol abuse were very common features of Soviet military life. As one soldier put it, 'even if you are not an alcoholic when you go into the Army, you are when you come out'.[181]

Viktor Belenko, a Soviet armed forces officer who defected to Japan in 1976, reported that his brother officers who were pilots, and even his ground crew, were drunk almost all the time. According to Belenko, ground crews in particular would drain the de-icing fluid from the aircraft, distil it, and then drink it. They often covered up their theft by the dangerous practice of replacing the de-icing fluid with water: if the de-icing tanks had to be used at high altitudes, the water would freeze on the wings and almost certainly result in a crash. The alcohol that was used in cooling and braking systems was particularly valued, not just because it was free, but also because it was purer than the alcohol that was commercially available; it became known as 'white gold' because of its great value on the black market.[182] The Afghan war, after 1979, offered a number of new opportunities, including access to marijuana; but alcohol retained its pride of place, together with a wide range of surrogates. Regulations permitted two bottles of spirits and four of wine but unlimited beer, and so beer bottles were emptied, filled with vodka and imported in some quantity. Apart from this there was shaving lotion and cologne, antifreeze and toothpaste, glue and brake fluid (heated up, for preference, 'with some nails in it'). And then there was shoe polish, smeared on a piece of bread and left out in the sun until the alcohol had separated off and could be consumed.[183]

Not surprisingly, there were many harrowing individual tragedies. There was, for instance, the case of the 19-year-old conscript who died of alcohol poison after taking part in a barrack-room drinking bout. It had followed an oath-taking ceremony, in which the victim's father – a respected police officer – had given the address. Afterwards, father and son had joined in a celebratory dinner at which a 10-litre jerrycan of illicit vodka had been produced by the parents of two other conscripts. Everyone joined in the toasts, and afterwards the celebrations continued in the barracks with what remained of the illicit spirits. The following day the young man was dead, his father refusing to testify that he had been the source of supply.[184] In another case, reported in the mid-1980s, an army driver had returned home after two years of exemplary service. He had given a lift to the regimental commander, and had been persuaded to buy some spirits. Drunk, he decided to take his girlfriend for a ride. He exceeded the speed limit, lost control and crashed; his girlfriend later died from the wounds she received.[185]

It is obviously difficult to reach firm conclusions about the extent of alcoholism in the Soviet armed forces on the basis of press reports and even large-scale programmes of interviewing. *Emigré* reports certainly suggested that in most units alcohol consumption occurred during off-duty hours, and that if soldiers became alcoholics it was many years after their two or three years of service.[186] Drinking on duty or appearing drunk for duty was relatively uncommon, though driving while intoxicated was a major cause of accidents involving motor vehicles.[187] The average pay of a conscript was a further limitation, equivalent as it was in the 1970s to half a litre of vodka every month; at least in Afghanistan it was the officers and NCOs who were drunk most often, sometimes during the day, rather than the rank and file.[188] The penalties for drinking were severe, including deprivation of rest-days and of further opportunities to visit the garrison town; it might also include up to fifteen days confinement in the guardhouse. There was little drunkenness to be seen in the garrison towns that were open to Western observers, and the towns themselves were heavily patrolled by military police.[189] Alcoholism, according to press and interview sources, nonetheless cut across all ranks and unit types; the conclusion of at least one careful study was that the rate of alcohol abuse and its associated problems was 'likely to be even higher in the Soviet military than in Soviet society at large', and that the problem as a whole was of 'epidemic' proportions.[190]

3.1 'The devil got out of his bottle and showed what tricks he could play'
(poster, Tashkent, 1970)

ВЫШЕЛ ИЗ БУТЫЛКИ ДЬЯВОЛ,
СВОИ ПРОДЕЛКИ ПОКАЗАЛ.

3

The campaign is launched

There was, in fact, a reasonably lengthy prehistory to the campaign against alcohol and its abuse that was launched by the Gorbachev leadership in the spring of 1985. Under Khrushchev, when levels of consumption were considerably lower, a Central Committee and Council of Ministers resolution of December 1958 had called for a more determined struggle against alcoholism and other 'survivals of the landlord-bourgeois order'; the main emphasis was placed upon education and propaganda, although restrictions were also introduced upon the sale of alcohol in shops and restaurants.[1] The preparation of homebrew had become illegal in 1948 (the law was strengthened further in 1960 and 1961),[2] and the criminal code that was introduced in Russia and the other republics in 1960 made clear that drunkenness was to be regarded as an aggravating circumstance and that persistent offenders were to be subjected to 'compulsory therapy' in addition to their sentence.[3] Under the apparently more indulgent leadership of Leonid Brezhnev, general secretary from 1964 until 1982, there were further and more determined attempts to reduce if not eliminate the alcohol abuse that had become a still more prominent feature of Soviet life. In 1966 the Presidium of the Supreme Soviet adopted a decree on hooliganism, introducing a system of fines for public drunkenness.[4] The following year a network of labour rehabilitation centres (*lechebno-trudovye profilaktorii*) began to be established, providing for the 'compulsory treatment and labour re-education' of persistent drinkers; the system was extended further in the early 1970s.[5]

A new and more comprehensive series of measures was introduced in 1972, following a resolution by the CPSU Central Committee and a separate decree from the Council of Ministers. The Central Committee, in its resolution, was again mainly concerned with education, the mass media and cultural and sporting facilities.[6] The Council of Ministers, in a series of more specific decisions, called for the production of vodka and other liquors to be reduced; stronger vodkas were to be phased out altogether and the output of wine, beer and non-alcoholic drink was to be increased to compensate.[7] These directives were passed into legislation by the Russian and other republican parliaments in June 1972 as part of a more considered attempt to 'eradicate drunkenness' and to create an 'intolerant attitude towards all its manifestations'.[8] Later in the year a network of 'commissions for the struggle against alcoholism' was established as part of the machinery of government at all levels of the Soviet system; and from 1976 a national narcological service began to operate.[9] In 1979 the Central Committee returned to the matter, calling for 'more decisive measures' including stricter observance of the regulations and 'more convincing and effective' anti-alcohol propaganda.[10] But efforts of this kind, it was later acknowledged, had little effect: the output of strong drink actually increased, so did the number of violations of the legislation, and many party officials had come to the conclusion by the late 1970s that the problem was simply 'insurmountable'.[11]

Indeed there was little evidence that Brezhnev and his immediate entourage took measures of this kind very seriously, at least so far as their own behaviour was concerned. His German counterparts, Helmut Schmidt and Erich Honecker, both confessed that they were 'afraid' to try to keep pace with the Soviet General Secretary.[12] His drinking, other visitors found, was 'far beyond moderation or any sensible control'. During the evenings he 'laced into vodka at a terrifying rate', and on holidays he had to be assisted to leave the room (the only one who could match him was Konstantin Chernenko, whose death in 1985 was attributed to cirrhosis of the liver).[13] Another of the most unrestrained drinkers within Brezhnev's circle was Yumjaagiin Tsedenbal, Mongolian party leader from 1940 almost without interruption up to 1984. His wife was Russian, his two children knew no Mongolian, and much of the family's life revolved around Moscow rather than Ulan Bator, Tsedenbal, by the time Yuri Andropov's personal physician came to know him, 'was already boozing rather than ruling'. During his visits to the USSR it was the task of the physician, Ivan Klemashev, to ensure that Tsedenbal was able to stand up on his arrival at Moscow airport, although he was 'almost never able to do so'. Further efforts were necessary to make sure the Mongolian leader could attend the diplomatic receptions that took place in Ulan Bator on the anniversary of the October revolution.[14] It was unlikely, given a leadership of this kind, that any campaign against alcohol abuse would be conducted with energy or inspire a great deal of popular conviction; and Brezhnev himself, in his last speech to a party congress in 1981, had to concede that it was still a 'serious problem'.[15]

Order and discipline under Andropov and Chernenko

The drive against alcoholism that was launched in 1985 was part of a wider campaign to strengthen public order that dated back some years before Gorbachev's accession to the party leadership.[16] One of the most important changes, during the brief period between Brezhnev's death and the accession of Gorbachev, was the acknowledgement that there was a series of problems that were deeply rooted in Soviet society and much more than capitalist 'survivals' (*perezhitki*). A developed socialist society, it had originally been argued, was characterised by the 'maturity of its social relations' and the 'high degree of its social and ideological unity'.[17] A society of this kind, the *Philosophical Encyclopedia* pointed out in 1983, could not free itself at once of the 'birthmarks of capitalism', such as drunkenness, hooliganism and bureaucracy. But they were at odds with the 'main tendencies of social progress', and most of the factors that encouraged their development had already been 'liquidated'.[18] Indeed there were 'no social roots for drunkenness and alcoholism' in the USSR, the academic literature was able to claim as late as the 1980s; it had even been suggested, rather earlier, that consumption was 'systematically falling'.[19] Brezhnev himself, in 1981, saw the resolution of problems of this kind as part of the larger process of the 'perfection of the socialist way of life' and the elimination of 'everything that hinder[ed] the formation of a new person'.[20]

These complacent formulations did not long survive the general secretary himself. His successor, Yuri Andropov, made one of the most important early contributions in an article on 'The teaching of Karl Marx and some questions of socialist construction in the USSR' which appeared in the party theoretical journal *Kommunist* in early 1983. The Soviet Union, he insisted, was only at the beginning of the long historical stage of developed socialism; the questions that arose in the course of its further development were 'far from simple'; and there should be no exaggeration of their closeness to the ultimate goal of full communism.[21] Chernenko, who succeeded him in February 1984, took the same view, urging that more attention be given to the complicated tasks that had still to be resolved than to what Lenin had called the 'distant, beautiful and rosy future'.[22] These emphases in turn became the basis for a specialist literature which acknowledged, more openly than ever before, that socialism had not necessarily resolved complex issues such as nationalism or gender inequality, and indeed that they were not necessarily resolvable within the framework of a single social system. Still more provocatively, it was argued that Soviet-type societies themselves contained 'contradictions' between social groups and that these could lead to 'serious collisions' of the kind that had occurred in Poland unless far-reaching democratic reforms were instituted.[23] The debate was suspended in 1984, but two years later it was one of those to which Gorbachev devoted particular attention in his report to the 27th Party Congress.[24]

The effort to overcome such divisions under Andropov and Chernenko took the form of a campaign to strengthen public order and morality, while at the same time permitting some broadening of the terms in which public issues such as alcoholism could be debated. One of the first targets was the late general secretary's family and friends: his son Yuri lost his ministerial post and his place in the Central Committee, his daughter was banished to Murmansk, his son-in-law was arrested on charges of large-scale corruption and close associates like the former interior minister Nikolai Shchelokov were dismissed from their positions and later disgraced.[25] More positively, there was a sustained attempt to strengthen discipline in the workplace and law and order in the wider society. One of the first clear signs of this new direction in official policy was the series of raids that the police began to make in early 1983 on shops, public baths and even underground stations in order to discover how many of those concerned had taken time off their work without permission. There was certainly some room for improvement. An official report in late 1982 found that of every 100 workers surveyed, an average of 30 were absent 'for personal reasons' at any given moment, in most cases to go shopping or visit the doctor;[26] another investigation, in 800 Moscow enterprises, found that in some cases no more than 10 per cent of the workforce were still at their places during the last hour of the shift.[27] Labour turnover, meanwhile, was rising; industrial accidents were becoming more frequent; and the quality of work was falling still further behind the levels of other countries.

An attempt to reduce the incidence of alcohol abuse was a central part of this wider campaign of social discipline. Andropov himself was a total abstainer.[28] His early writings and speeches, in fact, made relatively few direct references to alcohol and its abuse, but they were very firm on those who 'parasited on the humanism of our society' and in their condemnation of crime and other 'antisocial manifestations'.[29] The Central Committee meeting over which he presided in June 1983 made it clear that the party's tasks were inseparable from a 'most energetic struggle with drunkenness, hooliganism and parasitism, speculation and the theft of socialist property, bribery and money-grubbing';[30] the decrees on labour discipline that were adopted under his leadership included new penalties for alcoholism in the workplace, extending to dismissal and monetary compensation for any losses.[31] Konstantin Chernenko, Andropov's successor, had referred several times to alcoholism in his early speeches[32] and he dealt with the problem still more directly as party leader. Speaking to an audience of civic activists in October 1984, Chernenko expressed his 'serious concern' about the very limited results of earlier campaigns against alcohol and its abuse. Alcohol, he went on, undermined health, the home and the workplace, and it cast a shadow over the whole society. A more persistent and well considered campaign, it was clear, would be necessary to 'free society from this great evil';[33] the speech itself had 'for the first time focused public leadership attention on the serious nationwide problem of alcohol abuse'.[34]

There were, in fact, some modest attempts to develop a campaign of this kind while Chernenko was still in power. A national anti-alcoholism movement was already forming, prompted by the concerns of public health workers and other professionals; one of the first was in the Siberian academic town of Akademgorodok, staffed by members of the Academy of Sciences and their students.[35] A more determined campaign against alcohol abuse was launched in the city of Ul'yanovsk, a year and a half before the Central Committee had issued its directives, under its energetic first secretary Gennadii Kolbin.[36] The Soviet Sociological Association, reflecting these concerns, established a section on 'deviant behaviour' whose principal emphasis was upon the problem of alcoholism.[37] There were calls, if isolated ones, for a policy of total prohibition, and for a national temperance society.[38] There was, in fact, some evidence that official policies were beginning to bear fruit during the early 1980s: alcohol-related crime had begun to fall, the consumption of alcoholic drink was falling, and liquor was accounting for a diminishing proportion of the total.[39] There was nonetheless a rising tide of letters to the party and state leadership, 'mostly from wives and mothers', calling for more detailed measures to be taken in the months that led up to Gorbachev's accession and for the institution of a fullscale campaign.[40] As a letter in *Pravda* asked in March 1985, shortly before the new measures were announced and perhaps not fortuitously, 'How long are we going to put up with drunkenness?'[41]

The campaign begins

There was little sign, in Gorbachev's early speeches, that the new general secretary intended to make the campaign against alcohol abuse his first public priority. In the acceptance speech he delivered to the Central Committee on 11 March 1985 Gorbachev paid tribute to his two immediate predecessors and then promised that the strategy that had been developed at the 26th Party Congress – over which Brezhnev had presided – and at subsequent meetings of the Central Committee would remain unchanged: a policy of the 'acceleration of the country's socioeconomic development [and] the perfection of all aspects of the life of the society'.[42] His first full address to the Central Committee in April 1985 again emphasised the importance of the 26th Congress and called for a 'steady advance' rather than a clear break with earlier policies. The party's general line, as he explained it, involved the 'perfection of developed socialist society', a formulation that was thoroughly Brezhnevian in tone. Gorbachev did call for 'further changes and transformations' and for the establishment of a 'qualitatively new state of society, in the broadest sense of the word'. It was changes in the economy, however, that would be decisive in any development of this kind, and the speech was largely preoccupied with familiar matters such as growth, innovation and labour productivity, with just a passing and very general reference to 'negative phenomena'.[43]

There were, nonetheless, some indications in the general secretary's earlier speeches that he would be concerned to recover the moral values that were, for him, implicit in Soviet socialism, and that he would seek to reduce levels of alcohol consumption in particular. Gorbachev's earliest reference to the problem was in an article published in 1971 in which he spoke of the 'drunkenness, hooliganism and other negative phenomena' that were still to be encountered among Soviet youth.[44] In 1975 he praised the work of party committees that were seeking to strengthen public order and to 'step up the struggle against drunkenness and alcoholism'.[45] In another article in 1976 he urged party committees to take an uncompromising view of drunkenness among other social ills;[46]

in 1977, under his leadership, the Stavropol' *kraikom* went so far as to adopt a special resolution on the struggle against alcoholism, which placed its main emphasis upon broadly based prophylactic work. Drunkenness, Gorbachev observed, influenced all aspects of social life: the economy, family life, people's morality and consciousness. Throughout the territory, half the crimes and up to 90 per cent of the acts of hooliganism were committed by people in a state of intoxication. Alcoholism was responsible for 70 per cent of the absenteeism and for almost a third of the divorces in the area. Party members and officials were among those who were involved in alcohol abuse; the courts were unduly complacent about it, and the police failed to collect half the fines that were due from the drunks who had to be placed in sobering-up stations.[47]

This, however, was Gorbachev's last reference to the problem of alcoholism before the campaign was launched in the spring of 1985. In his speech on the Lenin anniversary in 1983 he censured those who sought to 'live off society' in general terms, and in an election address in 1984 he mentioned theft, bribery and speculation as violations of socialist morality but not – specifically – drunkenness.[48] In a major speech of December 1984, his last before election as general secretary, Gorbachev directed attention to the unequal distribution of income and benefits as a source of popular alienation from the regime;[49] his acceptance speech of March 1985 raised similar issues.[50] There was no reference to alcoholism in his address to the Central Committee in April, delivered at a time when the Politburo had already decided to launch a determined campaign against it, and just a passing reference in a speech in Leningrad in May – 'bureaucratism, parasitism, drunkenness, wastefulness, extravagance and other negative phenomena'.[51] It was not, in fact, until a visit to Siberia in September 1985 that Gorbachev gave any extended consideration to the issue, and then in response to persistent questioning. The campaign, he told locals, had overwhelming popular support. There might be a case for banning the sale of alcoholic drink entirely or forbidding its sale to known offenders if local people wanted to do so; and there would be a 'stern reckoning' with those inside the party itself who refused to change their habits in the light of these new requirements.[52] The measures, he told a meeting of Stakhanovites later in the month, had been 'warmly welcomed'; there were already 'encouraging results'; and though there was a 'long, hard struggle' ahead, he promised that the new policy would be followed through 'undeviatingly'.[53]

The evidence that is available suggests that it may have been his wife, Raisa, who influenced Gorbachev to take up the issue of alcoholism as the first public priority of his administration. Raisa Gorbachev in turn appeared to have been influenced by the fate of her brother Yevgenii, who used to accompany her to dances and protect her from over-attentive admirers. Yevgenii completed his military service and then entered university, studying, like Raisa, in the philosophy faculty at Moscow University. He began to write children's stories and novels with what his sister thought was a 'touch of Kafka' about them, although they failed to find a publisher. Yevgenii married twice and had a son, but had latterly been living alone and was understood to have taken a cure for alcohol dependence at a psychiatric clinic in Orel. It was this tragic experience – a 'constant source of pain for more than thirty years'[54] – that appears to have prompted Raisa Gorbachev to urge her husband to initiate the anti-alcohol campaign at a time when the consumption of drink was already acknowledged as a serious social problem.[55] The testimony of most participants is that Gorbachev himself, though no abstainer, was an active supporter of the sobriety campaign from its inception.[56] Others – including former prime minister Nikolai Ryzhkov – have suggested that he was initially impressed by the arguments against the form in which the campaign was conceived and only later became a convert, concerned above all by the country's 'moral atmosphere'.[57] Gorbachev himself, years afterwards, was inclined to minimise his own contribution;[58] at the time, in discussions with foreign journalists, he was clear enough that alcoholism was a 'national tragedy', that the figures were 'appalling', and that everything should be done to 'save the people, especially the Slavic people'.[59]

The strongest advocate of the sobriety campaign within the leadership itself was Yegor Ligachev, a Central Committee secretary since 1983 who had been promoted directly to the Politburo in April 1985 without passing through the customary candidate stage. Ligachev had publicly identified himself with the Gorbachev candidature and his support, he later claimed, had been decisive in his election.[60] Ligachev, from 1965 to 1983 party first secretary in Tomsk, was a teetotaller himself and had for some time given explicit attention to the problem of alcoholism. It should be ventilated more often as an issue in the newspapers, he wrote in 1978.[61] Party members and officials who drank should not be spared, he declared in 1983.[62] He sought to introduce a total ban on the sale of alcohol in Tomsk itself.[63] And in April 1985, before the campaign had been formally launched, he told a meeting in the Central Committee offices that the previous year 199,000 party members and 370,000 Komsomol members had been brought before the authorities because of alcohol abuse. An atmosphere must be established in party bodies, he went on, of 'general condemnation of drunkards', ending the 'liberalism' that had been shown towards those who compromised the party by their conduct. Party members who drank, in particular, could not be allowed to retain their responsible positions.[64] Ligachev had not, in fact, been a member of the Central Committee commission that had been examining the problem since 1984, but the question came up repeatedly in the

3.2 'Wouldn't you rather an apple, Adam?'
(*Krokodil*, no. 27, 1985)

Secretariat and his formal responsibilities and personal antipathy to drunkenness came together at this point to incline him towards 'radical', even 'severe and administrative' measures.[65]

Ligachev was supported by Mikhail Solomentsev, a reformed alcoholic who was chairman of the Party Control Committee and therefore responsible for discipline.[66] They operated, when the campaign got going, as a team: Ligachev, through the Secretariat, issued instructions to lower-level party officials on the 'elimination' of alcohol, while Solomentsev through his Committee punished those who failed to implement the directives sufficiently decisively.[67] Most other members of the leadership appear to have taken a less sharply defined position with regard to the campaign, and several offered more resistance in their memoirs than had been apparent at the time. Boris Yeltsin, for instance, wrote subsequently that he had crossed swords with Ligachev about a decision to close a Moscow brewery and to curtail the sale of drink still further. 'His entire campaign against alcoholism', Yeltsin recalled, ' was simply amazingly ill-conceived and ridiculous. Nothing was taken into account, neither the economic nor the social consequences.' Ligachev just 'plunged ahead without proper thought, and the situation got worse every day and every month'; Gorbachev let matters take their course; and Yeltsin himself came under attack for querying statistics that appeared to suggest the campaign was already enjoying some success. Ligachev was in any case the second most powerful member of the leadership and it was difficult to resist his dispositions. 'I could not reconcile myself to his obstinacy and dilettantism', Yeltsin recalled, 'but I got no support from anyone'.[68] Yeltsin did not, in fact, become a member of the leadership until after the campaign had been approved, and when he became Moscow party secretary in December 1986 he pressed the campaign forward with some enthusiasm: alcohol consumption fell by 40 per cent, and nine-tenths of all the wine shops in the capital were closed down.[69]

Several other members of the leadership later identified themselves as opponents of the campaign, including the Azeri leader Gaidar Aliev, who 'resisted, so far as [he] could'.[70] Within government itself opponents included finance minister Vasilii Garbuzov, who refused to sign the resolution and shortly afterwards retired, and a first deputy chairman of Gosplan, who was threatened with dismissal and expulsion from the party after he had three times declined to add his signature.[71] Georgian first secretary Eduard Shevardnadze, the representative of a wine-drinking republic with minimal levels of alcohol abuse, 'voted for the decisions, though inwardly I disagreed'.[72] The most serious opposition when the campaign was discussed by the Politburo on 4 April 1985 came in fact from Nikolai Ryzhkov, at this time a Central Committee secretary (he became prime minister later in the year). According to his own testimony, Ryzhkov was 'in favour of taking measures against alcoholism, and agreed that the nation was going to ruin, but I was categorically against the methods being proposed. At first I thought they were joking when they said that "drunkenness would continue so long as there was vodka on the shelves". Then I realised they were dead serious.' Ryzhkov pointed out the unfortunate experience of prohibition in other countries, and suggested that the measures should be limited to the restriction of drinking in public places and at work. He also favoured 'economic methods' (that is, higher prices) and education to try to reduce the incidence of abuse. He warned that if they were moving towards prohibition it would be necessary to ration sugar, as there would be an upsurge of moonshining. Ryzhkov was supported by Vitalii Vorotnikov, at this time prime minister of the Russian republic, and by Vladimir Dolgikh, a Central Committee secretary, but it was their opponents who carried the day.[73]

A report of the Politburo meeting appeared in the press the following day, 5 April 1985, which made clear that a full-scale campaign was about to be launched.[74] In view of the 'numerous proposals from working people' that had been received by central and local agencies, the report explained, 'the Politburo thoroughly discussed the question of combating drunkenness and alcoholism'. The Politburo agreed that the elimination of these 'abnormal phenomena' was a 'social task of extreme political importance', and approved a set of measures – socio-political, economic, administrative, medical and other – with a view to 'eliminating them from Soviet life'. Special emphasis was placed upon the need for 'consistency' in combating drunkenness, which suggested that the campaign would be sustained – unlike its predecessors – with some determination. Party, state and other bodies were to coordinate their efforts towards this end, and 'extensive anti-drinking publicity' would be developed. The meeting approved proposals for legislation designed to reduce the incidence of alcohol abuse; it also approved a 'complex of measures that [were] to be carried out for this purpose by the USSR Council of Ministers and the ministries, departments and law-enforcement agencies'. Sobriety, *Pravda* declared on 18 May in welcoming the decisions, must become the 'norm of our life'; *Izvestiya* thought the decisions were 'stern but just', taking into account the opinion of the 'overwhelming majority of Soviet people'.[75] *Krasnaya zvezda* promised the support of the armed forces; *Literaturnaya gazeta*, for its part, called on Soviet writers to recruit 'thousands and millions of people' to the drive to eliminate drunkenness and alcoholism from all aspects of daily life.[76]

The legislation on sobriety

The Politburo's decisions were made public in a Central Committee resolution, 'On measures to overcome drunkenness and alcoholism', which was adopted on 7 May and published, after the fortieth anniversary of victory in the Second World War had been celebrated, on 17 May 1985.[77] Under contemporary conditions, the resolution began, the creative potential of socialism and the advantages of the Soviet way of life were being revealed 'more and more fully'. This made it more important than ever before to observe the principles of communist morality and to overcome harmful habits and survivals of the past, 'above all such an ugly phenomenon as drunkenness and the abuse of alcoholic beverages'. The fact that the problem of drunkenness and alcoholism had become more acute over previous years could only give rise to serious concern. Earlier measures to combat alcoholism were being implemented unsatisfactorily. The approach being taken was one of 'short-term campaigns', without the necessary organisation and consistency. The efforts of party, state and other bodies were poorly coordinated. A large part of the population was 'not being instilled with a spirit of sobriety' and was 'insufficiently informed about the harm that the use of alcoholic beverages causes to the health of present, and especially future, generations and to society as a whole'. The media had been supporting the idea of moderate or 'cultured' drinking and had been showing 'all kinds of drunken parties and drinking rituals' in a positive light.

What did the Soviet people think about all this? The 'overwhelming majority', according to the resolution, took the view that the use of alcohol did a great deal of economic and moral damage and that it was intolerable in the life of their society. In their letters to the central and local authorities they had indeed demanded that 'effective measures' be taken to eradicate drunkenness, alcoholism and (at the same time) home brewing. Considering the overcoming of drunkenness to be a 'social task of great political importance', the Central Committee had decided to require party bodies at all levels, ministries and councils of ministers in

Moscow and the republics, local soviets, trade union and Komsomol organisations, and factory managers to work out and implement a 'set of comprehensive and well-defined organisational, administrative and educational measures aimed at the resolute intensification of the anti-alcohol campaign and the heightening of its effectiveness'. The whole campaign was to be given a 'genuinely mass, nationwide character' and an effort was to be made to create in every workplace an 'atmosphere of intolerance towards all violations of labour discipline and order'.

The resolution went on to list a series of more specific directives. First of all, the use of alcohol at public banquets and receptions was 'completely inadmissible' (Soviet diplomatic gatherings lost their customary sparkle and foreigners made their excuses before 'quickly withdrawing').[78] Party bodies were to take a more demanding attitude towards members who abused alcohol or failed to take part in the struggle against its influence. Party and state officials, managers, trade union and Komsomol officials who had a weakness for alcohol and who permitted the holding of drinking bouts were to be dismissed from their posts, and individual party members were to be held strictly accountable up to and including expulsion from its ranks. It was the 'duty', the resolution made clear, 'of every Communist and every official to set a personal example of active struggle against drunkenness and of struggle for the eradication of home brewing everywhere'.

More generally, the State Committee for Science and Technology, the Academy of Sciences, and Academy of Medicine and the Academy of Pedagogy, in conjunction with the ministries most directly concerned, were to prepare a 'nationwide, comprehensive programme for the prevention and overcoming of drunkenness and alcoholism'. The programme was to take account of the social, economic, demographic, educational, legal, psychological and medico-biological dimensions of the problem. Party, trade union, public health and other bodies were to step up their anti-alcoholic work in workplaces and student dormitories, regarding this as an 'indispensable condition for strengthening labour and production discipline and public order and for improving the lives of working people and members of their families'. It would be their job 'skilfully and persistently' to explain to the population at large that the use of alcohol destroyed their own health and that of future generations, and caused great material and moral damage to the wider society. The trade unions, more specifically, were to ensure that drunks were deprived of bonuses and of holiday entitlements, as they were entitled to do under the existing legislation on trade unions and labour collectives.

More positively, efforts were to be made to improve the leisure facilities that were available, particularly to young people, helping to ensure the 'sensible use of free time'. The existing network of special-interest clubs was to be extended, particularly on a residential basis. Every use was to be made of the facilities that were under the administration of the trade unions to develop tourism and excursions, amateur arts, scientific and technical work and fruit and market gardening. Alcoholic beverages were not to be sold in sanatoria, vacation homes or rehabilitation centres, at tourist bases or on collective outings, or on any form of public transportation. Alcohol was in no circumstances to be sold to those under the age of twenty-one. The Komsomol and its committees were to regard the struggle against alcohol abuse as 'one of their main tasks'; they were to be 'implacable towards all attempts to introduce teenagers to alcoholic beverages' and were to ensure there was no consumption at young people's parties and similar functions, while attempting more generally to secure the complete elimination of alcohol at all levels of schooling and in young people's hostels. The Ministry of Education, in conjunction with other bodies, was to develop and introduce a 'uniform system of anti-alcohol education' for young people at all kinds of educational institutions.

The media, as always, were to give a lead. Newspapers, radio and television, the creative unions and the Knowledge Society (which was responsible for public lecture campaigns) were to 'resolutely improve anti-alcohol propaganda, instil in people a spirit of sobriety and an intolerant attitude towards drunkenness, and graphically and convincingly disclose the harmfulness of alcohol, even in small doses'. Not only its harm to individuals, but its 'negative effects on all aspects of public life – the economy, everyday life, and people's morality and consciousness' were to be highlighted. Theatres, cinemas, television and radio were not to permit programmes that showed drinking bouts and drunken parties in a favourable light. More attention was to be given to new traditions and ceremonies which excluded the use of alcohol entirely, and a constant stream of information was to be supplied about the measures that were being taken to overcome drunkenness and about their effectiveness. Better use was to be made of the sporting facilities that already existed, and every assistance was to be given to individuals or groups that wished to construct simple facilities of their own. Every workplace should have its own sporting facilities, and should make every effort to encourage their use by local people. The construction of new facilities and the refurbishment of those that already existed would be taken into account during the preparation of the next five-year plan, which would cover the later 1980s.

The resolution dealt finally with a number of the coercive sanctions that could be applied to reduce the consumption of alcohol and particularly its abuse. The Ministry of Internal Affairs, the USSR Prosecutor's Office, the Ministry of Justice and the bodies under their control were instructed to eliminate the 'serious shortcomings' in their work with regard to public drunkenness. They were to put a 'resolute stop to violations of the regulations governing trade in alcoholic beverages', and must 'eradicate homebrewing and speculation in alcohol'. They were themselves to conduct anti-alcohol propaganda, and were to assist families and workplaces in re-educating alcohol abusers. The laws on combating drunkenness and homebrewing were at the same time to be 'strictly and steadfastly implemented'. A national temperance society, with its own journal, was to be established in order to encourage 'mass participation' in the campaign against drunkenness. From 1986

3.3 B. Semenov, 'One for the road!'
(poster, 1989)

onwards, quite apart from this, there would be annual reductions in the output of vodka and liqueurs, and the production of fruit and berry wines would completely cease by 1988 (more precise instructions had been agreed but were not at this time made public).[79] To compensate, there would be a 'substantial increase' in the production and sale of non-alcoholic beverages and of jams, fruits, grapes and berries in fresh, dried and frozen form.

This comprehensive set of directives was supplemented over the months that followed by more specific instructions at both national and republican level. The Soviet government itself responded almost immediately with a package of 'measures to overcome drunkenness and to eradicate homebrewing'.[80] The resolution was intended to 'resolutely intensify the struggle against drunkenness, alcoholism, homebrewing and the manufacture of other homemade strong alcoholic beverages'. Based on the Central Committee resolution, it translated its directives into more precise legislative language. Measures were detailed, for instance, to reduce the level of alcoholism in public places, making use in this connection of the *druzhinniki* or police auxiliaries as well as comrades' courts and other informal agencies. The State Committee for Publishing, Printing and the Book Trade was instructed to increase the output of popular-scientific literature, posters and pamphlets directed against the abuse of alcohol and intended for various groups of the population. Radio and television programmes were to be prepared which made clear the 'social and moral damage done by drunkenness' as well as the methods that were effective in combating it. Ministries and republics were to make specific provision for theatres and other cultural and athletic facilities in their preparations for the new five-year plan. Up to 3 per cent was to be deducted from the income of housing associations for the construction of local sporting facilities. The supply of metal-working and woodworking tools, film materials, artists' brushes and other requirements was to be increased, and a gradual changeover was to be effected to a system in which hard liquor was sold only in specialised shops or departments. On working days, alcoholic beverages could be sold only after 2 o'clock in the afternoon.

These general directives were made still more explicit by a decree of the Presidium of the USSR Supreme Soviet and by comparable decrees by the presidia of the various republican parliaments. The decree adopted by the Russian republic, by far the largest,[81] laid out a series of specific penalties for any infraction of the law. Public drinking, or the 'appearance of persons in public places in a drunken condition that offends human dignity and public morality', was to attract a warning or a fine of between 20 and 30 rubles. Any further offence within the same year would involve a fine of up to 100 rubles (nearly two weeks' wages at the time of the decree), or corrective work for a period of up to two months. Drinking in the workplace, or turning up for work in a state of intoxication, was to attract a fine of 30 to 50 rubles for each offence. No-one below the age of eighteen could be employed in the production, storage or sale of drink; parents or other persons who induced a state of intoxication in a minor could be fined up to 100 rubles, or in more serious cases could be punished by up to five years' imprisonment. There were comparable penalties for those who violated the regulations governing the sale of alcohol, or who bought up and resold vodka and other alcoholic beverages. The manufacture or possession of various forms of homebrew, or simply the possession of the equipment that was necessary to produce it, could entail up to two years' corrective labour or a fine of up to 300 rubles. Drunks could be detained in police custody, and those who were found to be in a moderate or serious state of intoxication would be placed in sobering-up stations and charged the cost of their overnight stay; those who evaded voluntary treatment could be committed to rehabilitation centres for up to two years. All these and other measures, finally, were to be coordinated by revamped commissions for combating drunkenness, which were to be formed in factories and other workplaces as well as at all levels of government.[82]

The Temperance Society

The Central Committee, in its May resolution, had 'considered appropriate the formation of an all-union society of the struggle for sobriety and the publication of its printed organ'.[83] A meeting was duly convened at the beginning of August 1985 by the Central Council of Trade Unions, the Komsomol, the Academy of Sciences and the Ministry of Public Health, at which it was agreed to found an All-Union Voluntary Society for the Struggle for Temperance (VDOBT). An organising committee was formed to take responsibility for further arrangements, and Yuri Ovchinnikov, a biochemist who was vice-president of the Academy of Sciences and a candidate member of the Central Committee, was named as its first chairman.[84] Interviewed in *Pravda* later in the month, Ovchinnikov suggested it was necessary to give the temperance movement a 'truly mass, nationwide character' and to 'create in every labour collective an atmosphere of intolerance towards drunkenness and all violations of labour discipline and order'. The Society, in this context, was to be the 'party's active helper', a

mass-participation autonomous public organisation that is called upon to promote the overcoming of drunkenness, the broad development of the anti-alcohol movement in the country, the introduction into everyday life of new, socialist customs and ceremonies that exclude the use of alcohol, and the successful implementation of measures to combat this socially dangerous evil.

What would the new Society actually do? It would, for a start, promote sobriety in factories and other workplaces, in cultural and recreational centres and at places of residence throughout the USSR. Members would be required to pay particular attention to individuals with a known weakness for alcohol. The Society would seek more generally to shape public opinion, and 'clearly and convincingly disclose the harm done by alcoholic beverages and their negative effect on public and personal life'. Its members would 'resolutely counteract all propaganda of alcoholic beverages' and would help to ensure compliance with the legislation that related to drunkenness and alcoholism, eliminating homebrewing and monitoring the implementation of the regulations that governed the trade in alcohol. They would also help to develop leisure-time facilities, particularly for young people. Membership of the Society would be open to any Soviet citizen who had attained the age of eighteen and who set an 'example of abstinence from the use of alcoholic beverages and of worthy behaviour in public and private life'; there would be no 'social drinkers' within its ranks, no schoolboys, and no collective affiliations. It was, in fact, a classic 'front', giving a nominally mass and voluntary character to the promotion of party purposes; as Ovchinnikov himself made clear, it would conduct 'all its work under the direction of party committees' and would be based itself upon the principle of democratic centralism.[85]

The Society was formally established in September 1985 at a conference in Moscow.[86] The Society, it was agreed, would be responsible for assisting the party in resolving a 'problem of enormous social and political importance'. It should become an organisation of 'uncompromising enthusiasts who set an example by totally renouncing the drug alcohol and waging an active struggle for sobriety'. Its nucleus would be made up of 'advanced representatives of the working class and the collective farm peasantry who [were] able to lead others by a personal example of sobriety and an active struggle for a healthy way of life'. Members would be expected to take a particular interest in 'so-called unhappy families', providing a persuasive case for the abandonment of alcohol which would facilitate a 'breakthrough in people's psychology and behaviour and the broad introduction into everyday life of new alcohol-free traditions and customs'. Whole families, villages, settlements and cities should be encouraged to join the struggle for a sober way of life (or in effect, to adopt a 'dry law'). A 'whole network' of alcohol-free zones had been created in Azerbaijan, for instance, with recreation centres, comfortable teashops and cafes, and 'dozens of street chess clubs'.

The conference established a formal structure for the Society, based on lines that had already been made familiar by the CPSU and other Soviet mass organisations. The Society, it was agreed, would be based upon branches set up in places of work or study, or in residential areas, provided at least five members were available to constitute them. The branch would also include temperance clubs operating within medical, cultural and other institutions. The branches would be directed in their activities by district, city, regional and territorial organisations of the Society, which would in turn, come under the control of republican temperance societies. The Society's highest organ would be an all-union conference, convened every five years, which would elect a Central Council. The Society would also have a monthly publication, a revived *Trezvost' i kul'tura* (Sobriety and Culture), aimed at a mass audience and intended to be a 'mentor for people organising a healthy life and sensible, interesting leisure-time activities and in introducing alcohol-free ceremonies'. Yuri Ovchinnikov was confirmed as the Society's first chairman. In his address to the conference he described the Central Committee resolution as a 'programmatic document' for all levels of state and society, declared that it had met with 'great approval' on the part of the Soviet public, and called for the Society to unite those who were 'real enthusiasts' for the total elimination of alcohol.[87]

Within a few months – by May 1986 – the Society was already claiming 350,000 branches and about 11 million individual members. There was a somewhat uneven spread: there were branches in most industrial enterprises in the Ukraine, but in fewer than half of the corresponding enterprises in the Russian republic. Workers and collective farmers accounted for only a third of the total membership, and there were very few young people and Komsomol members.[88] This was still a remarkable rate of expansion, and the Society continued to grow: by early 1987 as many as 14 million members had been enrolled, and they were organised in 450,000 branches throughout the USSR, including over 70 per cent of all workplaces. About a quarter (24.7 per cent) of the Society's members were also members of the CPSU, and nearly half (47.8 per cent) were women; young people and Komsomol members now accounted for 23.4 per cent of the total membership, and workers for a substantial 39.7 per cent.[89] Complaints persisted that members were being recruited collectively in factories and institutes; party members were being told they had to join; and even those who drank, and said they intended to continue, were being recruited in some places[90] (workers in Penza, for instance, were told they could still drink 100 grammes of vodka 'if they had to').[91] Recruitment had been encouraged by rumours that the Society's members would not be sent to sobering-up stations if they were found in a state of intoxication. Would it end up like the lifesavers' society, asked readers of the Society's journal, which had an all but universal membership although only half of them could actually swim?[92]

The Society in fact developed a wide range of activities. It organised courses, and visits to museums, and lectures. Following earlier Soviet practices, it ran an 'agitational steamer' on the Volga and an agitational train named after the Leninist Komsomol; it held exhibitions and put out brochures. By the end of 1986 over fifty films had been forced out of the commercial repertoire because of their overly indulgent treatment of alcoholism, and cuts had been enforced in over 100 television programmes.[93] The first issue of the Society's journal, *Trezvost' i kul'tura*, appeared in January 1986; it already had 600,000 subscribers – 'rather more than we expected', according to its editor Stanislav Sheverdin.[94] The new journal, he promised, would include 'essays, articles, reportage, interviews, reviews and juridical consultations on anti-alcoholic themes'; its other themes included dressmaking and break-dancing, cartoons, crosswords and a photoclub.[95] There could be no 'harmless doses', a doctor wrote in one of its early issues, addressing himself to the supporters of 'cultured drinking'.[96] Nor was there any truth in the rumour that alcohol would increase resistance to radiation, it was explained in the aftermath of the Chernobyl explosion.[97] Equally, it was untrue that vodka improved one's sexual performance: quoting *Macbeth*, the journal explained that it 'provoked the desire but took away the performance'.[98] The Society also provided other services, among them a 'help-line' operated by its members in Tallinn.[99]

3.4   A. Rudkovich, 'Fight drunkenness!'
(poster, 1985)

What were the new temperance clubs like, and what did they actually do? Some people had much too narrow a conception of clubs of this kind, V. Morozov explained in *Komsomol'skaya pravda*, supposing them to be associations of 'ascetic fanatics or former alcoholics'. How wrong they were! In fact aiding former alcoholics was 'just a small part of the clubs' multifaceted work', which centred around the 'struggle for sobriety everywhere, at work and in everyday life'. They encouraged new and more sober ceremonies when people got married or went off on military service. The Dnepropetrovsk temperance club had prepared slide shows on sobriety for factories, schools and colleges; it held discussions on the history of temperance, and organised sporting and literary events in which 'conversations and debates are followed by the serving of tea, performances by amateur-art groups, and dancing'. They also organised nature trips and educational excursions, and distributed literature and practical recommendations of various kinds.[100] By early 1988 there were 5,000 sobriety clubs throughout the USSR, about 3,500 of them in the Russian republic.[101]

The repertoire of institutions devoted to the promotion of sobriety was completed when in early 1986 the Council of Ministers established an 'all-union research centre on the medical-biological problems of the prophylactics of drunkenness and alcoholism'.[102] The establishment of the centre followed a letter to *Pravda* from Professor Yuri Lisitsyn, a member of the USSR Academy of Medicine, in which he had called for a 'large research centre that would not only study the clinical, biological, immunological and other aspects of alcoholism, but would deal with this problem in a comprehensive fashion, as one requiring the combined efforts of demographers, statisticians, sociologists, psychologists and especially representatives of social-hygiene and public-health efforts'.[103] The new centre was based within the Serbsky Institute of General and Criminal Psychiatry (notorious, in fact, for its treatment of real or imaginary 'dissidents'); its purpose was to research the 'biological bases of the formation of a harmful attraction to spirits', hardly the broadly based remit that Lisitsyn had originally suggested.[104] Efforts were being undertaken at the same time to ensure that these new institutions were staffed by professionals with a properly combative attitude towards alcohol and its abuse. In particular, the unofficial chief spokesman of those who favoured 'cultivated drinking' rather than total abstinence, Eduard Babayan, a department head at the Ministry of Health and the country's chief narcologist, was severely reprimanded by the Party Control Committee for his 'lack of principle and inconsistency in assessing the harmful effects of alcohol on people's health' and removed from his duties.[105] The only way forward for people like Babayan, explained a member of the Temperance Society, was 'genuine public self-criticism';[106] the advocates of total abstention, meanwhile, had from this point onwards an almost unchallengeable ascendancy.

4.1 T. Nemkova, 'Happy is he who doesn't drink'
(poster, 1989)

Лучше
ПРЯНИЧАТЬ
— ЧЕМ
БРАЖНИЧАТЬ

ВИНА НЕ ПЬЁТ

4
_____

The campaign advances

Soviet campaigns, at least until the later Gorbachev years, had a number of distinct and well understood characteristics.[1] The first stage was for 'serious shortcomings' to be identified, supported by a series of apparently independent research findings and by a flood of real or if necessary fabricated letters in the press from ordinary citizens – ideally workers and mothers – demanding that 'something be done'. This prepared the ground for the second stage, which was the adoption of a resolution promising to eliminate the shortcomings that had been brought to the leadership's attention in this way, and setting out the equivalent of a 'general line' (the Central Committee resolution on alcoholism was a very clear example of this kind). The third stage, which is the subject of this chapter, sees the campaign pressed vigorously forward. Local officials, responding to the lead they have been given, compete to report the most rapid and striking successes. The central authorities, confirmed in their wisdom by these reports, are encouraged to raise their original objectives. The campaign is hailed as a decisive turning point in the press; it is taken as the theme of academic conferences and symposia; and it serves as the basis for citizen 'initiatives' of all kinds, responding with apparent enthusiasm to the strategy mapped out by a far-seeing leadership.

In the case of the campaign against alcoholism this third stage involved a number of different elements. The Sobriety Society, as we have seen, expanded rapidly, and its journal acquired a mass circulation. Opinion polls found a remarkably high level of agreement with the leadership's timely initiatives. The churches concurred; so did teachers, writers and trade unions. Statistics were published that appeared to demonstrate the campaign was having its intended effect; and a series of individual 'success stories' in the press supplied appropriate role models. This upbeat approach prevailed throughout 1985 and most of the two years that followed: this was, in effect, the 'heroic period' of the campaign.[2] Leading activists, propelled to public prominence, began to argue that the elimination of alcohol and not simply the limitation of its abuse was an immediate and practicable objective; members of the leadership, encouraged by the reports they were receiving, urged the same more radical policy. The fourth phase, involving the gradual intrusion of stubborn realities and an acknowledgement that 'not everywhere' had it succeeded, saw the campaign merged into a set of looser, less specific objectives emphasising a healthy way of life; its proponents, as in the 1930s, lost their political positions, and simple 'administrative' approaches lost ground to a more nebulous 'complex approach' not very different from the policies in place when the campaign originally began.[3]

Pressing the campaign forward

Enforcing the new laws was, in the first instance, a task for the police and court system; and from the outset they made clear that their powers would be exercised vigorously. A plenary session of the USSR Supreme Court in April 1985, before the campaign had been officially inaugurated, urged judges at all levels to 'employ all legal means to discourage drunkenness and alcoholism and to apply compulsory alcoholism treatment to chronic alcoholics'; lenient officials were to be disciplined, and those responsible for juvenile drinking were to be 'held accountable'.[4] Discussing reprieves in June, the Supreme Court decided they could be revoked if the offender was involved in the 'consumption of alcoholic beverages in public places, appearances in public in a drunken state that is offensive to human dignity and public morality, violation of labour discipline by appearing at work in a drunken state [or] consumption of alcoholic beverages on the job'.[5] At a further session in October the Supreme Court warned that a number of courts were still not 'waging a proper struggle against speculation in alcoholic beverages and against the drawing of minors into drunkenness', and made clear that there must be 'very resolute measures' to combat speculation in alcoholic beverages. Officials involved in drinking on the job must be held criminally responsible; chronic alcoholics must, where appropriate, be deprived of their parental rights or evicted from the family home; and they could properly be dismissed from their employment.[6]

Responsibility for enforcing the law rested in turn upon the police and other state or voluntary agencies. There could be 'no place for indifference' in a struggle of this kind, Boris Kravtsov, minister of justice, told Moscow radio.[7] The prosecutor general, Alexander Rekunkov, promised the 'unremitting work' of his officials to ensure that the legislation was implemented 'firmly and strictly', and that there was a 'real reduction in violations of public order'.[8] They would be taking still more 'urgent measures' against drunks and their activities, added interior minister Vitalii Fedorchuk, formerly head of the KGB in the Ukraine. In the past there had been a 'one-shot' approach to matters of this kind, with persistent signs of 'liberalism' within the ministry itself. This time, he promised, the new legislation would be applied 'strictly and unswervingly'. Who had not seen the brisk trade in liquor that went on near construction sites, industrial enterprises, dormitories and kindergartens? All of this would be ended. Not only this: the atmosphere at shops and other retail outlets would be improved, ending a situation in which drunks tended to gather around them, 'offending public morality by their behaviour'.[9] The task, Fedorchuk told *Kommunist*, was to eliminate drunkenness entirely from Soviet life and to establish sobriety as a 'conscious and universally observed norm of the socialist way of life': an objective to be achieved, not only by police action, but by the 'determined efforts of the whole society'.[10]

Speaking later in the year, the first deputy minister of internal affairs was able to tell Moscow radio that the police were already taking the 'most resolute measures' as part of an 'irreconcilable and even more energetic fight' against speculators and home brewers in particular. There were four times as many prosecutions as in the previous year,[11] and many exemplary punishments. There were death penalties for murders and other crimes committed under the influence of alcohol, and 'show trials' for habitual drunks at the factories at which they worked.[12] There were, of course, all kinds of efforts to evade the law in these circumstances: like the worker arrested by the police outside his enterprise for trying to smuggle out some industrial alcohol in a rubber tie (others were caught using hot water bottles); or the manager of a liquor store who bought 300 bottles of cognac ostensibly 'for her own use'.[13] Whatever the pretexts, Fedorchuk insisted, there would be 'no indulgence' in any matters of this kind.[14]

Much more, indeed, had to be done within government itself. The Ministry of Public Health was an early target. There had been 'flagrant violations' of the regulations that applied to patients with chronic alcoholism and 'major shortcomings' in the organisation of inpatient services, *Pravda* complained; all of this, in turn, was attributable in large part to the lax supervision that had been exercised by senior ministry officials, several of whom were sanctioned by CPSU disciplinary agencies.[15] The Russian Ministry of Inland Water Transport was another offender, the Party Control Committee reported in September 1985, with unusually high levels of absenteeism on its Yenisei line directly attributable to alcohol abuse.[16] The Ministry of Trade, a year later, was blamed for 'serious shortcomings' in the way in which sales were monitored, and for the failure to implement plans for a reduction in the sale of alcoholic drink. Some republics had been allocated higher sales targets for the first half of 1986 than they had actually recorded in the second half of the previous year; alcoholic drink was still being sold near industrial enterprises and schools, and restaurants were allowing liquor to be served to mark 'all kinds of celebrations, weddings, retirement farewells, and so on'. There were speculative sales of drink, and illegal sale to juveniles was taking place on a 'massive scale'. The trade minister was 'severely reprimanded' and the deputy trade minister and party secretary were cautioned.[17]

Official action took many forms. One of the most obvious was price control. In August 1985, as the first step, the prices of fruit juices were reduced, but the prices of vodka, cognacs, fruit and berry wines were increased substantially; the prices of beer and ordinary wines were unaffected.[18] Almost a year later, in July 1986, there were further increases of between 20 and 25 per cent in the prices of vodka, liqueurs, spirits and cognac, and rather lower increases in the price of fortified wine, with compensating reductions in the prices of a range of household and consumer goods.[19] The state plan, covering the period up to 1990, envisaged progressive reductions in the output of alcoholic drink and increasing allocations for cultural and sporting facilities.[20] The trade unions agreed a 'complex' of organisational, administrative and educational measures, including the dismissal of officials who had allowed drinking sessions to take place or had any weakness of their own.[21] The Komsomol called for the 'unconditional observation' of the Central Committee resolution, and members themselves were obliged to set an example in their 'healthy and sober way of life'.[22] There was action of a rather different kind on the cultural front, including changes in the operatic repertoire. Soviet radio shortened a scene of revelry in Verdi's *La Traviata*, and two operas were removed entirely from the Moscow repertoire because of their emphasis upon drinking; there were calls for Pushkin and Omar Khayyam to be censored.[23] There was even a cut in the film version of Sholokhov's *Fate of a Man*, at the point at which a Soviet soldier had downed a glass of vodka as a symbolic gesture of defiance towards the advancing Germans.[24]

What about the party itself? There had, in fact, for some time been proposals that members should be total abstainers. Four veterans, in the mid-1970s, wrote directly to the Central Committee about the alarming growth in alcohol abuse in the country at large, and among party members in particular. They suggested specifically that the party rules should contain a provision making it clear that drunkenness and party membership were incompatible. There was no reply from party headquarters to their suggestion, but the veterans circulated a letter, inviting comments and cooperation. Terrible things were going on in the Gorky region, they were told, but only the non-drinkers were alarmed by them. A village electrician told them how difficult it was to be that *rara avis*, an abstainer, and not for health reasons but out of conviction. Once some drunks had been so angered they had almost killed him, by trying to throw him on a bonfire. There was particular resistance to the idea that party members should be required to be total abstainers: a great many people would be excluded from it, and anyway, the veterans were told, there was no serious alcohol abuse within the party's ranks. There was no attempt to victimise the authors of the letter, as had happened in earlier times; indeed, the Central Committee eventually conveyed its gratitude to the authors, two of them Civil War veterans, for their 'concern for the fate of the party and the people. And that was that . . . '.[25] Calls for total abstinence were voiced in other sections of the party or Komsomol press, but without any obvious effect.[26]

The 27th Congress was due to consider a new version of the party rules, and in the discussion it was proposed that alcoholism should serve as grounds for expulsion.[27] There was no direct reference to alcoholism in the draft of the Party Rules that was published in November 1985, but the version agreed at the Congress included a requirement that party branches concern themselves with the Soviet patriotism and social activism of members, 'and with their sobriety'. The new version of the party programme, also adopted at the Congress, committed the CPSU to an 'unrelenting struggle against crime, drunkenness and alcoholism'.[28] Among educational and ideological measures, the party committed itself in addition to the 'steady and consistent eradication' of drunkenness together with other 'manifestations of alien ideology and morals and all negative phenomena'.[29] In its resolution on the Central Committee report the Congress noted the 'exceptionally great importance of the work to affirm a healthy way of life and to eliminate drunkenness and alcoholism which had been developed on the initiative of the Central Committee and actively supported by the Soviet people'. In the struggle with this evil there could be 'no relaxation'.[30]

Gorbachev's own report welcomed the struggle against alcoholism and drunkenness. 'In the name of the health of society and the individual', he declared, 'we have taken resolute measures – we have joined battle against tradition shaped and implanted over the centuries.' Already drunkenness had been pushed out of the workplace, and there was less of it in public places. The situation in families had improved, there were fewer on-the-job injuries, and public order had been strengthened. But there was still a need for extensive, persistent and varied work to ensure a definitive break with habits that had been established over a long period. 'There must be no indulgence here!' he concluded, to 'prolonged applause'.[31] Prime Minister Ryzkhov, in his report to the Congress on the new five-year plan, promised that the policy of reducing the production and sale of alcoholic drink would be maintained: this would facilitate a change for the better in the structure of consumption, and it would be reflected in the five-year plan and in the annual plans that were based upon it.[32] The guidelines approved by the Congress duly directed that there should be a 'persistent struggle against drunkenness and alcoholism, and also against habits harmful to people's health'; as compared with the draft published the previous November the guidelines also called for the establishment of 'sobriety as a norm of the socialist way of life'.[33]

The issue of alcoholism was raised by rank-and-file as well as more senior speakers at the Congress. A railway worker, Galina Kostenko, was concerned by the harm done by drunks, loafers, self-seekers and sloppy workers on the Baikal–Amur line on which she worked. A miner, Yuri Shatalov, welcomed the 'timely measures' that had been undertaken by the Central Committee, and was certain alcoholism would eventually be eradicated. A Ukrainian farm worker, one of the Komsomol members and Pioneers chosen to address the Congress, promised to add her efforts to the struggle to eliminate the 'weeds' of drunkenness, such as idle talk and negligence. M. I. Zhelnina, a hospital manager from Pskov, brought the warm thanks of local people, and especially women, for the 'determined struggle' that had been launched against the 'dangerous evil' of alcoholism.[34] Fewer party leaders mentioned the campaign; the Georgian first secretary, Dzhumber Patiashvili, one of those who did, spoke of sobriety as a sign of health, not only among individuals, but in social and family relations, and Mikhail Solomentsev, one of the campaign's initiators, spoke animatedly about the way in which 'some people' had been allowed to evade similar requirements in the past. Gennadii Kolbin, first secretary in Ul'yanovsk, spoke of the pioneering efforts that had been undertaken in his own area. There were assurances from Kaimran Bagirov and Semen Grossu, first secretaries in Azerbaijan and Moldavia, that viticulture in their republics would be reoriented so as to 'benefit the health of Soviet people'; the Uzbek first secretary, Usmankhodzhaev, told delegates there had even been suggestions in his own republic that the campaign was evidence the 'word of Allah' had finally reached the Kremlin leadership.[35]

The party's commitment to sobriety, in these early stages, was more than a matter of formal provision. Members, for a start, were expelled for the abuse of alcohol. Party and state officials in Orenburg region, for instance, instead of 'resolutely combating harmful traditions and habits and serving as an example in establishing a sober way of life', had concluded a district party conference with a banquet at which alcohol had been served. The district first secretary, his deputy, and the chairman of the local soviet were expelled from the CPSU entirely; the other participants were subject to party sanctions of a less drastic kind.[36] Another scandal took place in Lipetsk, at a retirement dinner for the deputy director of the local hospital at which alcohol had been served and costly presents handed over to mark the occasion. There were severe party reprimands for four of the revellers, all of whom were dismissed; the deputy director would have been expelled from the party altogether, but she had given the colour television she received to a children's home and escaped with a warning.[37] In Perm', where the regional council had authorised the sale of alcohol near factories and railway stations, there were 'severe reprimands' for the three party members who were responsible.[38] And still larger numbers could be involved: in Vinnitsa region, for instance, 74 party officials were expelled in connection with the campaign,[39] in Belgorod 182 were expelled and 220 severely reprimanded, in Tambov 253 were expelled in 1986 and another 353 the following year,[40] and in Ul'yanovsk more than 1,000 were expelled over three years.[41]

Reviewing progress in September 1985, the Politburo agreed that the establishment of sobriety was a 'most important party and state task' that must be accomplished 'firmly and unswervingly'.[42] In a more extended statement published a few days later the Central Committee claimed that the campaign had received the 'full approval and support of the Soviet people' and that efforts to implement it were 'gaining momentum every-where'. Officials were being required to set an example; a national temperance society was being established; laws were being tightened; and consumer demand was moving away from alcohol and towards juices, foodstuffs and other consumer goods. But the campaign was 'just beginning', and there were 'no grounds for complacency'. A certain section of the population 'among those having a weakness for alcoholic beverages' was still resisting the attempt to strengthen more sober attitudes and practices. There were still party officials who had failed to understand the 'exceptional political and social significance' of over-coming drunkenness and alcoholism, and who limited themselves to 'one-shot' campaigns that were not sufficiently directed against 'specific wrongdoers – drunkards, home brewers and speculators'. Party members should themselves set an example, and party committees should develop an 'aggressive struggle against drunkenness and alcoholism'.[43]

Some members of the leadership were even more insistent on rapid results. Ligachev, the campaign's chief sponsor, spoke in September 1985 of a 'powerful social movement for the elimination of drunkenness' which was 'gaining strength' and acquiring 'concrete organisational forms' such as the newly established temperance society, which must develop a network of local affiliates 'as quickly as possible'. The 'positive results' of the campaign, Ligachev insisted, were the outcome, not simply of the restrictions that had been imposed, but of a 'positive choice in favour of the sober way of life'.[44] Speaking to local party officials in July 1985, he explained that the struggle with alcoholism was not a 'short-lived campaign' and insisted that there be no 'leniency' towards members who violated the party's decisions on these matters.[45] Ligachev was present at a conference in party headquarters in June 1986 at which several areas had been criticised for being content with the 'first, partial results' of the campaign, and for having 'recently slackened off their work'.[46] Ligachev attended a conference later in the year which noted that the work that was being undertaken to 'normalise the moral atmosphere in the country' was 'gaining momentum', with crime, absenteeism and road accidents all reduced. But there were no grounds for complacency, particularly in the face of the increase that had occurred in illegal distilling and in domestic alcoholism; and there were 'serious shortcomings' in the work of law enforcement bodies and medical institutions, which in some cases were placing too much emphasis upon purely administrative methods.[47]

All members of the leadership, however, were concerned to defend the first results of the campaign, both in party meetings and in direct exchanges with the public. Ligachev, for instance, gave the annual address on the eve of the anniversary of the revolution in November 1986. Just a year and a half had passed since the resolution, he noted: and yet wine and vodka consumption were down by a third, absenteeism was down by the same proportion, and crime had fallen by a quarter. The economic benefits from these changes were close to compensating for the loss of revenue that had been incurred. But could the gains be measured only in rubles? How many lives had been saved, and how many families preserved? Relying on the support of an 'absolute majority of the Soviet people', Ligachev promised, the party would 'steadfastly eradicate drunkenness, alcoholism and drug addiction and affirm a sober way of life'.[48] Gorbachev, speaking to journalists in March 1986, told them that ordinary people, in their letters to the party and to the newspapers, had warmly supported the leadership's proposals.[49] The campaign, he told

4.2   Children at a Leningrad school showing their anti-alcoholism posters on national TV, 1987
(Novosti)

the Central Committee in June, was one of the party's 'most urgent tasks', and it was their duty to 'carry out the mandate of the Soviet people'.[50] Speaking to local people in Vladivostok, he took a similar line. Women, he told his audience, had been writing to tell him that at last their husbands had seen their children, and they themselves had seen their husbands. The number of fatal accidents had fallen by a fifth in a single year, and there were fewer divorces. 'Do you grasp what I'm telling you?', he asked them: 'we cannot retreat on this matter'.[51]

From policy to practice

Government directives have always been central to public campaigns against alcohol abuse; and they were particularly important under Soviet conditions. In a state-owned economy, enterprises could simply be instructed to reprofile their production. Prices could be raised and lowered. Shops and restaurants could be required to open at particular hours, and to sell – or not to sell – particular products to particular sections of the population. The courts, the police and even the armed forces could – in a system with a single ruling party – be required to carry out the directives of the leadership, even if they appeared to have been poorly conceived or to infringe the liberties of the citizen. And yet party members were a small minority – less than 10 per cent – of the total adult population. Workplaces could be controlled through trade unions and management, but it was less easy to reach into the home environment. Towns were easier to monitor than the countryside; and smaller towns fell less often under the scrutiny of the leadership than large ones, above all the capital. It was clear, for these reasons, that the campaign would have to take effect in families and neighbourhoods if it was to be successful, and that it would have to engage the support and cooperation of the public at large. Drunkenness would only be eliminated, as Gorbachev explained, 'if we throw ourselves into the task wholeheartedly. If we carry it out tirelessly, determinedly, accepting no compromises'.[52] How did things appear to be going, a year or two into the campaign?

Better in some areas than in others, as early investigations made clear. And not well at all in the central Russian region of Yaroslavl', where by September 1985 there was already concern that it had been a 'one-off campaign'. All kinds of plans had been drawn up, journalists found, but they were vague and almost always identical. *Sovetskaya Rossiya*'s reporters were 'astonished' by the scenes that met their eyes in the town of Uglich on what had been declared an 'alcohol-free day'. Not a single store was selling liquor, but the doors of a local restaurant were 'barely holding up under the press of those wanting to enter'. It was only midday, but there 'wasn't room to swing a cat in the crowded room'. The tables were packed with the 'flabby, pale faces of people who had come to "clear their heads" of hangovers'. On Sundays the stadiums were empty, and well-equipped gymnasia were under lock and key. In the Uglich Watch Factory's half-empty Palace of Culture journalists spoke to its director, V. Shishkin, who was making preparations for an alcohol-free wedding. Unfortunately, Shishkin explained, 'we can't find a couple to marry.' Alcohol consumption in the region had fallen off sharply in June, immediately after the Central Committee resolution: but in July and August it had risen to levels that were even higher than those of a year before, in a region in which levels of consumption were already well above the Russian average.[53]

There were further problems in the Vinnitsa region in the Ukraine, according to an investigation that was organised by two committees of the USSR Supreme Soviet. There had been little attempt to put the resolution into effect, legislators reported in February 1986, and there had been no significant decline in alcohol consumption. There were only 'feeble efforts' to increase the responsibility of managers and officials, and in many workplaces there was a 'permissive attitude' towards habitual absenteeism and a lack of principle in meting out punishment for violations of the law'. The addiction services available to the public were most unsatisfactory, and the courts had 'not always been effective' in ensuring that offenders were punished with the full rigour of the law. Not only in Vinnitsa but in other regions as well there had been no real effort to expand the output of non-alcoholic drink, and the rules governing the sales of wines and liquors were being 'flagrantly violated'.[54] There were similar shortcomings in Bryansk, according to a report that appeared in December 1985. The regional authorities had reported a 'hard and determined offensive' against alcoholism to their superiors; it emerged that local drinkers had, in fact, enjoyed a 'strange invulnerability', and that local efforts to reduce abuses had been a 'fiasco'. Levels of alcohol consumption were meanwhile among the highest in Russia, with consumption of moonshine 'particularly widespread'.[55]

There were several more spectacular cases. A 'collective binge' in the Udmurt republic, for instance, was reported by Moscow radio in November 1985, based upon the experience of a group of seasonal workers who had been travelling there to assist with the harvest. 'Hardly had the platform disappeared from view through the passenger car windows', it was reported, 'than vodka appeared on the tables.' Some of the workers started to sing; 'the vodka flowed freely, but a sense of responsibility on the part of those in charge was in rather short supply'. The police were finally obliged to intervene: two of the revellers were detained, but the others were left to help local farmers in a 'virtually irremediable condition: for two days they wandered around like flies in winter, barely able to walk, let alone perform any work'.[56] There was a further scandal in the oil town of Tyumen', where alcohol was being sold in the refreshment bars of local party and government headquarters.[57] Had the campaign been wound up, asked several letters in the papers? In Podol'sk, wrote I. Tarasenkov, 'things are the same as before: vodka is sold from 8 in the morning until late at night . . . We have appealed to the city party committee, but in vain.'[58] In many other places, it appeared, the struggle against alcoholism was already losing its urgency: a few shops had been closed, the drunks had been given a 'good warning', a few had been sent to the doctor, and that was that. Now all over the country drunks had 'started again to organise noisy drinking parties, where they were proposing toasts to the thaw in the anti-alcohol campaign'.[59]

Cases of this kind, however, were still in a minority; much more common, in the first year or two, were reports that gave a very different and much more encouraging impression. Moscow radio reported a particularly striking success in the Kirov region, 'until recently . . . one of the hardest-drinking regions of the Russian Federation'. By May 1986, when the report was broadcast, the party had assumed control and there had been noticeable results, including a 'sharp fall' in alcohol consumption. The crime rate had fallen, and so had the level of hooliganism. Above all, there had been a 'change in attitude – to be drunk in the street [had] become a cause for shame'.[60] There was good news from Kursk, where sobriety was 'becoming the norm of life'.[61] In Donetsk, miners had 'decided, as a brigade, to give up drinking altogether'; now they were all abstainers who spent their spare time on the sports field.[62] At the No. 1 Motor Vehicle Combine in Moscow drivers were being 'checked almost as scrupulously as cosmonauts' before they took to the road.[63] In L'vov, community meetings were being held at which notorious drunks, 'finding their words with some difficulty', were affirming their commitment to total sobriety; there were fewer drunks on the streets, the children's play areas had been repaired, and chess clubs were operating again.[64] In Sochi, the restaurants and bars were selling record numbers of 'fruit and milk cocktails, juices, non-alcohol drinks, ice cream and confectionery'.[65] In Yaroslavl', the number of drunks detained in local sobering-up stations had fallen so much some of them had to be closed for lack of 'patients'.[66]

Whole areas had turned over a new leaf, according to a report in the party press from the secretary of the party organisation in a bloodstock farm. What welcome changes were coming over the village! The streets were cleaner, there were new houses, a sporting complex had been built. But most of all, there had been a cultural, even spiritual improvement; people taking a greater part in public life, and above all, taking a much more uncompromising view of drunkenness and the social ills to which it gave rise. The local party had decided to take the matter seriously. Anti-alcoholic propaganda, it was agreed, would be 'aggressive'. Violators would be exposed in their workplaces. A raiding party was formed to root out homebrewers, who were subjected to 'show trials' and exemplary punishment. A village meeting agreed to list the 'lovers of spirits' in the local shop, and to refuse to sell them vodka or wine. Later it was agreed not to sell alcohol in any form in the area. Medical workers arrived, explaining the harmfulness of drinking 'even in small doses'; more positively, a choir was formed, and a folklore ensemble. And what was the result? Homebrewing had been eliminated, drunkenness itself was on the way out, and 'for the past two months there had not been a single case of an appearance at work in a state of intoxication'.[67] In a Tula metallurgical factory there was a very similar picture: offenders were displayed on a noticeboard and if necessary dismissed; the factory, meanwhile, 'fulfilled and overfulfilled the state output plan'.[68]

Homebrewing was beginning to yield its place in other areas as well, according to a report that appeared in June 1985 from the village of Yastrebovo in Belgorod region, where 'for some time large numbers of the male population' had been 'noticeably unsteady on their feet'. The police and a volunteer force soon identified the problem: 'the house of Baba Sonya, a very active and profit-motivated distributor of intoxicating poison among the local population'.[69] There were also voluntary surrenders of homebrewing equipment, as *Izvestiya*'s correspondent discovered in the Chuvash republic. Several thousand stills had been turned over: 'every kind of infernal machine', from washtubs and milk cans to samovars and tea kettles, held together by coils of glass, stainless steel and 'several kilometres' of non-ferrous metal. There were more than a hundred different designs, some of them 'real inventions'. In one village the chairman of the rural soviet had led the surrender, followed by the chief engineer, the bookkeeper, the veterinarian and the police auxiliaries. 'Have you ever seen such a thing', asked the older women, crossing themselves, 'people turning in a source of drink of their own free will?' In some villages, it emerged, nearly every home had been making its own brew. Most were surrendered voluntarily; others were recovered from ravines and garden plots. When homebrewing was at its peak, the correspondent was told, 'some of the villages reeked so strongly of home-made spirits and beer that even the chickens walked around drunk'.[70]

There were several, rather more individual successes to report. There was a 'certain milkmaid' in the Saratov region who had been 'wasting away' through her alcoholism; colleagues sought to persuade her of the error of her ways, 'particularly on payday', and now she was one of the best milkmaids in the area who had 'fulfilled the five-year plan ahead of schedule'.[71] A military academy graduate from Perm', G. Kirov, had been a respected commander at the early age of twenty-six and 'life seemed fine'. Then suddenly he fell ill, and was pronounced unfit for peacetime service. He found it difficult to settle down in civilian life, and began to drown his sorrows in vodka. He was on a downward slide when he met a 'remarkable person and genuine Bolshevik' who had persuaded him to seek a cure. Now he had taken no drink for several years, and worked on a livestock farm; he was one of the first to join the local branch of the temperance society.[72] Or there was 33-year-old Yurik. At ten he was already sampling vodka and from that age had become attached to the 'green serpent'. He drank everything he could get: eau de cologne, varnish, glue, window cleaner, even brake fluid. Unable to understand he was slipping into an abyss and with 'friends' who were unable to help him, he dropped out of college and found it impossible to keep a job. Doctors gave him weeks to live. Then, at last, he gave it all up, started running (friends joked that he was 'training for the Olympics'), and in seven years hadn't touched a drop. He was now the moving spirit in a Riga temperance club.[73] The temperance journal featured a series of such stories in a column, 'I have given up spirits', a number of whom claimed to have been literally 'born again'.[74]

Some other cases were even more directly biblical in the account they offered of redemption through love. There was Suzanne, for instance, who had met Oleg at a friend's party. A drink was proposed. To her surprise, Oleg refused: if his girl didn't drink, neither would he. The evening went well. But her joy was premature. She began to see Oleg more and more frequently, but he was always drunk, and then he vanished entirely. A week later she received a postcard, urging her to forget him and find happiness with someone else. It had come from a hospital. Somehow or other she found the hospital, and then found his bed. 'Why did you come?', he asked. She would have left; but already she knew – she loved Oleg, and he loved her. She decided to stay. Then Oleg asked her to sit closer, and told her: 'Help me. Save me. If you leave me, I will die.' What could she say? But she was overwhelmed with joy at the thought that Oleg needed her, and that she could help him to live a normal life. Oleg spent two months in the hospital, with Suzanne in attendance every day. He proposed marriage; she accepted. But what about the festivities? Would he agree to a non-alcoholic wedding? He did, despite the remonstrations of some of their relatives. And best of all were his words: 'Darling, what would have happened to me, if it hadn't been for you . . . '. A year later their joy was complete when a son was born; he could never guess, wrote Suzanne, how difficult it had been for his parents to find simple human happiness.[75]

The temperance journal, seeking to inspire by example, carried a series of interviews with the famous and respected on their decision to abstain from alcohol. The chess player Gary Kasparov told the magazine he had 'never experienced a wish for spirits'.[76] The writer Vasilii Belov, a USSR people's deputy, directly advocated a 'dry law'. How, he asked, could a narcotic substance be consumed in a 'civilised manner', as some had suggested? People, he believed, 'wholeheartedly accept[ed] the resolution of the Party Central Committee and government' and looked forward to 'even more resolute, even more radical measures'.[77] In a later interview he directly criticised members of the Politburo – Lev Zaikov, Alexander Yakovlev, Alexandra Biryukova, even Gorbachev himself – for their indifference or even support of 'cultured drinking'.[78] Another writer, Valentin Pikul', was interviewed in early 1986; there was a poem by Andrei Vosnesensky; and Chingiz Aitmatov followed in 1987.[79] Andrei Sakharov was interviewed some years later: the Nobel prizewinner, in a brief conversation, confirmed that he neither smoked nor drank.[80] Another prominent figure to be featured was the pop star Alla Pugacheva, who was a specially invited guest at a Soviet–US conference on alcoholism and drug addiction; rather later they interviewed Elton John.[81] The writer Anatolii Rybakov, famous for his controversial novel *Deti Arbata*, agreed that the 'uncontrolled alcoholisation' of the country from the 1950s to the 1970s was 'to a certain extent' the outcome of the Stalinism of earlier years, and of the 'psychological climate' that had been created.[82] Some wrote directly to *Pravda* to express their thanks for the 'uncompromising war on drunkenness' that had been declared under its auspices. When the decree had been published, wrote V. Abramov, a cloakroom attendant from Leningrad, he and others had expected a short-lived campaign and that after a week or two everything would revert to normal. Now it was clear they had all been 'deeply mistaken'.[83]

And we've got the figures to prove it

Soviet statistics were often called 'success indicators' and success was usually what they indicated. It was certainly essential to a successful campaign that there should be some early evidence of progress, both to confirm that the strategy had been well conceived and to reinforce the morale of those who were conducting it. Alcohol statistics were particularly suitable for recording successes of this kind. Figures for total output were the responsibility of the state itself, and could be reduced by government directive. Figures for the output of homebrew and other unauthorised forms of alcohol were necessarily estimates which could easily be manipulated. Alcohol was normally one of a number of circumstances connected with industrial accidents, road deaths, suicides and so forth, and again the figures could be adjusted so as to demonstrate whatever was necessary. Local officials, in no doubt about what the central authorities wanted to hear; were strongly encouraged to exaggerate their successes and underreport their failures; and academics were encouraged to frame their survey questions in a way that was likely to elicit a suitable response (how, in any case, could you ask people if they drank illicit alcohol, or if they made it themselves?).[84] Statistics of this kind are, of course, of varying validity in many countries;[85] combined with the pressures of a Soviet campaign, they soon began to cooperate.

The first priority was to reduce the level of production of alcoholic drinks, and this was relatively easily achieved. Interviewed a few months after the decree had been adopted, the Ministry of the Food Industry was able to report that liquor output was being cut 'drastically', first of all vodka and low-grade wine, but in addition the output of champagne, grape wines and beer had been reduced. The cutback in production was already ahead of the requirements of the Council of Ministers decree; the factories that had discontinued the production of alcoholic drink were being converted to fruit juices and confectionery; others still would process fodder for animal husbandry. There had even been progress in developing a low-alcohol wine and champagne, although unfortunately

4.3   'What do you mean an illegal meeting – they've brought the portwine!'
(*Krokodil*, no. 33, 1988)

'some of the substances that give the wine its taste and aroma [evaporated] from it along with the alcohol'.[86] The first statistical yearbook of the Gorbachev administration appeared in October 1986; interviewed in the press, the head of the Central Statistical Administration drew attention to the figures that had for the first time been provided on the sale of vodka and liquors. Production of these items had totalled 281 million decalitres in 1984, but just 238 million in 1985. During the first year of the campaign, from June 1985 to May 1986, the output of vodka and liquors had declined by 33 per cent, of grape wine by 32 per cent, of fruit and berry wines by 68 per cent, and cognac production by 44 per cent.[87] Not only were production and consumption falling: so too was the potential for future production. The area of fruit and berry plantations fell from 3.4 million hectares in 1980 to 2.9 million in 1988, and the area of vineyards fell in parallel from 1.3 to 1.1 million hectares in 1988.[88]

Further batches of statistics strengthened this reassuring impression. The output of alcoholic drinks, for a start, continued to fall sharply (see Table 4.1). Champagne, cognac and beer held their ground, but by 1987 the production of vodka, other hard liquor and wine was less than half the level that had been attained in 1980, and very much less than the levels that had been projected in the original decrees. The estimated output of home-made wines also fell, though less dramatically.[89] The sale of alcoholic drink through the state and cooperative retail network, including public catering, fell by half between 1984 and 1988;[90] levels of consumption were already a third or even a quarter of the corresponding figures for France, Italy, Belgium and Austria, and the Soviet Union, once among the leaders, now ranked second last in Europe in its total alcoholic consumption.[91] Per capita sales in terms of pure alcohol were just 3.7 litres in 1988, as compared with 8.4 litres in 1984; the share of alcoholic drink in all retail sales fell from 16.7 per cent in 1984 to 10.7 per cent in 1987; and the share of family income that went on alcoholic beverages, for all social groups, fell very substantially.[92] Alcoholic beverages more generally fell from 4.3 per cent of all consumer purchases in 1980 to just 2 per cent in 1988.[93]

There was good news of various other kinds as well. Crime was down, for a start. The campaign against drunkenness and alcoholism, the USSR Supreme Court was told, had led to a 'substantial decrease' in convictions for premeditated murder, rape, hooliganism and other serious crimes connected with drunkenness (there had however been no noticeable reduction in convictions for less serious crimes, and convictions for

Table 4.1. *Production of selected alcoholic beverages, 1980–1988 (million decalitres)*

	1980	1985	1986	1987	1988
Vodka/spirits	295	238	147	123	142
Wine (grape)	323	265	141	147	179
Champagne (m. bottles)	178	248	195	235	258
Cognac	9.4	7.0	6.7	9.5	11.8
Beer	613	657	489	507	558

Source: Derived from *Narodnoe khozyaistvo SSSR v 1989 g.* (Moscow: Finansy i statistika, 1990), p. 497.

homebrewing had increased as a result of greater vigilance).[94] According to the Central Statistical Administration, crime of all kinds fell by 25 per cent during 1986, road accidents were down by 20 per cent and absenteeism at work fell by about a third; serious crime in Russia alone was down by 36 per cent in the three years since the launch of the campaign.[95] The proportion of all crimes that were committed in a state of intoxication fell at the same time, from 53 per cent in the early 1980s to 49 per cent in 1985.[96] Absenteeism was down by more than a quarter as a direct result of the campaign, according to official sources, and there were fewer dismissals as a result of violations of the labour law.[97] And there was a fall in the number of drink-related fatalities on the roads: there were fewer accidents, fewer deaths and fewer casualties.[98]

Perhaps most important of all, the first years of the campaign brought about a considerable improvement in public health statistics. The death rate, for a start, fell in 1986 for the first time for many years. The mortality rate in 1984 was 510 per 1,000, but it fell in 1986 to 432 – a 15 per cent improvement, largely attributable to the campaign against alcohol abuse. Deaths caused by accidents at work – often associated with alcohol – fell by a third, and fatal heart diseases, which were worsened by drinking, fell from 143 per 100,000 in 1984 to 125 in 1986.[99] Deaths from alcoholic poisoning were down by more than half in just two years;[100] deaths that were associated with alcohol abuse more generally fell by the same proportion.[101] More positively, the birth rate went up; so did the proportion of all births that were healthy, and the proportion that survived the first year of life.[102] There were fewer divorces, and fewer that were associated with alcohol abuse.[103] Life expectancy, reflecting these and other changes, began to stabilise and then to improve; the average expectation for women increased by more than a year between 1984 and 1987, and for men it went up by more than three years.[104]

Although almost all of the relevant indicators pointed in the same direction, there were still considerable regional variations. Levels of mortality remained highest, as before, among the Slavic and Baltic nations, and lowest among the peoples of Central Asia and the Caucasus; yet in every case there was an improvement.[105] The figures reported in the press were, almost inevitably, an overstatement of the improvement in public health that had in fact occurred. The reduction in the number of alcohol-related divorces, for a start, could scarcely be explained by changes in legislation over the previous few months; the number of divorces actually increased in 1986, and the fall in the number of cases related to alcohol appeared to owe something to the work of specially established 'reconciliation commissions' as well as to a clear reluctance on the part of the authorities to accept petitions couched in these terms.[106] And there were cases of actual falsification of the data.[107] The increased cost of state-produced alcohol, together with the reduction in its availability, led at the same time to a massive increase in illegal distilling of perhaps 40 per cent in 1986 alone. This meant that the fall in total alcohol consumption had been more like 23–25 per cent than the 50 per cent reported in official sources; but this was still a reduction greater than any other country had achieved other than at times of war or total prohibition.[108]

In some ways most important of all, there were signs of real change in public attitudes. Earlier studies had shown relatively little support for the kind of decisive measures that had now been taken; there were 'overwhelming majorities' against any restrictions upon consumption, according to the surveys taken at the time, with just 5 per cent of men and 13 per cent of women, in other studies, favouring a policy of prohibition.[109] There was, throughout, a deep ambiguity in popular responses: people were willing to condemn alcoholism as a social evil, and yet reluctant to make the personal commitment to sobriety that its elimination would have required. The temperance campaigner, Fedor Uglov, conducted a regular experiment on this basis. After his lecture, he asked who would support a dry law: 'as a rule, the overwhelming majority'. He then asked who would be ready, the next day, to accept its requirements for themselves. 'After a long pause in the auditorium only a few, mainly female hands [were] hesitantly raised'.[110]

Attitudes of this kind appeared to be changing, if the surveys conducted after the campaign had been initiated were any guide. By late 1985, 11 per cent of those who were asked had given up drink altogether, and 34 per cent were drinking less.[111] Another survey, conducted a year after the campaign was launched, found that 8 per cent had given up alcohol altogether, and another 30 per cent, particularly those with families, had cut down on the amount they consumed (a recalcitrant 15 per cent said that 'nothing had changed for them during the year and that their attitude towards alcohol remained unchanged'). The measures themselves were widely welcomed: 49 per cent agreed with them, 26 per cent said they should be even stricter, and only 1 per cent disapproved. Only 12 per cent had not recently seen an instance of drunkenness; but half of those polled thought the atmosphere in workplaces was much improved. Drinking was still a mass occupation: 78 per cent of the urban population drank on holidays, and approximately the same proportion served drink on family occasions; 16 per cent celebrated paydays and bonuses in the traditional manner, and 15 per cent celebrated a new purchase in the same way. There was moreover a 'widespread view' that alcohol was not harmful, and one in ten thought the limited use of alcohol was actually good for them; a large majority (65 per cent) was nonetheless convinced that this time alcoholism would finally be 'liquidated'.[112] In Kiev, there were 'hundreds of letters' from grateful citizens in support of the new policy.[113] In Sverdlovsk, 18 per cent of men and 31 per cent of women supported a total ban;[114] in a district of Novosibirsk, as many as 85 per cent of those who were asked favoured a total ban on sales;[115] in Tomsk, 89 per cent took the same view.[116]

A particularly thorough investigation in the Urals city of Chelyabinsk, carried out after the 1985 decree and again in 1987, found that a great number of liquor shops and beer bars had closed, 'sobriety zones' had appeared, propaganda in favour of a healthy way of life had been intensified, and local people had begun to 'develop a critical attitude to the use of alcohol'. Over the two years, 13 per cent of the industrial and agricultural workers who were surveyed had given up spending on alcohol altogether, while another 35 per cent had substantially reduced their expenditure. Nearly half of those surveyed noted an improvement in the level of absenteeism, 42 per cent noted better labour discipline, and 32 per cent reported better labour productivity. There was also a better 'moral-political climate', with a significant fall in the number of family conflicts. In 1985 56 per cent of those they asked thought they could not celebrate a special occasion without the use of alcohol; by 1987 the proportion was down to 31 per cent, and 11 per cent had made it a

4.4   A. Lozenko, 'Drunkenness is suicide'
(poster, 1988)

rule to organise family celebrations without alcohol. There was some feeling that the campaign had already begun to lose impetus, particularly in the towns, but there was nonetheless strong support for the measures themselves, particularly in rural areas. Overall, 86 per cent of those who were asked supported 'severe sanctions' against drunks, and an increasing proportion sought 'more decisive action'.[117]

Early results, in fact, were so encouraging that a very wide section of opinion both inside and outside the USSR was persuaded to believe a remarkable success might be within their grasp. The Ministry of Health had insisted from the outset that the aim was not a 'strengthening of the struggle with alcoholism and drunkenness, but a complete emancipation from this socially dangerous evil'.[118] The struggle to eliminate its influence, the deputy chairman of the journalists' union insisted, would go on until drunkenness and alcoholism had been 'completely eradicated'.[119] Village meetings were encouraged to take the initiative, limiting the sale of drink still further, sometimes naming particular individuals to whom it was not to be sold or banning its sale altogether.[120] Local officials took up the cause, competing with each other to introduce 'dry months' in the areas for which they were responsible';[121] the leadership, for its part, left no room for doubt about what it wanted to hear, calling (as Ligachev did in late 1985) for sobriety zones to be established and 'the sooner, the better', or even for total prohibition.[122] Foreign correspondents accepted that there had been 'positive and sometimes spectacular results' after a single year, with the new laws 'fairly widely observed'.[123] Other reports acknowledged that the resolutions were 'having some effect', and that the whole campaign was more than the short-term effort that had been expected at the time.[124] For the most committed abolitionists there was a real prospect, for the first time in Russian history, of the permanent elimination of alcohol consumption within five years, or at least (as a Ukrainian government minister publicly predicted) by the year 2000.[125]

5.1   Waiting for opening time, 1988

5
_____

The campaign retreats

If the third stage of a Soviet campaign was typically an affirmation of success 'in principle', the fourth stage generally began with an acknowledgement that central objectives had 'not everywhere' been achieved and that there was a greater need to move 'from words to action'. The Central Committee itself marked the beginning of this new stage with an authoritative statement on the progress of the campaign which was published in June 1987, following a Politburo discussion.[1] Although a substantial amount of work had been done to establish a sober way of life, the necessary efforts were 'not being conducted everywhere with the proper perseverance, aggressiveness and consistency'. Party and state officials had lost interest in the campaign (some were 'themselves partial to the vice'), and there had more generally been a failure to understand that its objectives could not be eliminated 'at a single stroke, by noisy, short-term campaigns'. There had been 'no breakthrough' in the work of government, and law enforcement agencies had failed to display the 'proper activism'. There had even been an increase in the output of drink itself. The 'noble cause of establishing sobriety as a norm of our life', the resolution insisted, 'would be sustained until its conclusion'; and yet there was already a substantial body of evidence that the campaign had run into difficulties so serious that its future was already in doubt.

Centre, localities and authority leakage

The campaign had certainly been launched, but was it being implemented consistently down the line? According to the reports that reached the Central Committee, there were some conspicuous exceptions. In Karelia, Krasnodar and Poltava, it was reported in

September 1987, local party and state bodies 'after achieving certain positive results' had lost interest in the campaign. Commissions to combat drunkenness had been set up, but many were inactive and some had ceased to operate altogether. The level of consumption of alcohol remained high, and there had been a slowdown in the planned reduction in the sale of drink. In Poltava, the sale of certain kinds of alcoholic drink had actually increased in the first six months of the year; in Krasnodar more wine had been sold, the commercial network for selling drink had been expanded by a fifth, and restrictions on the sale of alcohol in restaurants had been removed. In Sochi, sales of wine, cognac and champagne had increased substantially. And in all of these areas, there had been little effort to expand the production of non-alcoholic drink and other goods to compensate for the loss of retail sales. The prevalence of homebrewing was a cause of particular concern. In Poltava, for instance, over 36,000 stills had already been confiscated, and sugar had all but disappeared from the shops. The police had shown undue leniency towards those who were guilty of violating the law; and in Krasnodar more than 200 had themselves been charged with alcohol-related offences. Nor was the party itself setting a worthy example; in Karelia 279 members had been apprehended in a drunken state, including 10 senior officials; there were even party officials who had homebrew delivered to them in their offices.[2]

There were similar problems in the industrial city of Perm', where the local party committee had not given an 'aggressive or large-scale character' to the campaign against alcoholism. Attitudes of 'complacency and liberalism' were still in evidence, and drunkenness itself was 'widespread'. Many were unaware that official policies had changed; and the chairman of the regional soviet had personally authorised the sale of drink near factories and cinemas, railway terminals and airports.[3] There was further criticism of party organisations in the Bashkir, Tyumen', Voroshilovgrad and other areas for 'relaxing their struggle against drunkenness and alcoholism'. The struggle against homebrewing was going badly, and coupons for the sale of intoxicating drinks had been introduced in a number of places 'under the guise of combating drunkenness'. This made even non-drinkers take to alcohol and led to speculation in the coupons themselves.[4] Alcoholics started to buy up coupons, or steal them; or they took their family's food coupons and exchanged them for alcohol coupons. In Petrozavodsk, even officials of the local temperance society had been supplied with coupons of this kind; in Chita, they were issued with voting papers; in Tajikistan, party officials manufactured their own.[5] Elsewhere only the 'most worthy' were given coupons, which had the effect of raising the prestige of drinking not reducing it.[6] In Tatarstan, it was later discovered, the party headquarters had incorporated an entire underground liquor factory.[7]

Party members themselves set a somewhat disappointing example. There was, for instance, a village called Novaya Budnya in Chernigov region in the Ukraine. In early 1987 an inspection team from the district administration called in to have a look at the sober life the local people were supposed to be living.

What the controllers found was something else – 'infernal machines' which, before their very eyes, ran sugar into brew and brew into full-proof moonshine. You would never guess [the report went on] who turned out to be the owner of the home-made miracle-working machine. It was M. M. Sodyl, a Communist and leader of a crop-growing team, a member of the local organisation of the Sobriety Society, and in addition a deputy on the Nedanchinsky village soviet. Believe it or not [the paper commented], at this 'teetotaller's' premises the controllers found 80 litres of moonshine and 17 litres of 45-degree first-grade hooch.

This, however, was a modest haul compared with what the controllers found on the premises of three of his neighbours, one of them also a party member: no less than 240 litres of semi-finished moonshine together with three sizeable containers ready for consumption. This was 'something of a record'.[8] A survey in Novosibirsk found that only 3 per cent of party members were active abstainers, rather fewer than among the local population as a whole; the local view was that 'a Communist is also a human being'.[9]

The Soviet ambassador to Bangladesh, Vitalii Smirnov, was one of those still prepared to argue in 1990 for total abstinence within the party. If the CPSU had been a party of non-drinkers, Smirnov told *Moskovskie novosti*, 'how high its authority among the people would have been!' Now that the constitutionally guaranteed leading role had been abandoned, the party would maintain its position only if members were able to reform their own behaviour. In this connection, he suggested adding a formal provision to the party rules to the effect that the Communist was 'obliged to lead a healthy way of life and under no circumstances to consume spirits or drugs'. The difficult years of revolution and civil war, Smirnov noted, had been the most sober in the party's history, and the ones in which the party had enjoyed its greatest authority. The drunkenness of the 1970s, by contrast, had led to stagnation and a serious loss of party authority, and in many of the countries allied to the Soviet Union their leaders – like Tsedenbal and the Afghan leader Babrak Karmal – had drunk to excess, corrupted their immediate circle and lost the trust of their own people. The CPSU, he concluded, should be a 'party of non-drinking Communists'; every Soviet person would want his son or daughter to be a member of such a party, and to fight for the realisation of its ideals.[10] Another view was that party members should, at least in most cases, be members of the temperance society, and that the rules should make clear that even 'cultured drinking' and party membership were incompatible.[11]

A subscriber to the temperance society's journal, who was also a party member, asked other readers what they thought of his proposal that the new version of the CPSU rules should include a provision that 'The Communist is obliged to lead a sober way of life.' Of the 222 replies he received only 3 were against, and many had a bitter experience to report. One of the party members who replied had been sent to a psychiatric hospital after he had denounced a city manager in Kaliningrad who 'took a drop'. Others testified to a 'wall of indifference' whenever they raised the subject. Four of them, for instance, had written a letter calling for a regime of sobriety within the party; the reaction of local officials was 'What is this? Making accusations against the Party? You obviously think it's in need of sobering up!' Marx, admittedly, had drunk; but 'Marx lived at a time when little was known about alcohol and its insidious effects.' For another correspondent, two-thirds of the party membership were drunks; yet another thought it 'time to call the whole Communist leadership to account for its sabotage of the anti-alcohol platform of the CPSU'.[12] Party members, it emerged, had kept their distance from the temperance society, and no more than a fifth of its members had joined up.[13] Overall, 4,700 party and Komsomol members were prosecuted for alcohol offences in 1987; in 1988 there were 7,000.[14]

There were disappointing results in other areas and institutions. There were 'serious shortcomings', for instance, in the Ministry of Health itself.[15] In the chemical industry there were signs that drunkenness was increasing, and there had been insufficient care in the storage of ethyl alcohol which had led to substantial losses through misappropriation.[16] In Moldavia – an important wine-producing area – the republic's state agencies and public organisations had 'grown lax' in their struggle against alcoholism; cases of drunkenness on the job had increased and every third crime was committed by an intoxicated person, 'a figure far above the national average'.[17] In Saratov the number of drink-related crimes had increased, as had the number of cases of grievous bodily harm.[18] In Estonia, the efforts that had been made by local soviets to reduce the level of alcoholism and home brewing were 'totally inadequate'.[19] Officials in the State Agro-Industrial Committee, it was discovered, had been planning an increase in the output of low-quality fruit and berry wines, and a 'considerable increase' in the production of cognac; 'strict reprimands' had to be administered.[20] In Moscow, a home-made still actually exploded in the home of one Shashkin, an official of the Russian Ministry of Light Industry.[21]

There was particular disappointment, in the CPSU Secretariat, with the way in which the media had sustained the campaign. There was no shortage of articles: over 100 in the central press and more than 50 television broadcasts in the last two months of 1986 alone. *Sovetskaya Rossiya* had been emphasising the regions where wine consumption was particularly high, in the north, Siberia and the Far East. The rural paper *Sel'skaya zhizn'* had been concentrating upon an all-union campaign 'For effective work and healthy living' and its implications for collective and state farms. The television news programme 'Vremya' had exposed a shop in Saransk where nearly all of its profits had been made from the sale of drink; on a return visit, in December 1986, the shop was selling fruit, soft drinks and confectionery, and making the same income. But there was still a 'whole series of omissions and neglected opportunities'. Coverage was unsystematic, and often focused on secondary aspects of the campaign. Journalists were reacting belatedly to the rise of home-brewing, and to the shift of alcoholism into the home. Government ministries were generally beyond criticism, even when they were delaying the transfer of enterprises to non-alcoholic production. And more generally, there was a lack of creativity or imagination in media treatment of the matter.[22] It was certainly true that media treatment of the alcohol problem had been falling off: there were fewer than half as many articles in 1988 as there had been in 1985, according to a comprehensive survey of the central and local press, and they were generally less detailed and analytical in their treatment.[23]

The pattern of public response

The decline in media attention was reflected in a popular perception that the campaign was beginning to wind down. *Pravda* found that this was definitely the view in a sanatorium in the Kuban' barely a year after the new policies had been initiated. 'The thaw has begun', remarked one of the guests, as he uncorked a fresh bottle. 'That's a fact', added his companion, in a slurred voice. 'The campaign is on the way out.' It turned out, on closer investigation, that the campaign against alcohol in the town had 'ended long ago'.[24] 'We thought that at last the drunken fog would lift and the family scandals caused by drinking would cease', wrote a group of mothers from Voronezh. 'And sobriety did reign in the city for a week or two. But the liquor merchants presumably couldn't stand the calm, and soon resumed their business'.[25] The effectiveness of the struggle had 'waned considerably', a Kishinev engineer told *Pravda*; people who had always had a weakness for the bottle were continuing to drink, even though it was harder to obtain.[26] In Volgograd even school pupils were drinking, and public transport reeked of alcohol; 'If you don't like the smell, get out and walk' one elderly passenger was told.[27] 'It seems to me', N. Alekseev of Moscow wrote to *Izvestiya* towards the end of 1987, 'that virtually the only result today of our "struggle against drunkenness" is the colossal lines outside the liquor stores. Meanwhile, people are drinking as much as they always have, only less openly'.[28] 'We launched the fight against drunkenness several years ago – a real, uncompromising and determined fight', another reader told the paper. 'It seemed that all we had to do was exert a bit more pressure, forbid certain things, impose some restrictions and raise the price of liquor, and that would be that.' What had been the result? Not universal sobriety, but a 'muddy wave of homebrew, eau de cologne, toothpaste and shoe polish and, horrible as it may sound, trichlorofon and dichlorofon, as well as drug addiction and addiction to toxic substances, with the inevitable result – poisoning'.[29]

A failure to implement the resolution seriously was one side of the problem; the other was a tendency to implement it with excessive zeal. As Galina Samoilova of Maikop told *Pravda*, there had been an innovation in her city: when buying wine or champagne she had to show her internal passport to a policeman, who made 'long and persistent enquiries' about why the bottle was being purchased. If, for example, she prepared the Georgian chicken dish *chakhokhbili* twice a month, the recipe for which required dry wine, she 'ran the risk of soon being placed on the register at the addiction-treatment clinic'. What had this to do with the real struggle against drunkenness and alcohol?[30] Sergei Zamoshkin, a lawyer, was on a business trip to a small southern town, where he saw some reports of people being punished for 'drinking beer in public places'. Where had they been drinking? In every case, 'near to the beer kiosk'. But where were they supposed to drink beer sold on tap, and when the local brewery wasn't equipped to bottle all of its output?[31] There were cases of police squads raiding weddings to make sure no drink was being taken; there were calls for *kefir* to be banned on the grounds that it contained traces of alcohol, and for liqueur chocolates to be made illegal as alcohol could penetrate in this way 'even into the families of abstainers'.[32] There were proposals that alcoholics themselves be isolated in special closed factories, or exiled to distant parts, or that they be put in prison for five years (*'perestroika*, like revolution, must be able to defend itself'). There were even suggestions that they be declared 'enemies of the people'.[33] Most alarmingly of all, there were suggestions that alcoholics be compulsorily sterilised, or at least that they be 'encouraged' to undergo a suitable form of treatment.[34]

There were also mistakes. As Vitalii Volkov, chief power engineer at a Donetsk mine, told *Pravda*, he and his colleagues had finished their shift at 5 p.m. and boarded buses to take them home to the city of Druzhkovka, 25 kilometres away. But five minutes went past, and then ten, and the buses stayed where they were. Then a policeman appeared at the door of each vehicle, and a team led by the vice-chairman of the local council got on the bus and demanded that every passenger breathe into a special glass 'for the purpose of identifying passengers in a state of intoxication'. There was not a hint in the resolutions on alcoholism, Voklov pointed out, that methods should be used which offended human dignity. At all events, a welder by the name of Sidorin, whose appearance for some reason looked suspicious to the people conducting the check-up, was taken off the bus so that an official report could be drawn up. Sidorin, as it happened, was a 'confirmed teetotaller – he doesn't even drink beer'. The mistake was discovered immediately after a medical check, but the man had been publicly insulted – 'moreover, to the great amusement of those who really do abuse alcohol'.[35]

The successes that were reported, moreover, were often illusory. There were alcohol-free weddings 'with a policeman at the door and vodka in the samovars', and ceremonies in which the bride's parents had been obliged to conceal the vodka in empty bottles of mineral water, 'occasionally confusing the contents'.[36] Non-alcoholic cafes were 'not infrequently' selling vodka and wine in the guise of Fanta or Borzhomi mineral water; drink could be kept in the grocery section of food stores and its sale reported as 'fruit', or it could be concealed in substantial quantities and then sold under the counter.[37] At a Moscow machine building factory, bottles were 'smuggled in through entrances, floated on rafts down river by the caseful, and hidden on station platforms'; there were cases of home brew 'actually being produced on the factory premises'.[38] Another strategy was to use intermediaries. Pensioners, for instance, occupied places in queues and then 'sold' them to more impatient colleagues. Vagrants, in a different strategy, began to 'persuade' old ladies to make the necessary purchases on their behalf. Chemists could hardly refuse to sell alcohol-based medicines in such cases, and as a result there was a constant shortage. 'No matter how much alcohol-based medicine we order', the shop managers complained, 'it's bought up by these boozehounds with the help of others.'[39] A similar tactic was for groups of workers to commission one of their number to

5.2   District Office, Sobriety Society
(*Krokodil*, no. 35, 1988)

stand in line while they did his work.[40] And there could be straight-forward deceit. Officially, for instance, the Pacific fishing fleet had gone dry: but when inspectors visited one trawler they found, in a single cabin, 576 bottles of vodka, intended for the second navigator's wedding.[41]

Public attitudes paralleled this gradual retreat. According to a survey in the summer of 1987, 33 per cent were in favour of continuing the measures approved two years earlier; another 33 per cent thought they should become more stringent; and only 9 per cent were in favour of a relaxation.[42] Support for hard-line policies of this kind, however, soon began to evaporate. In 1987, according to the same survey, only 17 per cent of the Soviet population thought it would be impossible to achieve success in the struggle against drunkenness, alcoholism and drug addiction. By 1988 the number of pessimists had doubled; and by 1989 the proportion of the population that did 'not believe that victory can be won over this social evil' was up to 58 per cent.[43] Surveys conducted in nineteen different regions in early 1988 found that as many as 85 per cent of those polled did not support the measures that had been taken to limit the availability of alcoholic beverages, and over 90 per cent were unwilling to make a personal commitment to abstain from alcohol.[44] The only group to be satisfied with the policies that were being pursued, ironically, were the alcoholics themselves: as a survey in Latvia found, 'in practice they were disturbed very little and they were quite happy with that'.[45]

Drinkers, it emerged, could be determined. In the Khakass republic they were prepared to sell their food and household goods, or even to offer the services of female members of their family to obtain a drink from street traders (a woman could apparently be 'negotiated' for up to 50 litres of wine).[46] And sometimes drinkers could take matters into their own hands. In Petrozavodsk, for instance, just before the 1987 New Year holiday, a crowd of 5,000 pushed back a lorry and smashed down the door of a wine shop; an old woman looking for refreshments for visiting relatives was crushed to death against the doorpost. It was the second such death the town had suffered.[47] There was another tragedy in the town of Privolzhsk, in the Ivanovo region, on the eve of a public holiday, when an 'enraged crowd forced its way into a milk store and down the stairs into its basement where wine [was] sold and crushed a 53-year-old man to death'.[48] In Poltava the windows of a local store were 'frequently forced open, foul language was heard and people were called some choice names'. Purchasers made their way home through a children's play-ground; then the 'bosom pals' would 'make themselves comfortable in the entrance halls of neighbouring houses and indulge in a good hard drinking bout'.[49]

There were similar scenes in Sverdlovsk when it was found that the supplies of alcohol promised for the New Year celebrations were not available. Hundreds of people had started queueing at the city's central food store as they thought they would be able to exchange their coupons for vodka without any risk of the exhaustion of supplies. After a wait of two or three hours, the crowd were told there would be no alcohol for sale. Disappointed shoppers began to move out of the shop and into the streets, positioning themselves on busy intersections so as to prevent the movement of traffic through the city. Impromptu meetings were held to protest not only against the failure to supply the promised alcohol, but also against persistent scarcities of food and other consumer goods. The crowds demanded that city representatives come before them to explain such shortages; within a short time the chairman of the regional soviet and the city party secretary appeared and tried to explain what they saw as the 'compelling and objective difficulties' that they confronted. Another 'spontaneous' meeting gathered in front of the city soviet, where an 'initiative group' had brought along a bus equipped with a public-address system, and began to make political demands including a call for a strike. 'The disturbances continued well into the night.'[50]

A survey of industrial workers found that 60 per cent would take no serious action when their colleagues were intoxicated: in the first place, they 'felt sorry' for them, they themselves were 'not without sin', and in any case they didn't think the matter was 'any of their business'.[51] By 1987, few were suggesting more drastic measures, and many more were expressing 'irritation' with the ineffective and counterproductive nature of the measures that had so far been taken.[52] Life, it seemed, had become dull. As Mrs Sidoruk wrote from Minsk, 'I always hated drunkenness. But suddenly it seems that no one celebrates holidays anymore. We used to make ourselves new dresses for the festivities. This year I didn't feel like making a single dress. Why bother?'[53] 'Thanks to the new reforms on drunkenness, ordinary working people have no holidays, and everyone walks around in a foul mood, like jackals', wrote Grigorii Smirnov on behalf of 114 fellow workers from Ordzhonikidze.[54] The restrictions that had been imposed on the sale of beer and vodka, workers from a Moscow factory told the Russian government, had 'only darkened our life'; no-one was calling on their friends, no-one was singing songs, life was a grim sequence of 'factory – home, alarm clock – factory'.[55] 'Who needs socialism without beer?', a Krasnodar reader asked *Argumenty i fakty*.[56]

'Give people back their smile!', urged a reader in *Literaturnaya gazeta*.[57] And there could be other reactions: as an anonymous reader wrote to *Izvestiya*, 'I usually read the paper after work, and I always have the same reaction to "sobriety" articles – I pour a glass of homebrew and drink to the health of their naive authors and to the failure of the anti-alcohol campaign.'[58]

The most common attitude, it appeared, was to deplore alcoholism in the abstract but drink oneself in moderation. When teachers, for instance, were asked if they could be teetotallers, 90 per cent replied in the affirmative. But only a minority thought moderate drinking unacceptable, and fewer than 10 per cent indicated that they had 'taken the pledge'.[59] A survey in Novosibirsk found similarly that 70 per cent were of the view that the consumption of alcohol in any quantity was harmful to human health, and to that of future generations in particular. But this had no direct consequences for those who held such views. The author, T. Vershinina, filled up a 'diary of contradictions' of this kind. One of the cases she quoted was a young woman, twenty years of age, whose guests had got drunk the previous New Year's Eve and accidentally burned their house down. The family had to spend the winter in a converted railway wagon, but still took the view that 'alcohol was essential for celebrations'. Or there was a woman in her fifties whose seventeen-year-old daughter had been knocked down and killed by a drunken lorry driver, but who nonetheless insisted that alcohol was a necessary part of social life. All kinds of excuses were advanced: 'If I don't die of alcohol, I'll die of a heart attack due to stress'; alcohol was a 'lesser evil than narcotics and other substitutes' (journalists were especially prone to this excuse); 'no one ever died of alcohol'; or 'there is so much worse going on all around that it is ridiculous to ask people not to drink'.[60]

Everyone, it seemed, was willing to condemn drunkenness in society at large; but if the drunk worked beside them they were more likely to suggest that he 'had a family' or was 'turning over a new leaf'.[61] Many were willing to argue, despite the evidence, that drink was harmless, and up to a tenth, in the same surveys, thought it could be positively beneficial.[62] Others were proud of vodka as the Russian national drink, and of the way in which it had displaced whisky in other countries.[63] Only one home brewer in twenty-five was exposed with the help of the public, the minister of the interior reported;[64] there were even cases in the press of an entire village or settlement 'harbouring "their own" maker of homebrew', with those involved often including the very people who were supposed to enforce the relevant articles of the criminal code, or of villagers 'taking their turn' at the local still.[65] Public attitudes, in fact, were deeply schizophrenic. As citizens, parents and rational beings, everyone supported the restrictions; but as consumers disinclined to spend their time waiting in queues, the same people were opposed to them.[66] Equally, the same people who told interviewers that they were 'total abstainers' were quite happy to drink wine and sometimes more than this on family and festive occasions.[67]

The boom in illicit distilling

It had traditionally been estimated that 30–40 per cent of Soviet alcohol consumption was in the form of *samogon* or a number of local equivalents (no official figures had been published since the 1930s, and it was likely that the authorities themselves had no reliable estimates).[68] *Samogon* was easily prepared, from grain, potatoes, fruit or even tomato paste as well as sugar;[69] the equipment required was quite widely available (even a kettle would do); and it was highly profitable for those who made it (on average, according to the Interior Ministry, a litre of *samogon* cost its producer about a ruble and a half and it could be sold for eight to ten times more than this.[70] *Samogon* was always a part of the rural scene, and a means of payment for minor services as well as a form of entertainment and consolation. It was 'common knowledge', the Soviet interior minister acknowledged, that a bottle of homebrew was 'often the basic form of payment for all sorts of under-the-counter services. Get a bottle ready if you need to have some firewood hauled, your garden ploughed or your house repaired.' In the Tula region, for instance, more than half of the people convicted of selling homebrew had made it in order to pay for everyday services.[71] About two-thirds of the rural population, surveys suggested, made at least periodic use of *samogon*; in urban areas the proportion was at least one in four.[72]

The introduction of a series of measures designed to restrict the output of alcoholic drink from legitimate sources, and to make it more difficult and expensive to obtain, had the result that has accompanied virtually every attempt to restrict the supply of alcohol: an explosion of illicit distilling, accompanied by an increase in all the forms of crime that were associated with a trade of this kind.[73] The phenomenon was certainly widespread. In one region alone 5,115 stills were handed in from 6,000 homes, and another 400 were found discarded in nearby orchards and ravines.[74] According to official estimates, illegal stills were already producing more alcohol than the state itself.[75] By 1988, according to the same estimates, illicit distilling exceeded state production by 40 or 50 per cent, and (in the view of others) had more than made good the cuts that had been introduced three years earlier.[76] For many members of the public there had been a positive 'epidemic' of homebrewing since the campaign had been launched, and the minister of the interior had himself to acknowledge that there had been a 'dangerous spurt' in activities of this kind.[77]

Official statistics found it difficult to take account of homebrewing itself, but there was no mistaking the sharp increase in the number of criminal charges that were brought in this connection. According to official figures, there were 30,000 prosecutions for homebrewing in 1985, 150,000 in 1986, and as many as 397,000 in 1987.[78] In 1986 and 1987 alone, 1 million stills were destroyed and 4 million litres of homebrew were seized.[79] According to the interior ministry, in the first six months of 1988 in the Russian republic alone there were 170,000 cases of illicit distilling, nearly three times as many as in the same period in 1987; nearly twice as much homebrewed beer and spirits had been destroyed, and four times the number of stills.[80] In the USSR as a whole 440,000 arrests for illicit distilling were made in 1987, which was twice the number arrested in 1986. In almost every part of the country arrests and prosecutions were almost twice as numerous in 1987 as they had been the year before, and in some cases the increases were spectacular. In the Yakut republic, for instance, arrests were up seven times, in Kamchatka nine times, and in the Irkutsk region almost ten times in a single year.[81]

Samogon, originally a countryside pursuit, had meanwhile moved into the towns. According to the interior ministry, by 1988 more than 40 per cent of illicit distilling went on in urban apartments. One man in the Bryansk region 'conditioned' about 170 litres of homemade beer in the attic of a five-storey block of flats; other were discovered carrying on the manufacture of *samogon* in a children's crèche, or under the cover of a Young Pioneer camp. In some parts of the Russian republic it had been discovered that activities of this kind were carried on in every third or fourth house.[82] Illicit distilling was also being carried on at the workplace; in some cases it made use of scarce materials and the latest tools and equipment, and all of this with the connivance of the workers and even management of the enterprise.[83] There were homebrewers with computer programs to 'fully automate the distilling process'; another ran an 'underground factory' with its own drivers, technicians and book-keepers.[84] There was a corresponding change in the 'social portrait' of the offender: paralleling its move into the town, homebrewing was increasingly being carried on by pensioners, housewives, shop assistants, hotel and restaurant staff and long-distance train crews.[85] Most home-brewers, according to official statistics, were women, though they were less likely to drink themselves and more likely to condemn such practices; homebrewers were also young, with more than half (52 per cent) under the age of thirty.[86]

Illicit distilling became well established at this time in areas of the country where it had previously been almost unknown. In Latvia, for

5.3 'Three hundred glasses of tea. The sugar – separately!'
(*Krokodil*, no. 15, 1988)

instance, there was no tradition of this kind; but when the restrictions were introduced, 'the people literally learned how to distil illicit liquor'. Soon the *samogonshchiki* were 'technically literate and able to distil alcohol from a great many raw materials'.[87] Homebrewing was well established in the Russian republic (72 per cent of all cases in 1987) and particularly in the major industrial cities of the Urals and Siberia, where there had preciously been no 'hotbeds' of this kind. The homebrew 'bug' was also spreading in the Ukraine, Belorussia, Kazakhstan, Lithuania and Moldavia.[88] In Chelyabinsk, more and more 'zones of illicit distilling' were appearing on the map of the region.[89] So great was the demand for homebrew that its price soared up to 70 rubles for a 3 litre bottle, more than the same amount of vodka in a state shop would have cost.[90]

One direct consequence of the upsurge in illicit distilling was a shortage in the supply of sugar as housewives competed with the moonshiners. In 1986 there was an 11 per cent increase in the sale of sugar as compared with 1985, and in 1987 a further increase. In two years the sale of sugar increased as much as it had done in the whole decade between 1970 and 1980.[91] These were enormous increases, and as the press pointed out, it was certainly '*not* for drinking tea'.[92] Once again, the increase was particularly remarkable in a number of areas. In Kamchatka, for instance, sugar sales increased by almost 40 per cent in a year, and there was a sharp increase in the sale of yeast.[93] In a district in the Smolensk region the consumption of sugar shot up by 65 per cent in the first quarter of 1987 although the area had been declared a sobriety zone.[94] One family of homebrewers that had been arrested in Kiev processed as much as 150 kilograms of sugar a day, which yielded 40 litres of *samogon*; a search of their house turned up twenty vats of homebrew, two huge distilling apparatuses and a very large stock of sugar.[95] In another case, half a ton of granulated sugar was retrieved from the home of an 'inveterate homebrewer'.[96] The USSR was the world's leading producer of sugar; and in 1987, it was estimated, about a tenth of this great output was used to make homebrew.[97] There was also an increase in the theft of fruit, used for making homemade wines.[98]

If sugar and other raw materials could not be purchased, they could often be stolen. In Dzhambul, a town in Kazakhstan, a criminal group involved in the theft of 140,000 rubles' worth of sugar was itself headed by the director of a local sugar factory.[99] As an interior ministry spokesman commented, many managers appeared unconcerned about losses of this kind, and factories lacked 'even elementary security, warehouses [were] not equipped with alarms and proper systems of records [were] non-existent'.[100] Equally, factory managers and the police could often be bribed. In Volgograd, for instance, 'criminal groups' bribed a range of officials including the head and deputy head of the regional police to enable them to take part in the 'organised' misappropriation of vodka and other spirits from a local drink-producing factory. Factory controllers visited from time to time, but as one of them was told, 'Don't be too keen, if you want to stay around!' Helping oneself to the odd bottle, it appeared, was routine practice; the factory bus-driver, for instance, managed to smuggle out 37 bottles of vodka and 6 litres of spirits. The only person who had recently been caught leaving the factory with illicitly obtained vodka, ironically, was the chairman of the factory's group of people's controllers, who were collectively responsible for maintaining these very regulations.[101]

Other raids were carried out in Dagestan, a southern republic renowned for its brandy. On one occasion three tankers containing purified spirit were detained by the police as they made their way into the republic capital; when challenged, one of the drivers handed fake documents to the police, and another was found to be carrying a pistol. It later emerged that a group based at liquor factories in Azerbaijan had 'contracted' with criminal elements in Dagestan to ship and then sell the 40 tonnes of pure spirit. Police raided the home of the driver who had been armed and found an expensive transistor radio together with ammunition for an automatic rifle, pistols and a hand grenade. Later the same day other members of the group were arrested, together with their printing presses and very large stocks of bottles and labels; and workers at a local factory were arrested trying to sell no less than 10,000 litres of misappropriated spirit. Dagestan, it was pointed out, had never previously been one of the regions in which illicit distilling was practised on a significant scale.[102] Over 1986 and 1987 about 1,600 'sugar' crimes were investigated, the number of yeast thefts almost doubled, and in 1987 alone there were about 7,000 cases of the theft of alcohol itself.[103] Bootlegging, moreover, was sometimes quite openly practised. In one case a woman was reported to be running an 'inn' which was floodlit at night to attract the passing trade; in another, *samogon* was sold by 'barmen on wheels', allowing topers to sit in their vehicles and 'drink in comfort' for a modest premium.[104]

These were not the only criminal implications of the campaign. The long queues outside liquor stores, for a start, were 'not just an ugly sight but a "high-risk zone" for lawbreaking'; there had been 'thousands' of convictions for petty hooliganism in these circumstances, according to the Ministry of the Interior.[105] Substantial numbers of the people waiting in line were 'not just drunks and parasites' – there were also pensioners and housewives who were buying the drink for resale. And there were 'drunken brawls in restaurants and cafes': in 1987 alone, about 4,000 citizens had to be taken from public dining establishments to medical detoxification centres.[106] The practice of 'family' homebrewing forced young people out on to the streets, where they more easily became involved in hooliganism of some kind. In Krasnodar, as many as 70 per cent of the children who were asked told investigators that homebrewing forced them out on the street, as there was no place left for them in the family. And some 90 per cent of the inmates in the Soviet Union's boarding institutions suffered from mental disorders caused by prolonged exposure to a troubled family situation, of which alcohol and homebrewing was often a part.[107]

The sanctions that were available to the law were clearly insufficient to halt this wave of crime. A 100 ruble fine, as a report from Tomsk pointed out, was 'nothing' compared with what the 'lovers of easy money' could obtain from their activities.[108] The penalty for a first offence was invariably a fine which was soon recouped, a legal conference was told, and the producer thereafter became more careful. In Belorussia, for instance, the 'lovers of easy profits' had located the underground production of alcohol in 'forests far from any prying eyes'. It was no easy matter to find these unusual 'public houses': even helicopters were ineffective as they were expensive and made too much noise, and only sniffer dogs seemed to offer much hope.[109] Determined homebrewers were also using ruined buildings, and some were going 'deep underground' and 'incorporating new technology': in Vinnitsa province a homebrewer was arrested who had set up a distillery in a forest thicket 'with a watchtower for observing the approaches through binoculars'.[110] Stills were set up in milling machines, concealed in barns and hayricks, and buried in vegetable patches and even in the manure heap:[111] a contributory factor, perhaps, in the distinctive flavour of a number of these preparations.

Denied access to alcohol, Soviet drinkers turned to a wide variety of substitutes (according to Latvian officials, there were nearly 150 such alternatives of varying toxicity).[112] Inexpensive colognes, lotions and mouthwashes were among the first to disappear from the counters of perfume stores. Even toothpaste, which contained no alcohol, became difficult to locate: it emerged that the glycerine it contained had a toxic effect when taken internally, and drunks were likely to confuse the symptoms of poisoning with intoxication.[113] Eau de cologne and alcohol-based perfumes had to be sold, like alcohol itself, after 2 p.m. Shop assistants complained that customers who bought hair tonic often gulped it down as soon as they were back on the street.[114] In Kuibyshev, on the Volga river, the director of a perfume shop demanded police help because customers insisted on buying eau de cologne by the boxload. Shop managers began to limit sales to two bottles per person, and only during licensing hours; the director of a household goods store in Perm', in the Urals, refused to accept glue deliveries because the moment it went on sale the shop was besieged by customers who often engaged in fist-fights.[115] In the Gomel' region of Belorussia, sales of window-cleaning fluid doubled between 1985 and 1986.[116] In the end, no cheap and reasonably available alcoholic preparations were left and it became difficult even to provide for routine medical operations like preparing the skin of patients before an injection.[117]

There were still more disturbing cases where those concerned with the illicit trade had actually lost their lives. Homebrew was itself a health hazard as it often contained metal oxides from the still and other 'trade-mark' additives from cheap tobacco to hydrochloric acid.[118] In a town in Krasnodar, for instance, a woman and two children died and a man was seriously injured when an illicit distilling apparatus exploded and set fire to a house.[119] At a cellulose factory in Archangel, in the far north, there was a serious case of mass poisoning after workers imbibed condensed alcohol wastes.[120] Six workers at a Moscow chemical factory were killed and hundreds were hospitalised when they drank stolen methanol; in a Voronezh combine nine died and ten were taken to hospital after they had sampled ethyl alcohol (the sobriety society chairman 'hadn't noticed' the incident, which had taken place on the shop floor in the middle of the working day).[121] A funeral wake turned into a full-scale disaster in the Ukrainian village of Zabolotoe, near the Polish border, after the consumption of black-market industrial spirit. The affair began when the local schoolmaster and a farm mechanic celebrated the delivery of furniture with a drinking spree. The mechanic died the next day and the schoolmaster fell ill, but fearing for his reputation, kept silent. He died a few days later and was buried without an autopsy. After the ill-fated wake, where the industrial spirit had been placed on the table with other strong drink, autopsies were performed on all the dead including the disinterred schoolmaster; altogether there were eight deaths and eighty hospital cases.[122] In 1987, 11,000 lives were lost in this way, almost as many as had been lost in the entire course of the war in Afghanistan.[123]

The Temperance Society falters

There were problems too with the All-Union Voluntary Society for the Struggle for Sobriety, the body that had been created to supply the campaign with a popular following. The Society was certainly an imposing institutional presence by the end of its first three years of existence, with 428,000 branches and over 14 million members; young people under the age of thirty accounted for more than a quarter of this total, and workers and collective farmers for more than a third.[124] The Society organised competitions for sobriety posters, put on temperance films, and monitored the implementation of sobriety legislation. The first all-union *reid* of this kind took place in association with the journalists' union in early 1986;[125] there were comparable exercises at lower levels, yielding thousands of offenders.[126] Apart from its own activities, the Society had given an enormous boost to the formation of temperance clubs: when it was founded there were about 250, but three years after the Society's establishment there were more than 5,000.[127] The Society, moreover, had direct representation in the Soviet parliament through one of the 750 seats that were allocated to public organisations in the new Congress of People's Deputies ('why only one seat?' members asked indignantly).[128] Nikolai Trubilin, deputy chairman of the Russian government and a former health minister, was duly elected against a single competitor, having promised to 'step up, not slacken, the struggle with the "green serpent"'.[129]

Despite its imposing size, leadership support and resources, the Society faced a series of difficulties. One of these was the lack of attention that was paid to its affairs by the bodies that had set it up, which took this opportunity to withdraw from the campaign.[130] Another was an increasingly hostile press, which blamed the Society rather than the population at large for queues, public disorders and speculation.[131] There was renewed support for 'cultured drinking': the poet Yevtushenko pointed out that a bottle could be 'good company' and deplored 'social shock therapy' of this kind; another writer in a trade union journal insisted that a glass of wine or even cognac on a festive occasion was 'not drunkenness' and that the harmfulness of beer, 'an ancient national tradition', had been 'greatly exaggerated'.[132] Another group of writers, some of them economists, put forward 'constructive' suggestions which invariably involved increasing the output and sale of alcohol.[133] Still others used the press or public platforms to blame the campaign for all kinds of shortages, even of money in their bank accounts.[134] The Society, its members complained, had 'become a kind of punch-bag';[135] it began to suffer from 'social isolation';[136] and there were even calls for its abolition.[137]

Still more fundamental was a persistent ambiguity about the Society's objectives, and in particular whether it favoured a moderation of drinking habits or total abstinence. Members of the Society, some local officials suggested, were required only to 'seek to achieve' sobriety (the rules were in fact reasonably clear that members had to represent an 'example of the sober way of life').[138] It was suggested by others that drunks should be allowed to join the Society so as to help them overcome their failings.[139] And what about the Society's own objective, which was to 'support the formation of a sober way of life'? Support whom, and in what circumstances? Wasn't the Society, in any case, supposed to be one of 'struggle' not just 'support'?[140] And what was its main 'success indicator': lower levels of public alcoholism or, as its officials sometimes suggested, an increase in its own membership?[141] Three years or more after its foundation, as a prominent activist pointed out, there was still no state programme for the elimination of alcohol abuse; more than this, the Society itself had offered no proposals that might serve as the basis for such a programme, or that indicated the particular place of the Society in its implementation.[142] The Society suffered a further blow when in December 1988 some of its members established a 'Union for the Struggle for People's Sobriety' headed by a controversial proponent of total abstention and member of the Academy of Medical Sciences, Fedor Uglov; and its purposes began to be obscured as Russian nationalists, anti-Semites and others sought to use it to advance their own agenda.[143]

One of the Society's enduring problems was that its members, often recruited indiscriminately or even against their will, failed themselves to set a suitable example of the 'sober way of life'.[144] In Odessa, indeed, it was the chairman of the local Temperance Society from whose home an illicit still was recovered.[145] In a collective farm elsewhere the chairman of the local sobriety commission had repeatedly been found in a drunken stupor at the wheel of his tractor. He had resisted arrest, and been placed under medical supervision; but there were no charges, he remained deputy chairman of the *kolkhoz*, and all that followed was a paid holiday in Yugoslavia.[146] In Chelyabinsk, all the members of a branch of the Society drank regularly, except one – 'and he ha[d] an ulcer'.[147] About a third of the Society's members were drinkers, it was suggested in *Pravda*, and many thousands had to be expelled;[148] or as another report put it, 'The drunks are still drinking. Only now with a membership card in their pocket.'[149]

Members themselves became increasingly disillusioned by the – as they saw it – overly formal and bureaucratic nature of the Society. The root of the problem, as an Omsk scientist put it in a series of 'polemical notes', was that the temperance movement had begun to develop in the early 1980s when the society was in a pre-crisis situation but the policy of perestroika had not yet been initiated. Almost inevitably the movement became oriented towards the 'policy of the "strong hand" and strong government, so that public order could be re-established and the country saved'. This, however, had led the movement up a 'blind alley': 'the fact is that "strong government" is the power of officialdom, and we have had more than enough of that particular blessing'. No social movement, thought Borovik, would ever emerge from the 'bureaucratic games' that developed in these circumstances: the only measures that were likely to be effective were those that reflected public opinion and democratic procedures. The Sobriety Society had itself become 'bureaucratised' and 'helpless'.[150] For Professor Zagoruiko, an activist and specialist on alcoholism from Novosibirsk, the Society had failed to defend the movement from its detractors and to rebut their arguments; it had become no more than a 'safety-valve for letting off social steam'.[151]

Another writer, V. Aristov, took much the same view as Borovik. The Society's activities, he complained, were still conducted from above in the 'administrative behind-closed-doors' style of earlier years; and its methods of work – hearing reports, passing resolutions, handing down directives – had lost their usefulness. Much more effective, in Aristov's view, would be a 'bank' of practical suggestions drawn from the experience of members and activists. Organised on a national basis, a fund of public initiatives of this kind was one in which every member and branch could play a part, and it would help the Society to find a role it could usefully perform.[152] Surveys found that the 'overwhelming majority', even of its members, had no clear idea of what the Society actually did.[153] In some cases it had become so inactive that it was 'almost an underground organisation', complained A. Surin from the Sverdlovsk region. He knew there was such an organisation in the area, he even knew the chairman, but what it actually undertook was 'a mystery to everyone'.[154] 'Hardly born, it already needs to be resuscitated' was the view of the Society of one of the members of its own Central Council.[155]

The Society, at the same time, began to develop a heavily bureaucratic mode of operation, demanding monthly reports from its branches under more than thirty different headings including weddings, births, anniversaries and so forth. How, it was asked, were branches supposed to respond to a question about the number of funerals that had taken place 'with the active support of members of the Temperance Society'?

5.4 'Here's the list of people in our district who aren't homebrewing' (*Krokodil*, no. 15, 1988)

And how could they count the number of birthdays that local people had celebrated in their own homes without alcohol?[156] It had become a 'typical useless bureaucracy that forced "volunteers" to join', ran a particularly caustic report in *Ogonek*. Three years after its foundation the Society had 450,000 branches overseen by more than 3,000 district and city offices, which in turn were supervised at the regional, territorial and republican levels. A Central Council managed the affairs of the Society as a whole from a 'lovely, columned edifice in Moscow', with a permanent staff of 6,500 financed by members' contributions; in addition there were 164,000 local councillors, who met regularly and claimed a generous *per diem*. Administrative expenses of this kind accounted for about a tenth of the Society's budget, and it was running at a loss. 'It bothers no one', complained *Ogonek*, 'that at least one-third of the Society's members drink, that branch chairmen frequently end up in sobering-up stations, and that workers are basically forced to attend Society lectures at factories.'[157]

In the light of this mounting and often valid criticism it was no surprise when in October 1988 the Central Committee Secretariat agreed to 'restructure' the work of the Society. For all its efforts, the Central Committee concluded, the Society 'had not yet become an authoritative organisation'. Founded on a wave of anti-alcoholic enthusiasm in 1985, it had been unable thereafter to make use of this 'credit of trust' and had failed to find ways of sustaining the struggle against alcoholism on a voluntary basis at a time when administrative measures were losing their effectiveness. Its large number of full-time staff had not simply failed to develop the Society's work, but had themselves become a factor in its bureaucratisation. Many members, even officials, were themselves far from convinced abstainers. A large number of branches were dormant, and others were limited in their activities to the collection of dues. The Secretariat, in its resolution, suggested that the Society's full-time apparatus should be reduced by half, at least at the republican and national levels, while retaining 'genuine sobriety enthusiasts' within its service.[158]

By 1989 the Society's full-time staff had been reduced by over 40 per cent, and a greater proportion of its energies was directed towards the formation of more broadly conceived 'centres of anti-alcoholic education'. New forms of rehabilitation treatment had been organised, which had been administered to over 1,000 people in Moscow alone.[159] There were changes in the Society's leadership: its original chairman, Yuri Ovchinnikov, died in early 1988 after a lengthy illness, and the

Central Committee recommended the appointment of Ivan Laptev, editor of the government paper *Izvestiya*, as his successor (he was duly elected in November 1988).[160] At a plenum of the Society in January 1989 a far-reaching decentralisation of its structure was agreed;[161] then in October 1990, at a second nationwide conference, the Society itself was transformed into an All-Union Society of Sobriety and Health with a somewhat broader set of responsibilities.[162] But there had still been no 'fundamental improvement' in the work of the Society, and with the gradual relaxation of restrictions on the sale of drink and rumours that the Society was about to be abolished altogether, 'pessimistic attitudes' increased among a 'significant proportion' of its members. Many, indeed, had ceased to play an active part of any kind in the affairs of the Society; branches were being wound up, and appeals were being made for the financial support of its publications. The task of renewing the Society, in the view of the Central Committee, would have to be 'stubbornly pursued'.[163]

6.1 F. Gubaev,
'At a wedding, 1990s'

6

_____

The impact of the campaign

In October 1988, just over three years after it had been launched, the Central Committee adopted a further resolution which in effect brought the struggle against alcoholism to a premature conclusion. Although the campaign had led to a 'healthier moral atmosphere in society', the Central Committee had to accept that 'radical changes ha[d] not yet been achieved'. It criticised the tendency to apply administrative methods and 'sensational, short-term efforts' to a complex and deep-seated social problem. Public opinion, the 'main force' in any struggle of this kind, had not been engaged in support of the campaign, and there had been much too great an emphasis upon prohibition and force. The output of drink itself had been reduced more sharply than the original resolution had specified and this had simply increased demand, leading to long queues, a rapid growth in illicit distilling, speculation, and greater use of a variety of substitutes. The sobriety society, for its part, had yet to prove itself a 'mass, authoritative organisation of active champions of the healthy way of life'. The resolution reaffirmed the struggle against drunkenness in principle; but party bodies were urged to make every effort to eliminate queues, in practice (although the resolution did not say so directly) by increasing the production of alcoholic drink and the number of places at which it could be sold.[1]

The ending of the campaign, at least in its original form, reflected a significant change in the balance of political forces that had originally been committed to its support. At a meeting of the Central Committee at the end of September 1988 one of the campaign's main proponents, Mikhail Solomentsev, had retired unexpectedly from the Politburo, together with three other figures from the Brezhnev era. At the same time it was announced that a series of commissions had been established under the auspices of the Central Committee, effectively bypassing the Secretariat, and that Yegor Ligachev had been moved from his important

position as secretary responsible for ideology to head the new commission on agriculture.[2] Ligachev himself thought the change of policy
a 'great mistake',[3] and it certainly allowed the opponents of the anti-
alcoholism campaign an opportunity to reopen the discussion. Ryzhkov,
in particular, reportedly 'exploded' at a Politburo meeting in late 1988.
'How much longer are we going to continue like this?', he asked his
colleagues, adding that he was proposing to cancel the campaign on
his own authority. It was finally agreed that the sale of dry wines,
champagne, cognac and beer in food shops should be permitted again,
but it was not until October and the retirement or demotion of
Solomentsev and Ligachev that the necessary instructions could be given.[4]

The campaign, in fact, had come under attack at leading levels from at
least the end of the previous year. The Russian prime minister Vitalii
Vorotnikov had supported the measures at the time of their introduction,
but had been 'categorically against attempts to turn a complicated,
multilevel campaign into a routine competition', with areas and enterprises competing with each other for the most rapid cuts in production.[5]
In November 1987, after consulting Gorbachev, he appealed to the
Central Committee to stop the law being implemented.[6] In early
September 1988 a much more substantial report was circulated by
Nikolai Ryzhkov, with assistance from the Ministry of Trade, pointing
out the 'negative phenomena' that had arisen in the course of the
campaign, particularly enormous queues but also illicit distilling and
other forms of crime.[7] On 8 September, acting on the basis of this report,
the Politburo relaxed the campaign, allowing wines, beer and cognacs to
be sold again in food stores, and on 12 October it went on to adopt the
more elaborate resolution that was published in the name of the Central
Committee as a whole later in the month.[8] The resolution spoke of a
'resolute intensification of the struggle for sobriety' and the 'impermissi-
bility of any deviation whatsoever' from the policies that had been laid
down in 1985; the minister of trade, interviewed in the press, explained
that there would in fact be 'adjustments' and that 'economic, educational
and other methods' would be given greater priority in the future.[9]

Almost every aspect in the campaign was vigorously contested, at this
time and in the months that followed. What, for instance, had happened
to the production and consumption of alcoholic drink over the campaign:
had it resumed its upward trend, taking account of *samogon*, or stabilised
at levels lower than those that had obtained when the campaign began?
What about the impact on the family and social life: had there been a
lasting improvement in the stability of marriages, in life expectancies, and

in health indicators more generally? And what forms of treatment, other than crudely imposed restrictions, had been found to secure worthwhile results? Looking back on the campaign in 1990, Ligachev, at least, saw no reason to apologise. There had been, he accepted, too great an emphasis upon administrative measures, and they had suffered from the 'illusion' that alcoholism could be eliminated in a single campaign; but the record sales of alcohol that were once again being recorded were a 'tragedy', even a 'slow Chernobyl'.[10] For Gorbachev, speaking at the 28th Party Congress a few days later, the campaign itself was 'not a mistake', although there had been misjudgements in its implementation.[11] Some went even further. For the writer Vasilii Belov, speaking to the newly elected Soviet parliament, the problem was that the resolution had not been implemented vigorously enough. It was, he insisted, 'not a bad decree', and ordinary people had become disillusioned with the Politburo because of the failure to ensure it was carried into practical effect.[12] And there was some pressure, at least from temperance campaigners, to bring to justice those who had subverted the campaign's original objectives and then administered this 'stab in the back'.[13]

For the campaign's detractors, by contrast, it had been blunder unequalled since the time of the Sumerians, two or three thousand years before the birth of Christ.[14] For economist and deputy Nikolai Shmelev, one of the most prominent early critics, the campaign had been undertaken with the best of intentions and it had led to a welcome reduction in alcohol-related accidents and crime. But, writing in *Novyi mir* in early 1988, he went on to argue that alcoholism had 'adapted to new conditions' and assumed 'more dangerous forms', such as the consumption of chemical surrogates and drugs. At the same time the state had been drawn into a '*samogon* war against the people' – a war it could hardly hope to win.[15] Speaking to the newly elected Soviet parliament in 1989, Shmelev argued that existing policies had done 'colossal damage' to market relations and to the budgetary system in particular, and went on to call for the resumption of a 'normal trade in spirits'; he spoke elsewhere about the loss of life from the consumption of surrogates, describing it as a 'second Afghanistan'.[16] For finance minister Valentin Pavlov, interviewed later, the campaign had been a repetition of the collectivisation of the 1930s, with all of its excesses;[17] for Vorotnikov, speaking to Western journalists, it had been a 'campaign of the command-administrative type . . . almost a campaign of terror'.[18] For the Komi first secretary V. I. Mel'nikov, speaking to the 19th Party

Conference in 1988, it was already time to call those who had launched the campaign to public account.[19] Others made the same demand in the Soviet parliament, and in the newspapers; for at least one journalist the whole campaign had been a 'bacchanalia of annihilation and destruction'.[20]

The production and consumption of alcohol

The limited availability of drink had certainly been unpopular, and the queues that had begun to form were the clearest possible indication that the attachment to drink was as strong as ever. Surveys conducted in 1988, shortly before the campaign was relaxed, found that people were often obliged to queue for up to three hours; in Moscow, on New Year's Eve, there was a line of 3,000 outside a single wine shop.[21] There were 'huge queues in the shops', Vorotnikov recalled. 'You couldn't visit a factory without being shoved into a corner and shouted at: "What are you doing, you can't do this to us." '[22] Gaidar Aliev, at this time a first deputy prime minister, brought photographs of the queues that were forming in Moscow to Ryzhkov, and then to Gorbachev and Ligachev, and reported on the hostile nature of the conversations that were taking place among disgruntled shoppers.[23] As the vice-chairman of Moscow city soviet explained, the long 'tails' that had been forming at wine stores and departments had led to 'justified criticism from Muscovites' and had 'nothing to do with embellishing the capital city' (the five-year target they had been given for reducing the sale of wine and vodka had been achieved in just two years, in line with the experience of many other Russian cities: Chelyabinsk, for instance, had 150 wine shops when the campaign began but within a couple of years there were only 4). From late 1988, however, the sale of champagne, cognac and wine was authorised on a wider basis, and the hours at which drink would be available were extended; only vodka, in future, would not be sold on Sundays.[24] The average Muscovite, it was calculated, was already spending up to ninety hours a year waiting to buy alcohol; and maintaining order in the queues at the city's liquor stores required 400 police and volunteer auxiliaries on a daily basis as well as a large number of patrol cars.[25]

The output and consumption of alcoholic drink, by this time, had already resumed its upward trend. Output had fallen sharply, by almost half in just two years in the case of vodka; but from late 1987 it began to

Table 6.1. *Sales of alcoholic drink in the USSR and Russian Federation, 1980–90 (official data, million decalitres)*

	1980	1985	1986	1987	1988	1989	1990
Vodka and liquor	293.9	251.2	156.6	123.6	136.9	179.5	210.0
Wine	485.1	386.8	189.5	156.7	184.7	204.8	164.8
Cognac	9.2	8.5	8.8	9.4	11.3	13.1	11.6
Champagne	14.9	21.9	20.7	20.6	21.8	22.4	21.3
Beer	620.7	687.8	496.9	514.6	564.8	608.1	627.8
In terms of absolute alcohol:	230.3	198.9	120.9	92.8	104.5	126.5	132.7
Per capita	8.7	7.2	4.3	3.3	3.7	4.4	4.6
Russia, per capita	10.5	8.8	5.2	3.9	4.4	5.3	5.6

Source: Adapted from *Narodnoe khozyaistvo SSSR v 1990 g.* (Moscow: Finansy i statistika, 1991), pp. 132–3.

increase again, and by 1990 it was approaching earlier levels. Beer, wine and champagne production had all fallen, wine particularly sharply; the output of cognac, by contrast, had steadily increased, but from a much lower starting point. Sales were also recovering, after a sharp fall in the early days of the campaign (see Table 6.1). Vodka sales, again, were down by half in just two years, but by 1990 they were close to the level that had obtained in the first year of the campaign. And by the same year the average citizen was spending a greater share of earnings on alcohol than had been the case before the campaign began, reflecting not simply a recovery in levels of consumption but also the higher prices that had been introduced. Including *samogon*, alcohol consumption from all sources was still considerably below the level that had been reached in 1984, still more so in 1980; but it was up, by nearly a half, as compared with 1987, the year in which the campaign had bitten deepest.[26] And levels of output and consumption were still increasing rapidly. In 1989 alone, according to official figures, the volume of alcohol produced was up 19 per cent, which was well above the increase that had been planned; in the Russian Federation, which was by far the largest of the republics, the value of sales was up by nearly a quarter in a single year.[27]

There was some disquiet about these figures in temperance circles. As L. M. Ovrutsky, a member of its board, pointed out in the sobriety journal, not a single one of the plan targets for consumer goods had been met, 'with the exception of the alcohol Mont Blanc'. Nor was it simply the case that the output of drink in general had increased. Beer, for instance, was up 7 per cent in volume terms, and wine 19 per cent. The sale of champagne had even fallen very slightly; but the sale of vodka and other forms of hard liquor had increased by a massive 32 per cent. Evidently, commented Ovrutsky, the pressure of the budgetary deficit had led to an unannounced decision to overfulfil the plan, and to do so by means of a record increase in vodka production and sales. If matters carried on in this way the 'next enormity' could be expected within three or four years. The plan results also contained information on levels of criminality, and these showed that the number of reported incidents had increased by a third; alcohol-related crime more particularly was up 17 per cent, very close to the increase in the sale of drink itself. At no time in modern history, Ovrutsky claimed, had a programme of extraordinary measures against crime been accompanied by a comparable 'normalisation' of the sale of alcoholic drink.[28] Was it coincidental, asked another writer, that for the first time in four years figures for the share of alcohol in retail trade turnover had not been published?[29]

The campaign, meanwhile, appeared to have had only a very limited success in its larger objective of encouraging a 'healthy way of life', including exercise and a wider range of cultural pursuits. There were more drunks about, for a start: the number of people found in public in a state of intoxication rose by 17 per cent in 1989 alone.[30] There were more drunks on the railways as well, including juveniles; the problem had 'in no way abated', an inspector told the sobriety journal.[31] There were more drunken drivers (the number of cases rose by a third in 1989 alone), and more alcohol-related deaths on the roads.[32] The campaign, equally, had no obvious impact upon levels of crime: indeed in many respects the network that was involved in the production and distribution of illicit drink made a direct contribution to a further increase. The number of all recorded crimes rose rapidly: up by 17.8 per cent in 1988, nearly a third in 1989, and a further 13.2 per cent in 1990.[33] The number of crimes committed while under the influence of alcohol increased in parallel – more sharply in the case of street crime, which rose by two-thirds in 1989 alone.[34] According to the Ministry of Internal Affairs, at a press conference that was reported in *Izvestiya*, at least one crime in every three by the end of the 1980s was associated with alcohol, including 72.3 per cent of all murders and attempted murders, 75 per cent of premeditated serious assaults, 69.9 per cent of rapes, and more than half of all robberies and thefts.[35] Nor were women immune from these trends. Over 267,000 were detained in 1988 for drinking spirits

6.2   D. Oboznenko, 'Opium of the people'
(poster, 1989)

and public appearance in a state of intoxication; the number of women receiving compulsory treatment for alcoholism doubled between 1985 and 1988.[36]

Two journalists on the trade union paper *Trud* described a typical day in the life of Moscow's only sobering-up station for women, an old two-storey building in an alleyway in the centre of town. Women arrived here at all hours of day and night, with their 'drunken, torpid, unwomanly faces, their clothes thick with dirt, the language foul and giggling hysterically. Morose. Hopeless. Wild.' By 12 noon the station had already received six admissions, and another twelve cases had been reported on the telephone. There was Ivana Babushkina, a 27-year-old technical assistant, who was unable to walk unaided at 8 o'clock in the evening and had been found in the middle of the road. Another woman was found lying in one of the doorways of an apartment block; another was sleeping in a market gateway; yet another was brought in from the outskirts of Moscow, 'a woman of pensionable age, carrying a dog in her arms'. Some 2,864 women altogether were apprehended in Moscow in a state of intoxication in the first six months of 1989; this was more than in the two previous years put together and almost 1,000 more than in 1986, the first full year of the campaign. Even in the Caucasian and traditionally Muslim areas female drunkenness was causing problems on a scale that had never previously been encountered.[37]

The wives of alcoholics had an equally hard time. As 'L.S.' of Moscow wrote to the popular education journal *Shkola i sem'ya*:

I am the wife of an alcoholic. You cannot imagine the torments that writing these three words have cost me . . . I have been married twelve years – and for twelve years I have always been putting my hopes in something. The last time I placed my hopes in anything was in the anti-alcohol decree, when the top leadership made it known that there would be no 'return to the old ways'. And sure enough there was a decrease in the sales of alcohol, and they stopped drinking at work.

But now, in 1990, it had begun again: 'at work, at home, with an excuse and without an excuse'. In fact, two-thirds of her husband's salary went on drink; she had to conceal the truth from her family and friends by taking a second job.[38] Another anonymous woman wrote from the Kemerovo region: 'Who can help me or even tell me how to raise children whose father is an alcoholic? How am I supposed to live when, with a nervous condition and so many other ailments that I can scarcely manage, I still have to be all right for work . . . I don't remember when I was last at the cinema, or in the country, or when I last enjoyed myself with the children.' But where could she turn? Her husband would refuse to visit the narcologist, there was no psychologist in her locality, and she was reluctant to seek a divorce. 'There's only one way out and that's for us to do away with ourselves.' Very often, it appeared, the wives of alcoholics were more in need of hospital treatment than their spouses because of what was called the 'coalcoholism' or 'codependence'.[39]

Had the countryside, at least, become sober? Not in the view of one of *Izvestiya*'s special correspondents, who filed an alarming report from a state farm in the Tula region where eight workers had died after drinking a poisonous alcohol substitute. As the paper explained, 'Tractor driver G.F. had crept into a storehouse and, having taken two bottles of the poisonous chemical "Gliftor", approached his boozing companions during the lunch break and invited them and his brother to a "drink". They then made their way to a workshop in the construction section. There another two workers got a share of his refreshment'. Alcoholic poisoning of this kind was 'anything but a rarity'; not surprisingly, perhaps, the farm itself was frequently short of labour.[40] There were similar scenes in the Tambov region, according to a report in the temperance journal. Three years earlier, a group of locals had written in a collective letter, their village had been declared a sobriety zone and a bookshop had been opened in what had been the liquor store. Life had become peaceful and happy, free of the 'obscene language in the parks and drunks in the House of Culture'. Then came instructions from above to resume the sale of alcohol. Supplies of drink appeared the next day in local shops; the day after that six workers failed to appear at the local collective farm, and now six milkmaids and three swineherds were alcoholics.[41] In Volgograd, even school pupils were drinking (one of the local wine shops was directly opposite the youth centre).[42] Once again, it was reported, boozers were 'swinging like pendulums', appealing loudly to 'their comrades (or mankind in general)' for support, and 'interspersing their "philosophy" with unprintable language'.[43]

There were scenes of almost biblical devastation among some of the native peoples of the far north, as a series of reports in the sobriety journal made clear. The first impression their correspondent had when he arrived at the village of Nogliki in Sakhalin, he wrote, was of a 'positive flood of alcohol available in the local shops'. The local people, the Nivkhi, had up to now lived 'free of the harsh and cruel vices of civilisation'. But now they had encountered a civilisation that existed 'exclusively in the form of alcohol, syphilis and commercial fraud'. Local traders took away salmon and caviar from the natives, leaving them with vodka, cheap wine, homebrew and even household solvents. Some became so drunk they fell off their sleds and had to be tied on; others slaughtered their reindeer herds, which began to disappear. Now one in twelve of the Nivkhi was a registered alcoholic, and not a single one had been successfully treated. The number of infant deaths had increased, as a result of parental inattention.[44] Nivkhi who joined fishing boats were almost forced to drink, in that they were met with *zakuski* and a drink when they arrived back from trips and were given alcohol on voyages to keep out the cold. New and infectious diseases were imported by the settlers, and the local population began to die out. Their language was russified, their land exploited for its natural resources, and the Nivkhi themselves were herded into towns where they adopted the unhealthy habits of their neighbours. By the end of the century the native language was expected to disappear entirely and the Nivkhi nationality would 'exist only on a passport'.[45]

Most vital of all, literally, were the figures on births and deaths. There were certainly some improvements to report. Diagnoses of alcoholism and alcoholic psychosis, for instance, had fallen and were continuing to fall; so too had the numbers of patients receiving treatment. Birth rates had risen, in the early years of the campaign, and the death rate had fallen. From 1987, however, and paralleling the relaxation of restrictions on the sale of drink, the birth rate began to fall again and the death rate mounted. The rate of natural population increase, the excess of births over deaths, had been 6.8 per 1,000 in Russia in 1986 but was down to 0.7 per cent by 1990 and by the following year the population was actually declining.[46] More of those born were suffering from congenital abnormalities than had been the case before the campaign began,[47] and deaths from alcohol-related causes, which had fallen in the 1980s, were also beginning to increase. Among the working-age Russian population nearly twice as many were dying of alcohol-related causes in 1991 as in the early 1980s, and life expectancy, which had risen briefly in the early years of the campaign, had resumed its earlier decline.[48] By the end of 1990 there was talk of a 'demographic disaster' after the improvements that had taken place in the early years of perestroika, with maternity hospitals 'literally empty' and a corresponding rise in the death rate as a result of wider social changes as well as the greater incidence of alcohol abuse.[49]

There was certainly some public opposition to the relaxation of the campaign so soon after it had been initiated. In the port of Nakhodka, for instance, they had started to sell alcohol in a fruit and vegetable shop close by a children's kindergarten. Local officials explained that the decision had been taken 'in the interests of the people' and 'for the convenience of citizens'. In practice, local people told the sobriety journal, the decision had been taken for the convenience of boozers, 'who now stretch out in groups alongside the vegetable shop from the early hours'.[50] There was a similar complaint from Saratov, where a wine shop had once again been opened up beside a kindergarten. In Stavropol' a wine and spirits shop had been established close to a school, a children's library and the 'Pioneer' children's cinema. In Semipalatinsk, mothers with young children had 'literally to push their way through a crowd of drunks' to gain access to the children's polyclinic. In a village in the Novosibirsk region children had even begun to give 'boisterous performances, playing at "drunken-uncle"'. In Chelyabinsk the hallways of local apartment blocks had been turned into drinking dens and public toilets, and in the summer 'whole companies' sat around under the bushes; if you tried to stop them 'stones and bottles come flying at your windows'. Approaches to local officials, and even to the Soviet government, produced no response. To whom were they to write now, local people asked: 'to the UN?'[51]

There were, in fact, some appeals for a change of course, such as a *cri de coeur* from the 'wives and mothers of Taganrog', or a letter from deputies in Chelyabinsk, or a heartfelt 'Open letter of Soviet people, concerned by the worsening of the alcoholic situation in the country', which appeared in the sobriety journal in 1990. The letter, addressed to the president, the Supreme Soviet and the mass media, warned against any weakening in the struggle against this 'dangerous evil'. In the initial stages of the struggle, as the letter noted, life expectancy had increased, public health and productivity had improved, and there was a 'real hope' that drunkenness might be overcome. Now, however, state bodies at all levels, without consulting with the people or taking any account of their own laws, were increasing the production and sale of alcohol, and the mass media had resorted to a 'no-holds-barred publicising and propagandising of alcohol and boozing which completely drowned out propaganda in favour of sobriety'. How, asked the signatories, could the cause of perestroika be brought to a successful conclusion

if at every step of the way in our daily life we are dogged by the malign and burgeoning spectre of drunkenness, when every year almost a million children are orphaned even though their parents are still alive, when annually in the country hundreds and thousands of children with drunken mothers and fathers are born with abnormalities, when crime with its sotted and often bloody hand holds Soviet society by the throat, when hundreds and thousands of people perish through traumas and accidents, and yet still we sustain multi-billion losses due to low-quality output, waste, damage to machinery and equipment, and lost work time?[52]

More generally there was a deepening pessimism, reflected in the polls, that the problem was capable of any kind of resolution: only 17 per cent doubted the success of the campaign in 1987 but 26 per cent did so by 1988 and by the end of 1989 an overwhelming 70 per cent had come to the conclusion that alcoholism would never be eradicated.[53]

Alcohol and public finance

Perhaps the most damaging criticism of the sobriety campaign, at least from the point of view of the authorities, was its unfortunate effect upon public finance and the budget in particular. This was certainly the gravamen of Ryzhkov's attack when he persuaded the party and state leadership to relax the campaign in late 1988. The result of official measures, he explained, had been not simply to reduce the output and sale of alcoholic drink, but at the same time to lower consumer spending as a whole. In 1985, when the campaign started, consumers had spent 5 billion rubles less on alcohol than they had done the year before. In 1986 spending had fallen by 15.8 billion rubles, and in 1987 by 16.3 billion: or over the three years, a total of more than 37 billion rubles. The spending power that had been released in this way had become available for the purchase of other goods: food, clothing, footwear, consumer durables and so forth. The supply of goods of this kind, however, had increased by much less than the extra demand: by only 12.4 billion rubles. A change in the balance of supply and demand on this scale, in its turn, had obvious consequences for the availability of goods and for reserve stocks, which had fallen considerably.[54] Indeed the whole of the disparity between goods and money incomes during these years, according to other calculations, could more than satisfactorily be explained by the 'vodka effect'.[55]

A fall in the availability of goods on this scale had obvious implications for the incentive to work (why make more effort if there was nothing on which the money could be spent?). The impact upon government income

6.3 D. Oboznenko, 'Bring back the good old Brezhnev days!'
(poster, 1989)

and expenditure was still more serious, as Soviet finance ministers made clear in successive statements. In November 1985 the head of Gosplan and the deputy finance minister, speaking to parliament, both underlined the importance of increasing the output of consumer goods to balance the loss of revenue that would arise from the fall in alcohol sales.[56] Finance minister Boris Gostev, presenting the state budget in late 1986, acknowledged that revenues had been lower than planned as a result, among other things, of the campaign;[57] a year later, in October 1987, he reported a further loss and a continued failure to increase the output of consumer goods to compensate.[58] Presenting another budget in October 1988 after official policies had changed, Gostev was able to report that the fall in revenues had been arrested and that turnover tax as a whole would increase in the coming year.[59] Nikolai Shmelev, a deputy as well as an economist, argued in these circumstances for the still more radical step of eliminating restrictions upon the sale of vodka and reducing its price 'as soon as possible'.[60] Others, in the press, were suggesting that the campaign had led to a budgetary loss of 10 billion rubles a year (or about a tenth of all indirect taxation), and arguing that there should be a cut in the price of liquor in order to cut the deficit, drive out homebrewing and eliminate profiteering.[61]

Shmelev was taken to task by other writers including V. Molkanov, the head of a local statistical bureau. Restrictions on alcohol sales and price increases had certainly aggravated the state of public finance, argued Molkanov. But there were compensating increases, such as better harvest yields. Sales of alcoholic drink had fallen relatively little since 1980, or even 1985, while retail trade as a whole had increased. It seemed more important, to Molkanov, to step up the production of consumer goods on which the spare rubles could be spent: the output of domestic appliances was barely half the level of demand, and of shoes only a third. And this was to take no account of the 'spiritual impoverishment, immorality and dissipation' that had earlier existed. Now, with the relaxation of the campaign, spending on alcohol was on the increase again, while the number of births and marriages had declined; even Molkanov, however, agreed that existing restrictions had to be 'liberalised'.[62] Other suggestions for restoring a budgetary balance included a special levy on earnings, and a reduction in the quantity of drink that was imported from abroad (there was a substantial and increasingly negative trade balance). But for others still drunks would pay whatever necessary, simply raising their charges for the household services they provided and stealing even more than they had done in the past.[63]

The campaign involved substantial additional costs, though most of these were less easy to identify. There was the cost of working time lost by people spending their time in queues rather than on the shop floor. There was the cost of policing the queues, tracking down illicit distilling, and incarcerating the offenders. There was the waste of raw material, particularly of grapes and other wine-making materials, which in 1986–7 had to be converted into fodder. Winemaking factories suffered heavy losses for which there had been no budgetary provision.[64] And there were the very heavy costs involved in the wanton destruction of vineyards. The total area of vineyards fell by about a quarter between 1985 and 1990 (the fall, admittedly, had begun before the campaign started); output was down more sharply still, and the production of wine itself was down by almost half over the same period.[65] The brewing industry, similarly, had been 'destroyed just when it was on the upswing', with a programme launched in the mid-1970s to install modern and often imported equipment in major cities and in some of the southern republics. The Czechoslovak firms that supplied the equipment 'simply couldn't understand why machinery capable of producing first-rate beer was distributed to dairies and margarine-producing shops as auxiliary equipment'. Sales of brandy had been increased, but this had been achieved by emptying casks that had been meant to age for a much longer period. Vodka production could be revived more easily, but there was a shortage of bottles as the factories that produced them had turned to other forms of output. As a 'last resort' distilleries had been ordered to 'pour vodka into beer and Pepsi Cola bottles'. Experts thought it would be five years before Soviet consumers could buy a bottle of champagne, beer or brandy without a 'mob scene'.[66]

Most serious of all, perhaps, was the shift of economic activity from public to private hands that had been a direct result of the campaign. To begin with, as Shmelev saw it, the measures taken had had some positive effect: a reduction in accidents at work, less drink-related crime, fewer drunks on the streets. But most drinkers had simply adapted to these new conditions and turned to alternatives, including chemicals and other surrogates; while the state, for its part, had become engaged in a struggle with the population, a struggle (as Shmelev pointed out in several places) that it could hardly hope to win given the simplicity with which *samogon* could be produced. How could every country cottage, and every apartment, have its own police guard? And the profitability of *samogon* was such that it was worth any risk to make it, which suggested in its turn that the country was on the verge of the 'full-scale underground production of spirits (as in America during the 1920s)' and a corresponding increase in organised crime. Shmelev's own calculations suggested that if two-thirds of the income from alcohol sales in the early 1980s had been generated by the state sector and one-third by homebrewers, the result of the campaign by the late 1980s had simply been to reverse these proportions. All of this amounted to a voluntary donation of state revenue to the homebrewers – a rare event in the history of the drink trade.[67] Shmelev welcomed the relaxation of restrictions that took place in late 1988; but it was unlikely at the high prices that continued to obtain that the massive production of *samogon* would be reduced and that the state would be able to recover the revenue it had lost.[68]

Shmelev's own remedy was certainly a bold one. The price of vodka, he suggested, should be roughly halved (to 3 or 4 rubles a bottle), and a 'broad network of well-appointed bars and cafes' should be established. This would hardly lead to an increase in drunkenness, as the cause of alcohol abuse was not the price of drink but the 'whole socioeconomic and spiritual situation of the country'. In the 1950s, for instance, when the price of spirits had been significantly lower and it had been sold almost everywhere, consumption had been a half or even a third of the levels recorded in the 1980s. A change of policy of this kind would help to undermine the homebrewers and ensure that spending on alcohol helped to generate income for the state and not for private producers. And if elderly peasants began to pay for minor services with money, rather than alcohol, it would reduce the production of *samogon* more effectively than anything the police force could hope to accomplish. The uprooting of vineyards – a precious inheritance and the result of many generations of labour – should also be ended. The struggle with alcoholism, certainly, should continue, but it should be a 'slow, persistent struggle', acting through the provision of consumer goods and a 'raising of the general cultural level of the population'.[69]

Applying sanctions

There were problems not only in securing the compliance of institutions and individuals, and the active cooperation of the sobriety society: there were also problems in applying the sanctions for which the law provided in the event of non-compliance. One reason for this was that some of the articles of the relevant legislation were in conflict with the Soviet constitution: the prohibition on the sale of alcohol to those under twenty-one, for instance, appeared to contradict the provisions that related to the rights and freedoms of the citizen.[70] The subjection of alcohol offenders to compulsory treatment was also a violation of the constitution, and in particular of articles 57 and 42. The first of these gave citizens the right to legal defence against any infringement of their personal freedom, 'let alone their honour and dignity'. Indeed, unless they had been deprived of Soviet citizenship, it was unconstitutional even to describe the people concerned as 'alcoholics'. Article 42, for its part, gave all citizens a guaranteed right to health: but this was violated by the practice of administering a compulsory course of treatment for alcoholism. Compulsory treatment, it was represented, was in effect a prison sentence; indeed it was worse, as prisoners did at least know why they were being detained. And it opened a wide scope for abuse, in that it could be used by the authorities for 'psychiatric repression against anyone who was found to be awkward', or by factory managers to get rid of persistent critics.[71]

Was it 'constitutional to drink', asked the sobriety journal in reply? Although there were 'imperfections' in the system of compulsory treatment, the constitution did also impose obligations, such as to work and to obey the law. The drunk, by taking alcohol, placed himself in a condition in which it became very difficult for him to discharge these obligations. Article 42, similarly, obliged the state to protect the health of its citizens, and to treat alcoholics as it would those who suffered from other illnesses. This was true even if alcoholics did not wish to be treated, and did not regard themselves as in need of treatment, as their condition was likely to affect the health of others. It was still important to ensure that the constitutional rights of alcoholics were treated with as much respect as those of other citizens.[72] In the event the Constitutional Review Committee, at a meeting in October 1990, ruled that compulsory treatment of this kind was indeed a violation of the constitution, and also of international conventions on human rights;[73] the law, later still, was changed to reflect these rulings.[74]

A related difficulty was that the laws on alcohol abuse were often obscure or inconsistent. The law, for instance, forbade the drinking of spirits in public places. But it did not define 'spirits'. Writing in *Sovetskaya militsiya*, a journal put out by the Ministry of Internal Affairs, two police officers argued that the law should be interpreted broadly so as to include the consumption of beer in public places, as it was a weak alcoholic drink. On this basis, it was argued, what was to stop measures being taken against lemonade, *kefir*, liqueur chocolates and other mildly 'alcoholic' items?[75] The law also used a variety of terms to refer to the same phenomenon, mostly without precise definition: 'drunkenness', 'drunken appearance', 'unsober state', 'state of intoxication' or 'state of serious intoxication' (all of these in the legislation of 1985); or 'chronic alcoholism' and 'inveterate drunkenness', in other legislation. Courts and lawyers then interpreted these various terms with some freedom.[76] In a case of this kind a man had been arrested coming out of a restaurant where he had quite legally been consuming alcohol. How was he 'offending public morality'?[77] The Soviet minister of justice himself commented on the case of a Moscow scientist, 'V.', who had entered a metro station early one evening after visiting friends and drinking a little wine. A policeman, standing beside the turnstile, caught a whiff of alcohol and demanded that V. accompany him to the station, where he was found to be 'half-drunk'. When, asked the minister, was a citizen drunk, and when was he sober? And what, in these circumstances, was there to prevent the police simply victimising a member of the public as he went about his lawful business?[78]

Apart from this, there were wide variations in the severity with which the law was applied. In reality, the justice minister explained, 'every region, town and even enterprise implement[ed] the legislation in its own way'. A worker, for instance, might be dismissed in one enterprise, while another worker, employed elsewhere in the same enterprise, might simply be reprimanded. This was a result of the fact that the law was applied, not by jurists familiar with its requirements, but by factory managers, trade union officials and others whose superficial knowledge of the law and whose wish to take account of the moral aspects of the case could lead them to decisions that were at variance with the law as it actually stood. Courts had begun to reinstate workers who had been dismissed improperly for violations of the anti-alcohol law, and this brought the law itself into disrepute.[79] More generally, there was an undue emphasis upon the sanctions of the criminal law. Some 90 per cent of those found to be 'under the influence', for instance, were not alcohol abusers and had no previous convictions.[80]

There were persisting doubts about the effectiveness of legal sanctions in any case. Suppose, for instance, that a father or a mother was being deprived of parental rights. Dozens of people were involved, the court might take what appeared to be a just decision, the children were saved, and the public breathed a sigh of relief. But this was often a decision 'on paper only'. The people who were sentenced were forgotten, and no one found the time to collect the children from their parents, 'who by this stage have really hit the skids'. The children still saw their parents ravaged by excessive drinking, but now they were free to do what they pleased – the court's decision had freed them from their parental responsibilities. Even the children who were placed in a home immediately after the court's decision took some time to free themselves of the 'nightmare' they had been through. And eventually they would have to return to their original home, where their parents would be behaving 'as shamelessly as before'.[81]

Things were no better in sobering-up stations (*vytrezviteli*) or in the more elaborate labour rehabilitation centres (*lechebno-trudovye profilaktorii* or LTPs) that had been developed in the 1960s as corrective labour institutions.[82] The internal regime at institutions of this kind had for a long time remained almost entirely secret. 'Fenced off from daily life not only by barbed wire but also by a skilfully fashioned curtain of secrecy', *Izvestiya* reported in 1988, 'those rehabilitation centres became just like detention camps, with a rigid regime and minimal rights for their inmates.'[83] As another correspondent pointed out, the rehabilitation centres were based upon a 'complex pass system akin to that of corrective labour institutions'. There was 'constant surveillance; a uniform; a strict regime; a limited number of visits; barbed wire; [and] guards, although without weapons'.[84] Inmates had their own version of the name of the institution in which they were held: 'Luche, chem Tam – Pomeret'' (loosely, they would be better off dead).[85] It was a strange kind of hospital, wrote *Sovetskaya Rossiya*, that was 'enclosed by barbed wire, with guards all around and where patients are treated by people with epaulettes'; it was the only 'hospital' to which people were sent not on the recommendation of their trade union committee but by the decision of a court, and without being guilty of a crime but simply because they were ill.[86]

One of the problems of the rehabilitation centres was that, in the absence of a proper judicial procedure, it was easy for mistakes to be made about commital. A man could be sent to an LTP, wrote *Sovetskaya Rossiya*, 'because his wife has slandered him for over-indulging. And the mother-in-law is apt to help by blowing the whistle. Nor is there any likelihood of a proper discussion where there is neither a court hearing nor lawyers. Everything is decided personally by the judge on the basis of representations made to the local police by members of the family or neighbours.' Indeed there was no end to the abuses in the LTPs: the compulsory labour of the aged and the sick, the deduction of one-third of earnings for the state, and the lack of leave and even pay for the 'patients'.[87] In a third of the cases examined in Moscow the necessary documentation was incomplete, and yet those who were wrongly sentenced to compulsory treatment had no right of compensation;[88] there were even cases where commitals took place so that 'plans' could be fulfilled.[89] The inmates of a women's centre in Ordzhonikidze appealed directly to *Sovetskaya Rossiya* on this basis. They wrote:

There is not one of us who is guilty of a crime against other people. We have not robbed or killed or brawled. If we are guilty of anything it is our weakness for drink and for this we ask the forgiveness of our husbands and children. We have been forcibly separated from them for long periods and have been subjected to a regime which is in no way different from that of a correctional colony. Why are we kept under guard like dangerous criminals? Help us, in the name of all that's holy, to get back quickly to our children![90]

One reason for change in the rehabilitation centres was indeed that the inmates had become increasingly difficult to regulate. There had been cases of 'group absenteeism from work', and in some of them, 'instances of hooliganism, attacks on . . . staff, pogroms and arson'.[91] Matters went still further at a camp near Rybinsk, where the inmates had confronted the duty officer one evening and demanded 'vodka and freedom'. They repeated their demands later in the evening, and then hacked their way out of the centre using iron railings and set out for Rybinsk, about 10 kilometres away. By morning they were entering the town, surrounded by police cars and by officers with riot shields 'in the manner of Crusaders'. After the promises of improvements most of them returned later to the centre, but about fifty were found to be missing; they included not only alcoholics but criminals with lengthy records.[92] Another strike took place at a centre in Krasnodar, where the 534 striking inmates 'peacefully and with restraint' demanded that the Russian government carry out treatment for alcoholism within the system of the ministry of health rather than the ministry of internal affairs, and on a voluntary basis.[93] A particularly spectacular riot took place at a rehabilitation centre in the Volgograd region some months later. Alarming news roused the police and local officials from their beds at about 3 a.m.: 'A long column of men was marching through the streets of the sleeping town of Kamyshin.' After some discussion with officials, the men returned quietly to their barracks; the cause of their complaint had been the brutal behaviour of the troops who maintained order at the centre.[94]

Like prisons in most other countries, the rehabilitation centres soon established internal forms of authority and began to predispose their inmates towards further indiscipline and crime. The atmosphere, according to the staff themselves, encouraged the emergence of 'ringleaders' who tried to impose their criminal proclivities on others. All who spent time in a rehabilitation centre had this fact marked on their work record, and believed – with some reason – that they had become 'second class members of the society'. The great majority – 70 per cent, in the case of a centre in the Volgograd region – returned there after a further offence; there were third, fourth and even sixth time offenders. The medical attention that inmates received was also outside the scope of the regular health service and inquiries were not welcomed.[95] And there were about 10 per cent of offenders for whom an isolation regime was completely inappropriate, who needed rather the attention of their 'nearest and dearest' if they were to reintegrate themselves into ordinary life.[96] If they had any justification, staff at the centres believed, it was that they gave a period of relief to the long-suffering families.[97]

Pressures of this kind led to some relaxation in the regulations that were applied in rehabilitation centres in 1988: insignia no longer had to be worn (this, it was felt, equated inmates with common criminals), their

6.4 A homebound Russian soldier, 1993
(Bettmann)

shops began to sell a wider range of goods, and inmates were given permission to go on leave 'not in a quilted jacket but in civilian clothes'. Almost all forms of organisation were suspended, apart from compulsory work; and inmates, with the permission of the head of the centre, were allowed to stay out until 8 p.m. when visiting family and friends. Relatives themselves were able to visit more freely and with fewer arrangements to distance them from the inmates. Inmates could even attend ordinary concerts and filmshows. Words like 'cell' and 'search' were withdrawn from use, although occasionally 'examinations' might take place; and staff had begun to address each other by their first names rather than as 'comrade'. Steps had even been taken to dismantle the barbed wire that had encircled the centres.[98] And there were changes in the committal proceedings, with the presence of a lawyer and the right of appeal. The aim, Moscow television explained, was to get rid 'as far as possible of the attributes adopted from corrective establishments', although it was hard to get the staff to 'tune in to a new and humane wavelength'.[99]

There was little evidence, before or after these changes, that the rehabilitation centres had much effect in achieving their ostensible purpose, which was the treatment and rehabilitation of alcoholics. The system of treatment, staff at the centres freely confessed, was most inadequate. Only 20 per cent of those treated led a sober life in the first year, and only 13 per cent remained sober by the end of the second year. Those who underwent treatment and went on to lead sober lives were 'numbered in single figures'. These were the figures for a single, better than average centre; for the country as a whole the rate of recovery was no more than 2 or 3 per cent.[100] It was widely agreed elsewhere that the rehabilitation centres had not fulfilled the hopes that had been placed in them. 'The administration of these institutions are more concerned with fulfilling production tasks than in treating patients, and there are not enough medicines, not to speak of more advanced forms of care.' The effectiveness of treatment in these circumstances was 'practically nil', and discipline was poor. The expediency of continuing with LTPs was in serious doubt, 'but the question is with what are they to be replaced?'[101]

The limited 'democratisation' of the centres, in fact, led in some respects to greater difficulties. About a third of offenders, for instance, failed to turn up at the end of their period of leave; some were at large for up to three months, and those who did come back on time often had difficulty standing up. Some offenders refused to work; cooks refused to serve lunch; in one case an inmate turned up for work in a state of intoxication and then 'presented an ultimatum, whereby if he was not allowed to have a hair of the dog he would go on strike'. In Rybinsk there had been two strikes about the blocking of leave and holidays by the administration; the centre was in any case in the grip of illicit distilling, as there was no difficulty in obtaining yeast and every inmate was allowed to buy a kilogram of sugar once a month in the local shop.[102] Another innovation of the late 1980s had been to establish experimental factories under the administration of rehabilitation centres. The Third Moscow LTP, for instance, provided the staff for a factory of this kind; but of the 1,200 formally registered, only 137 actually turned up and these could 'snooze the whole of the working day'. The workshops were empty, the equipment rusting, and the foremen, who were ordinary employees, not only drank themselves but debauched the inmates in their charge.[103] There were even cases where offenders were sent to work in factories producing alcoholic beverages.[104] And how were offenders to be treated for their alcoholism in any case when they returned to the rehabilitation centres late at night after the working day had ended?[105]

It was no surprise, in these circumstances, when the rehabilitation system in its existing form was wound up by the Russian Supreme Soviet in 1991. The decision followed a ruling that the Committee of Constitutional Supervision had made the previous October and was intended to prevent any 'unjustified restriction of the rights and freedoms of citizens'. All chronic alcoholics who had been sent to rehabilitation centres simply because they had refused compulsory treatment or because they had continued to drink after a course of treatment were to be released. Commissions would be formed for this purpose, composed of doctors as well as local government officials, and with a member of the procuracy in attendance to ensure that there was no violation of procedures; and any case in which a release had been denied could be challenged in the courts. In the meantime, and until a more comprehensive law had been adopted, the only basis for detention in a rehabilitation centre was to be the systematic violation of public order, or any infringement of the rights of others that was connected with drunkenness or drug abuse.[106] The system had been at its peak in 1988, but by the time of the decision to dissolve it there were still 272 institutions with over 112,000 inmates, together with 26 special institutions for women offenders and 1 for the under-age; the last inmates were discharged in the summer of 1994, some of the wives protesting to the last against the premature release of their alcoholic husbands.[107]

7.1 New Year, 1992
(Bettmann)

7

Russia, alcohol and the policy process

There was certainly no sign, in the early post-communist 1990s, that alcohol had relinquished its place in Russian public or private life. The Russian president, Boris Yeltsin, admitted that he allowed himself a glass 'or maybe two' of cognac on a Sunday evening with his family, or some beer after visiting the bathhouse;[1] but there was continuing controversy when he appeared to have fallen, in obscure circumstances, into a Moscow canal,[2] and his unsteady performance during a first visit to the United States excited parliamentary comment.[3] There was further criticism in early 1993 when Yeltsin, defending himself against impeachment, spoke uncertainly before the Russian parliament and had to be assisted from the hall. 'We have a drunk President', declared a centrist deputy from St Petersburg; another agreed that the president had created a 'strange impression'.[4] Celebrating the withdrawal of Russian troops from Germany in 1994, the Russian president had to be steadied as he left the reception and then attempted to lead the Berlin police band in a 'spirited rendition of Kalinka'.[5] Nor was it simply Yeltsin whose conduct was affected by such circumstances. During the attempted coup of 1991 at least two of the conspirators were in less than full possession of their faculties; former Prime Minister Pavlov later admitted he 'might have had a drop'[6] and Gennadii Yanaev, briefly the acting president, was unable to recognise the people who had come to arrest him.[7] Even Western social scientists found alcohol a complicating factor in their investigations: as many as 2 per cent of those who were asked, in a survey in early 1992, were unable to respond because of their intoxication.[8]

What, in fact, was the place of alcohol in Russian social life in the early and mid-1990s? To what extent had it been affected by a change of economic system and not simply of government, and by a painful process of adjustment that had widened inequalities and left millions in poverty?

Had temperance campaigners acknowledged their apparent defeat and modified their tactics in a society in which a mass public movement could no longer be created 'from above' with a press that could be relied upon to be supportive? Had they found different and more effective means of treatment, if slower ones, than prohibition and compulsion? Above all, for students of public policy more generally, what were the lessons to be drawn from the apparent failure of a centrally directed programme of social change, sponsored by a government in a society in which it was (at this time) unusually powerful? The campaign against alcohol abuse was the last but also one of the most comprehensive to be conducted in what was still the Soviet Union: it followed campaigns to collectivise agriculture in the 1930s, to develop the Virgin Lands in the late 1950s, or (on a more modest scale) to extend the Shchekino chemical plant's system of increasing labour productivity and Zlobin's brigade method in construction in the 1970s.[9] But the campaign against alcohol abuse was one that took place against a background of attempts to reduce alcoholism in other societies, and at other times; and it can be seen in the still wider context of 'implementation studies', examining the varied success of governments in converting their general objectives into observable changes in the behaviour of mass societies. It is this broader perspective – the campaign against alcohol abuse as a case study in the implementation of public policy – that informs this final chapter.[10]

Implementation studies take their origin from an awareness of the gap that often develops between the objectives of central government (for instance, to reduce black unemployment in Oakland, California) and the extent to which those objectives are actually achieved at local level by the officials who control the programme concerned. Under the 'top-down' model, governments are assumed to have clear objectives, a hierarchical control structure, an optimal allocation of responsibilities between the various levels of administration, a means of measuring performance, and a system of management that identifies any deviation from central objectives and corrects them whenever necessary.[11] In practice, it emerges, there are likely to be a series of 'implementation gaps' as the original objectives are converted into policy by subordinate agencies and by local officials (often, in the literature, described as 'street level bureaucrats').[12] The causal assumptions of a policy, moreover, are critical to its success. How has the 'problem' been conceptualised, and by whom? And are the means chosen those that reflect an adequate diagnosis of the problem in the first place? An analysis of implementation, in addition, must 'encompass the policy problem (and the variety of affected actors), not just the initial policy decision'.[13] To what extent, for instance, are the interests of all the groups that were likely to be affected taken into account? And how consistent are their objectives with each other, and with those of government? The study of policy implementation helps us to explain the persistent failure of central government to achieve its objectives in late Soviet Russia; there are, in turn, many ways in which a study of policy implementation under the unusual circumstances of communist rule can help to advance a body of literature that has almost entirely assumed the open, bargaining cultures of the developed West with their strong well-organised interests, their independent press and judiciaries, and their active and well-informed citizenry.

Russia, alcohol, post-communism

If a reduction in alcohol consumption had been the central objective of the campaign there was little evidence, by the early 1990s, that it had achieved a real measure of success. Taking *samogon* and state sales together, the level of alcohol consumption had recovered to the level that had prevailed before the campaign had been initiated.[14] Levels of consumption had meanwhile been falling in most Western countries, leaving Russia, by 1993, ahead of France as the world's heaviest drinking nation, with an average consumption of a bottle of vodka for every adult male every two days.[15] A higher proportion of this consumption, moreover, was in the form of spirits: as much as 90 per cent, compared with 60 per cent in the early 1980s.[16] Alcoholics, by 1990, were spending twice as much as they had done before the campaign began, and family budgets were hit twice as hard.[17] Drinkers were younger than ever before, and girls were (for the first time) drinking more than boys.[18] Alcohol had become an industrial incentive, as when two districts in the north Caucasus were invited to compete for 10 tonnes of 'Zhiguli' beer, presented by a local cooperative to the one that first completed the harvest.[19] In Kirov, local officials offered the price of a cheap bottle of vodka for each stray dog that was handed in;[20] elsewhere, doctors offered a bottle of vodka for every three blood donors and were overwhelmed by the demand.[21] In Kamchatka, a food processing factory started to pay its workers in vodka because of a continued shortage of currency.[22]

Something of the effect of these figures was apparent in reports that reached the Russian parliament about the state of public health. A report in late 1993 from the State Statistical Committee made it clear that the problem of alcoholism had 'reemerged with new vigour'. Consumption had risen by a third over the previous five years, and the consumption of vodka and other liquors had nearly doubled';[23] so too had the incidence of *delirium tremens*.[24] There were towns, like Lipetsk, where doctors reckoned that half the local male population was alcoholic;[25] nationwide about 30 per cent of the working population were reckoned to abuse alcohol in the early 1990s.[26] There were increasing numbers of deaths from frostbite and exposure, 'almost all' of them in a state of inebriation; there were more deaths inside the sobering-up stations themselves.[27] The absence of a state monopoly on production and sale, moreover, had weakened controls over the quality of the alcohol that was publicly available for sale. By 1994 it was estimated that half of the alcohol sold was illicit, and that up to 70 per cent of the drink sold by street traders was not simply illicit but positively dangerous.[28] In Syzryan, 17 died when they mistook methanol for alcohol and went on a binge;[29] more than 400 died in the Far East after consuming Chinese alcohol to which ether and other toxins had been added at up to fifty times the permissible level.[30] In Omsk, spirits that should have been used to dissolve rubber were sold to unsuspecting locals;[31] in Tver', hardened drinkers literally turned violet when they swallowed a lacquer polish based upon coloured methylated spirits.[32]

There were other, often familiar signs of the alcohol problem that had resurfaced by the mid-1990s. Crime, for instance, had steadily recovered, and just as many crimes were committed in a drunken state as before the campaign had begun; the proportion of drunken murders had even increased.[33] The number of drunken driving incidents that took place in 1990 was two and a half times greater than had taken place in 1985, at the start of the campaign.[34] In family life the main source of domestic difficulties was identified as alcohol,[35] and the main reason given for divorce, once again, was the drinking of the husband.[36] Alcoholics were selling their flats, under the privatisation programme which allowed them to do so, and abandoning their children;[37] there was even a case of the sale of a three-month-old baby for two bottles of wine.[38] There were 'wine riots': in Chelyabinsk, where irate shoppers seized control of a department store until they were served; in Perm', where workers threw up a barricade on the main street;[39] and in Moscow, within 300 metres of the Kremlin, when rumours of a vodka delivery turned out to be ill-founded.[40] Coupons were being counterfeited,

7.2 The dangers of illicit alcohol
(*Izvestiya*, October 1994)

stolen or resold,[41] and turned in this way into a 'form of convertible currency',[42] or given as birthday presents because there were no other goods in the shops.[43] In industry, meanwhile, up to 25 per cent of working time was being lost because of alcohol-related illness or death, and more than half of all accidents were connected with drinking;[44] there were cases of this kind even at nuclear power stations.[45] And it was unlikely that the laws would be enforced effectively, with up to 30 per cent of the police force affected by the same problems.[46]

What were the larger costs of the campaign, asked Vladimir Yarmosh, former head of spirits production in the Russian government and now the chairman of 'Rosalko'? A 'far from complete list' would include the '60–70 destroyed liquor factories and thousands of hectares of uprooted vineyards, outbreaks of homebrewing and hopeless shortages of sugar', as well as a 'new, "drunken" queue in which all the country [had been] standing'. In 1985 there had been 310 liquor distilleries; in just a few years 'almost a hundred' had been either destroyed or converted to other uses, with a more than proportional fall in output. The May 1985 decision, Yarmosh pointed out, had not been discussed with the producers who had then the responsibility for implementing it. The best he could do, with a few 'patriots', was to save about seventy distilleries by re-equipping them to produce *kvass* and lemonade. Indeed there was more than a shortage of drink: there was a 'bottle catastrophe' as well, with liquor plants receiving about a quarter of what they needed and a disastrous shortage of corks, with Armenia no longer in a position to supply them. There was another 'catastrophe' with packaging, which had previously been made by prisoners. Better social conditions, Yarmosh believed, were the key to any real improvement; but this would take decades, as the May 1985 resolution had thrown them back at least a generation.[47]

Public policy, in these circumstances, was confused and contradictory. First of all, the state monopoly was ended and prices were freed, as part of the liberalisation introduced in January 1992.[48] The new Russian criminal code, published in draft at about the same time, continued the move towards deregulation by legalising homebrewing;[49] in Kirgizia, in late 1991, the law had already been changed to allow private as well as state-run distilleries.[50] Imports began to reach the Russian market in significant quantities: there was 'Kutuzoff' and 'Suvorov', 'Alexander I' and 'Catherine II', even 'Yeltsin' and 'Gorbachev' (which apparently made those who tried it 'talk uncontrollably about *perestroika*').[51] By early 1994 as much as 60 per cent of all the vodka sold in Russia was imported.[52] But there were countervailing moves back towards a state monopoly, with distilleries licensed and retail sale limited to outlets approved by a new federal authority.[53] As in the nineteenth century, it was argued that this would protect consumers from a wide range of illegal and sometimes dangerous substitutes; at the same time it would help domestic producers, and improve public revenues (as much as 89 per cent of the value of domestically produced alcohol went to the state, while importers paid only for the right to sell and bootleggers paid nothing at all).[54] Producers, some of whom had ceased production, had reason to be grateful,[55] but retailers thought it unlikely any new policy would be implemented and continued to trade regardless, and customs duties were easily evaded.[56] Several cities and regions moved separately towards local monopolies;[57] and the Russian government itself banned all alcohol and tobacco advertising in the mass media.[58] There were even calls, in 1994, for a new 'state programme for the elimination of drunkenness and alcoholism'.[59]

The public was also in a state of some confusion, if surveys and civic initiatives were any guide. There were still attempts to stop and then reverse the 'poisoning of the Russian people': the open letter to President Gorbachev sponsored by the temperance society produced a significant response, with about a million signatures,[60] and in November 1990 the leading prohibitionist, Fedor Uglov, wrote directly to Gorbachev to convey his concern. 'If urgent and decisive measures are not taken soon', he told the Soviet president, there would be 'grave consequences for the people and the country as a whole which would be early and irreversible.'[61] Temperance campaigners in Chelyabinsk called for Nikolai Ryzhkov and other members of the Soviet government to make a 'personal commitment' to sobriety;[62] the open letter had now attracted 2 million signatures and messages of support were still pouring into the society headquarters.[63] Why was the question not being raised in the Soviet and Russian parliaments, Uglov asked in 1991? Could legislators not see that alcoholism was 'destroying the country, ruining the people and damaging its genetic pool'?[64] His own book *Iz plena illyuzii* had sold 5 million copies very quickly; its main target was the common misconception that there could be 'cultured' or moderate drinking.[65] Now, despite the 'alcoholic genocide' of the Russian people, more than ten different newspapers had refused to publish his writings. What was this but a 'carefully planned campaign' for the 'alcoholisation of our people'?[66] Uglov was still prepared to call, in the early 1990s, for 'obligatory sobriety for all':[67] in other words, a complete end to the state sale and production of alcoholic drink, and 'extraordinary measures' against homebrewers. Writing elsewhere (and in a book he had to finance himself) Uglov called for a year's imprisonment for public drunkenness, and five years for the production of *samogon* (with the confiscation of equipment); the promotion of alcohol or tobacco consumption should also become a criminal offence.[68] If not, he wrote in *Pravda*, the Russian people in just fifteen or twenty years would be an 'obedient herd of half-wits'.[69]

It was not only figures like Uglov, the 'spiritual father of the modern sobriety movement',[70] who were concerned about the rising tide of alcoholism. There was an equally categoric assessment from Igor Bestuzhev-Lada, an eminent and relatively liberal academic at the Institute of Sociology. Drunkenness and alcoholism, Bestuzhev-Lada told the sobriety journal, were 'no less serious a social problem than food or energy'. It was a question, he went on, 'of the life or death of our society': either alcoholism would be overcome, or 'what will happen to us is what happened to the majority of people who have disappeared or are disappearing from the face of the earth because of the "green serpent"'. And just as it was necessary to work out a long-term strategy for food or energy, so too a programme of this kind was necessary for the 'de-alcoholisation of society'. It should, Bestuzhev-Lada suggested, include a complex of measures: not only the reorientation of production towards consumer goods, but also the improvement of leisure facilities, better narcological care, a pricing policy that would undermine illicit distilling, and a campaign of law enforcement that would 'hit the biggest and most blatant predators as hard as possible'. There should also be measures against public drunkenness, and attempts to make drinking less glamorous in the mass media, and an improvement in the work of the sobriety society so that it would be a 'real people's volunteer corps'. Last, but most important, was a democratisation of society itself, with the emergence of a citizenry that was able to take decisions for itself and accept responsibility for them. It was a change in social relations of this kind, he suggested, that would be the 'main cure for alcoholism'.[71]

The social origins of alcoholism

Bestuzhev-Lada was not the only student of alcoholism in Soviet and Russian society who was reaching for more complex diagnoses of what was a very ambiguous 'problem'. 'It is the system that should be cured, not the alcoholics', as some readers suggested to *Pravda*. Ordinary Russians were fed up with empty promises and endless 'experiments' with no sign of (for instance) the long-promised improvement in their sports facilities.[72] A Moscow worker, Sergei Kochergin, wrote to the temperance journal to explain his position. He was, he explained, a drinker, he always had been and he had 'no intention of changing his habits'. He and his pals used to gather in a basement hangout, the

'Mochalka', which was near the Sandunovsky baths in Moscow. It was a sort of 'men's club', Kochergin explained; usually the same sort of people were there, with vodka only a sort of 'background' against which people could relax and express their feelings. There were never any fights or debauches. Now the Mochalka had been closed. But people drank even more at home. Everyone, Kochergin thought, needed a way of unburdening themselves: life was a series of situations in which – at a meeting, or in the director's office – one thing could be said, while – in the newspaper, or in life itself – something quite different was taking place. 'On the television – everything is fine. But go into a shop anywhere on the Volga or in Siberia – empty shelves.' Or take his neighbour, a shop assistant, with his apartment filled with under the counter goods – where was the justice in that? At least in the Mochalka it was possible to speak about such things. Goods and services, meanwhile, were 'measured in bottles', in a 'new political economy'; nobody wanted rubles for them.[73]

Replying to the correspondence that ensued, Kochergin had to reassure some of his readers that he did, in fact, exist: 42 years old, and a Moscow factory worker since the age of 16. There were three kinds of reply. The first simply abused him: he was 'undoubtedly an alcoholic', wrote L. Klimova from the Kuibyshev (now Samara) region, even an 'enemy of peace and socialism'. Others called him an 'enemy of the people' and demanded his immediate incarceration in just the same way as people had been herded into collective farms in the 1930s. As a pensioner from Sverdlovsk (now Yekaterinburg) put it, 'Only one thing is needed: discipline. Stern Stalinist discipline. In Stalin's time there was vodka everywhere, in all the shops, it was sold without restriction, but there were no drunks about. They were afraid.' Others still, in a rather different response, pointed out the lack of any reference to human qualities like conscience, honour, fairness or mercy in their daily lives. As Kochergin himself pointed out, hardly any of the promises made by factory managements had been fulfilled; indeed it was hardly considered a fault to engage in deceit of the workforce. Not that you could fill the shops overnight, but at least what there was could be more equally distributed. When millions of workers saw equal treatment, wrote I. Kutimsky from Irkutsk, 'then the question "To drink or not to drink" will come off the agenda'. But what had actually happened? Those who more than any others cried 'Don't drink, don't steal' were themselves the first to do so. What was left for ordinary people? 'Work, work, and once again work.' And for what? 'So that someone else could get rich.' What was that but 'slavery'?[74]

There was a similar evaluation in the interview that took place with Ven'yamin Yarin, a prominent USSR people's deputy who was by profession a metalworker from Nizhnii Tagil in the Sverdlovsk region. For a start, Yarin pointed out, alcoholism was of great value to the management: 'It's easy to order a drunk about, as he has no idea of social questions; he doesn't need a flat, rent, decent living conditions or humane working conditions.' Alcohol, again was a 'continuing and reliable source of income'. The restrictions introduced in 1985 were limited, and in any case they were 'soon taken over by functionaries in the *raikoms, ispolkoms* and so forth'; their motto appeared to be 'If you can't feed them bread, give them champagne even if the deluge follows soon after.' Coupons had been introduced in Nizhnii Tagil, but the only result was that those who never drank vodka were trading in their coupons to obtain it: in effect, the authorities had 'legalised alcohol abuse'. Nor was this all that had to change: the resolutions on democratisation adopted at the 1988 Party Conference, for a start, had to be implemented in full. And there were nearly 50 million poor, one of the 'main reasons for alcohol abuse'. It was social justice of this kind, for Yarin, that must be among the main prerequisites for a successful campaign.[75] For others, the campaign would succeed when people believed they were no longer working pointlessly but for their families, and could buy what they wanted in the shops: then they would be less likely to waste their money on drink.[76]

For others still, the 'years of stagnation' of the 1970s had taken a heavy toll, with the 'moral vacuum' to which they had given rise. The 'apathy, fear and anxiety' of these years, it was pointed out, had 'frequently led to stressful situations and to various illnesses'. People 'naturally reacted by seeking some way of relieving themselves of their tensions, uncertainty and tiredness, and sought some means of restoring their "spiritual balance"'. Alcohol supplied that means.[77] There were suggestions, in other discussions, that the Brezhnev years should be known as the 'epoch of developed alcoholism' (the official doctrine of the time spoke of 'developed socialism') or as a *period zastol'ya* (of drinking sessions, a play on the word for stagnation). There had been a 'wave of drunkenness' at this time, wrote *Sovetskaya Rossiya*, which was connected in its turn with the 'indifference' that people encountered in their daily lives and with their 'desire to escape from miserable reality into a world of drunken fancy'. The leadership of the time, indeed, had 'deliberately encouraged the people to intoxicate themselves, so that they might not think about politics or notice the mountain of problems that had been accumulating'.

All of this argued a policy that took account of the 'material and spiritual content of human life' – necessarily a lengthy process.[78] Others spoke of the 'privileged existence for some and a low standard of living for others' which encouraged crime as well as alcoholism itself. There should be 'free, unlimited access to wine and vodka' to undermine this criminal underworld;[79] but for many what was needed was a still larger process of 'regeneration', or what a meeting in the Moscow Patriarchate described as a 'higher level of spirituality in the society, with high moral norms among all its members, and the restructuring of interpersonal relations in a spirit of humanity and mercy'.[80]

There did, in fact, appear to be some ways in which individual cases of alcoholism could be assisted. Charitable and religious work was one of these. There were rock concerts to raise funds for the struggle against drugs and alcohol;[81] and the Orthodox Church became more closely involved, providing 'spiritual and moral assistance' for the treatment and rehabilitation of alcohol abusers as well as hospital visits and assistance to self-help groups.[82] The Church itself began to establish 'sobriety fraternities', of which there had been over 2,000 in the prerevolutionary period, although it was only after 1990 and a change in the law that the churches were able to engage legally in charitable activities of this kind.[83] Other churches became involved, such as the Seventh Day Adventists.[84] Another change was the development of a widespread network of forms of treatment, some of them innovative and all of them based on civic initiative rather than central decree. One of these was 'Alcoholics Anonymous', which was allowed to establish itself in Russia in the late 1980s after decades of resistance. By 1990 over 200 were attending its sessions in Moscow, and there were sessions in another twelve cities.[85] There were also private services of various kinds.[86]

An approach that enjoyed a particularly strong following was the 'Dovzhenko method', widely used by the temperance society, and reported to achieve a high rate of success; Dovzhenko had himself cured several thousand, and success rates of 90 per cent were commonly claimed.[87] Dovzhenko, a Ukrainian doctor who had originally been a merchant seaman, had been applying his methods since the early 1980s, in the first instance without official support. The director of a narcological centre at Feodisiya operating under the auspices of the Ukrainian Ministry of Health, his treatment sought to 'encode' a hostility towards alcohol through what he described as 'stressopsychotherapy'.[88] Dovzhenko's success owed something to special circumstances: his patients had volunteered for his form of treatment, they had to have abstained from drink entirely for at least two weeks beforehand, and treatment lasted for six months as compared with an average elsewhere of four.[89] Some were, nonetheless, prepared to see him as a 'miracle worker' who rescued 'hopeless cases', and Dovzhenko himself claimed that 'nearly everyone' who attended his sessions gave up drinking altogether.[90] Valid or otherwise, Dovzhenko's methods were widely applied by pupils and colleagues, as well as by 'charlatans' with no real authority or competence.[91] Gennadii Shichko, a Leningrad doctor who died in 1986, was also favoured by the temperance society; a network of 'Optimalist' clubs, applying his psychotherapeutic methods, began to develop from the early 1980s.[92] And there were attempts to develop a 'therapeutic theatre'.[93]

Equally, there were a number of popular 'methods' that did not obtain the approval of the Ministry of Health.[94] A particularly egregious case concerned a 'certain Stolbun', who practised a treatment based on ethyl chloride at his clinic in Leningrad. The ethyl chloride, it emerged, was 'applied to parts of the body that are not usually mentioned in polite society', and in the company of other men and women, 'only half-dressed', who were receiving the same treatment. Stolbun himself provided a series of lectures that dealt with the 'origin of obscenities' and 'phallic cultures'. The directors of the clinic claimed that their method stimulated the 'nerve centres that create feelings of love for the homeland and for the opposite sex', suggesting that it be used for 'mass work with the younger generation'; they had been experimenting in this way for about ten years in the belief that they were resisting a 'schizophrenis-ation' of the entire population. Stolbun himself was a schoolteacher who had failed his medical examinations, and his success rate was less than that achieved in regular addiction centres; many of his patients suffered subsequently from personality changes, and some of them turned to drink.[95] Other problems arose with the development of more commercial approaches: doctors began to advertise in the press, promising to cure alcoholics of their dependence and attracting patients who in some cases were prepared to pay considerable sums so that they could obtain a certificate that they could hand to the local police.[96]

If there was any general agreement it was that alcoholism had deeper, much more complex origins than had been thought to be the case, and that nothing less than a 'fundamental *perestroika* of the consciousness of the individual and of society, of the relationships of all strata of society and of every person to drinking, drunkenness and alcoholism' would be necessary.[97] It was equally clear that further research – even an All-

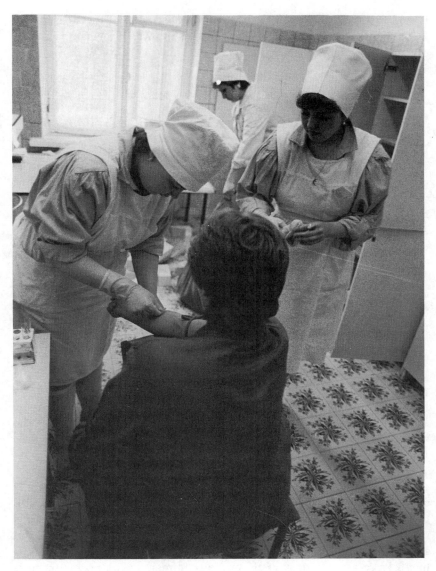

7.3 Treating an alcoholic, 1990
(Novosti)

Union Scientific Research Centre for the Discovery of the Reasons for Drunkenness and Alcoholism[98] – would be required if the campaign was ever to be brought to a successful conclusion.

Russia, alcohol and the implementation of public policy

In the triad of policy formation, policy implementation and policy evaluation, the study of implementation was until recently the neglected element.[99] Crucial, in this sequence, was policy formation: how decisions were made and by whom, and the forces that appeared more generally to have contributed to the outcome in question (it was accepted that to speak of 'decisions' was often an oversimplification). Policy implementation, by contrast, suffered from the assumption that decisions were 'automatically carried through the implementation system as intended and with the desired end results'.[100] There was, again, always an awareness of the difficulties that public agencies might encounter in seeking to put more general directives into practical effect. Nevertheless, it was not until the 1970s and Pressman and Wildavsky's study of the apparent failure of a large federal job-creation scheme to achieve its purposes (in this case, the improvement of employment opportunities for blacks in Oakland, California) that 'implementation studies' became accepted as a distinct field in public policy analysis. It was defined, by Pressman and Wildavsky, as the 'process of interaction between the setting of goals and actions geared to achieve them'; their book had the subtitle *How great expectations in Washington are dashed in Oakland, or why it's amazing that federal programs work at all.*[101]

Earlier approaches to implementation emphasised its 'top-down' character: it was essentially a study of how policies determined centrally were put into effect at lower levels. An approach of this kind has also been labelled a 'policymakers' perspective', as it deals with the attempts made by policymakers to implement their own priorities.[102] Optimally, in such circumstances, the administrative system would be a unitary one, like a large army with a single line of command. The norms or rules enforced by the system would have to be uniform, and there would be perfect obedience or forms of control to ensure that central instructions were put into effect. There would also be perfect coordination between administrative units, with perfect information concerning the situation in hand, and no time pressure.[103] Translated into the context of political action, this means that policies should be as unambiguous as possible, and that there should be as few stages as possible in the sequence of action that was required from each subordinate level of government. There should be no 'outside interference' by other agencies, and there should also be 'control over implementing actors'.[104] Others have emphasised the importance of the causal assumptions upon which policymakers have based their actions, finding in 'study after study' that this was the 'critical variable explaining program outcomes'.[105]

Approaches of this kind were challenged, in the late 1970s, by an alternative body of literature which posited the formation of policy by local officials: the policy, indeed, might in practice be the 'sum of negotiated settlements among street-level bureaucrats and target groups – largely irrespective of what is written in the law books'.[106] As an example of this approach Weatherley and Lipsky studied the Comprehensive Special Education Law of 1972, which became effective in Massachusetts in 1974. A crucial role in implementation of a large and complex bill of this kind was played by the local officials who were responsible for administering it on a day to day basis, or (in Weatherley and Lipsky's terminology) by 'street level bureaucrats'. At this level, time and resources were always limited: this resulted in a considerable degree of autonomy for local officials, who could choose their own priorities and ration services in the way they wished. As Lipsky argued, 'the decisions of street-level bureaucrats, the routines they establish, and the devices they invent to cope with uncertainties and work pressures, effectively become the public policies they carry out'.[107] An alternative approach, 'implementation as evolution', concentrates upon the interaction between central goals (which are often diffuse) and central officials (whose effective authority is limited), on the one hand, and local officials and the mass public on the other, whose ability to modify, renegotiate or stultify official policy had previously been underestimated. Seen in this perspective, implementation is best considered as a 'policy/action continuum' in which an 'interactive and negotiative process is taking place over time' between those responsible for formulating a policy and those responsible for putting it into effect.[108]

Although it was not directly influenced by this literature, the study of policy formation and implementation in the former Soviet Union offered many parallels. Under 'totalitarian' conditions, with a single ruling party based upon democratic centralism, policy was ostensibly based upon an official and unvarying ideology. There could be no legitimate opposition to central directives, and the authorities could ensure compliance by their use of the army and police. They controlled the mass media and law courts, and – under conditions of state ownership and planning – they were in practice the only employer, placing all the working population in a position of direct material dependence. Nevertheless, even here the 'bottom up' perspective had a certain relevance. The central authorities, it emerged, were often divided in their views: between defence and heavy industry, and the light industrial and consumer sectors; between different republics and regions; and even philosophically, on issues like the class character of international relations or the nature of 'pluralism'. The ideology, in any case, had little direct application to the policy choices of an industrial superpower. And lower levels of government, overburdened by commands from above, could often select their own priorities. Indeed they were encouraged to do so, in the 1970s and 1980s, by an increasingly assertive mass public, which could exercise some pressure by letters or other forms of intervention, or even by riots and demonstrations. The characteristic response of Soviet 'street level bureaucrats', in such circumstances, was 'formalism': not overtly challenging central directives, but offering little more than verbal support.[109] The result – not just in the USSR but in other communist systems – was a characteristic process by which 'high level "decisions"' were turned into 'modest programs', and sometimes into 'non-decisions'.[110]

A reasonably well understood accommodation had developed along these lines by the early 1980s. The authorities, for their part, would usually refrain from force. They would take public opinion into account (or at least give that impression), as when the Politburo cancelled the much-criticised plan to divert the Siberian rivers in 1986 (with large and unpredictable environmental consequences) and to construct an unpopular war memorial on the outskirts of Moscow.[111] Under Gorbachev there were moves to extend these processes of consultation into a more open media and a limited degree of electoral choice, balancing party leadership 'from above' with popular initiative 'from below'. There was a law on 'all-national discussions' in 1987, a law on referenda in 1990.[112] The courts became more independent, the CPSU itself less centralised. The forms of popular pressure developed in parallel: first a loosely structured 'informal' movement, and then (from 1990) a legal multiparty system. And there was increasingly the 'politics of the street', particularly a series of large-scale demonstrations to support the ending of the Communist Party's political monopoly in 1990 and more generally to support Boris Yeltsin. In parallel, a series of 'unscheduled "on-the-job discussions"' developed into an unofficial labour movement, and then in 1989 into the largest series of strikes that had been seen since the 1920s.[113]

If all of this was reminiscent of 'implementation as evolution', by a continuous process of negotiation between parties whose influence varied over time and across the policy agenda, there was a further more specific feature of Soviet policy formation (and of that of many communist-ruled nations): the campaign.[114] Its origins lay in the earliest years of Soviet rule, in the operations that had been mounted to recruit volunteers into the armed forces, into basic literacy classes, or into the network of nominally voluntary associations that began to develop in the 1920s.[115] Elections, as they became routinised, acquired most of the characteristics of campaigns: they involved the mobilisation of the mass population to meet centrally determined objectives, including an elaborate and not entirely onesided process of discussion and information. More elaborate campaigns were mounted on important occasions like the adoption of the 1936 constitution, nominally 'discussed' by over 50 million adults in its draft form.[116] In 1977, when a new constitution was adopted under Leonid Brezhnev's leadership, 80 per cent of the entire adult population was reported to have taken part in a discussion of this kind.[117] Rather earlier, in the 1930s, the collectivisation of agriculture had been the subject of a nationwide campaign, and a detachment of workers, the '25,000ers', was mobilised to assist; a Stakhanovite movement, to emulate the record-breaking miner, was developing at about the same time. In the 1950s the Virgin Lands became the subject of another campaign; and in the 1970s and 1980s, a whole series of much more limited campaigns or 'experiments' was conducted in factories, farms and construction sites throughout the USSR.[118]

Campaigns, on this evidence, passed through a series of well understood cycles. As we have noted in earlier chapters, a public issue would first of all be identified by a series of calls for action from ordinary citizens, prominently featured in the official press. Mrs Goryunova's letter to *Pravda* in March 1985 was a perfect example. She herself was an installation worker at an electrical machinery factory, and a wife and mother; and the paper was able to report a 'broad response' a few days later, most of them agreeing with the need for a 'decisive struggle'.[119] There was, in fact, no need to manufacture a level of public concern, if the numbers of letters that reached the newspapers in response to articles on these subjects was any guide;[120] the prominence given to them in the official press was nonetheless a clear sign that at least a substantial section of the leadership had decided some action was necessary. The next step was for the leadership to 'respond' to this cue, acknowledging a legitimate public concern: as it did in the resolution of 17 May 1985 that launched the anti-alcoholism campaign, or as it did in launching an elaborate 'food programme' in 1982 after a flood of uncomplimentary letters on the subject had reached the Central Committee, or as it did in the early 1980s when the Andropov leadership sought to respond to public anxiety about crime and public order.[121]

In the third stage, with leaders emphasising that this was 'not just another campaign',[122] the whole effort advances vigorously. Local officials compete with each other to report 'successes' to the centre: establishing, as they were encouraged to do, as many 'sobriety zones' as possible, closing down wineshops more rapidly than had been planned, and promoting a mass following for the temperance society even if the newly conscripted members were moderate drinkers rather than abstainers. Stories of individual redemption filled the press, and figures like the temperance campaigner Fedor Uglov were propelled to public prominence, offering what appeared to be a scientific basis for the campaign's most fervent supporters within the leadership. Fourthly and finally, as widespread evasion or even falsification became clearer and as the unfortunate side-effects of the policy became more apparent, it was acknowledged that 'not everywhere' had the required changes been made, and that a 'more complex', long-term strategy would have to be adopted. The campaign against alcohol abuse, as in the late 1920s, became part of a more diffuse movement in favour of a healthy lifestyle and the specific legislation was reversed or quietly abandoned. Party secretaries and other 'street level bureaucrats', long accustomed to cycles of this kind, had in practice already transferred their attentions to more pressing and – from the point of view of their advancement – promising objectives.

Soviet campaigns, accordingly, had their internal dynamics. They could be divided into management campaigns, or more disruptive 'innovation campaigns'.[123] Those who identified the campaign at an early stage could expect to be rewarded: a notable example was Gennadii Kolbin, party first secretary in Ul'yanovsk when the campaign began, who was widely interviewed on the innovative programme of action that was already under way in his region – *Pravda* alone carried two reports in the second half of 1985, and the Ul'yanovsk approach was widely praised at the founding congress of the temperance society.[124] Kolbin shortly afterwards became first secretary in Kazakhstan, and later still chairman of the USSR People's Control Committee. Equally, those who made no effort to endorse the campaign's objectives risked their position, as did the ministers and party officials who continued to hold well-watered banquets after the decree had come into effect. Those who most uncompromisingly articulated the new line could also expect to be rewarded: Uglov, in this connection, was sometimes compared with Trofim Lysenko, the charalatan whose illiterate but politically congenial recommendations to the Khrushchev leadership had inflicted great harm on Soviet biology and all who practised it.[125] Supporters of 'cultured drinking' were hounded out of their positions and denied a public platform as the campaign's proponents established a stranglehold on the mass media; they lost their positions in turn as the campaign faltered and was finally reversed. All of this was part of what was called the 'treadmill' or 'cycle of reform':[126] a series of policy initiatives and changing slogans that left real life in almost exactly the same place and discredited the

7.4   Conducting hypnosis treatment, 1990
(Novosti)

leadership that had sought to introduce the original changes as well as the policies themselves.

The campaign and the problem of implementation

Viewed from this perspective, there were several reasons why the anti-alcohol campaign had failed to achieve its original objectives – and had in many cases worsened the situation it was supposed to alleviate. Set against the requirements of a 'top-down' model of implementation, it was certainly clear that *the policy was ambiguous*. Did it, for instance, mean total abstention, or simply an undertaking to reduce consumption as far as possible? Was the sobriety society one of abstainers or of those who hoped in due course to become abstainers? Did the policy itself extend to light wines and beer, or only liquor? Ligachev, the campaign's chief promoter, was a convinced teetotaller, and yet (speaking to the Constitutional Court in October 1992) he spoke approvingly of a glass of good wine.[127] Others had been still less consistent, publicly deploring alcohol abuse while (like Brezhnev) taking a personal part in its 'elimination' in his dacha with his closest associates.[128] And how, in any case, was 'success' to be measured: in a reduction in consumption, or an improvement in public health, or more positively in an increasing number of total abstainers? There had, in fact, been divisions between 'moderate drinkers' and abolitionists since prerevolutionary times (as in other countries); in the end, as we have seen, it proved impossible to reconcile them within the ranks of a single organisation.

Nor was there much doubt that the *political leadership was divided*. There were open supporters of the policy, like Ligachev and Solomentsev. There were opponents, at least within the context of leadership discussions, and most notably Ryzhkov. Gorbachev himself, on the available evidence, did not initiate the process that led to the resolution of May 1985, just after his accession to the general secretaryship, but he did not oppose the case for a public campaign and then identified himself with it wholeheartedly after it had become party and state policy, arguing in the most cataclysmic terms about a threat to the 'gene pool' of the Slavic peoples[129] and defending the loss of revenue that had been sustained as 'not really a loss' given the improvement in public health and in other areas of social and economic life that had taken place.[130] Nonetheless, he had no personal commitment to sobriety and it was not a personal priority when set against the domestic and international tasks that confronted the new general secretary. Later, as we have seen, he sought to ridicule the idea that he had ever been associated with the campaign – 'they tried to make an abstainer out of me', he told reporters in 1992.[131] The campaign depended critically upon the temporary ascendancy of Ligachev and Solomentsev within the leadership; once the balance of influence had moved against them in late 1988 the campaign was almost immediately a casualty.

Not only was the leadership divided: *so too was the temperance society* that had been intended to mobilise grassroots support for the new policy. In principle, all the society's members were committed to a sober way of life; but there were tensions on strategy and tactics, with a 'fundamentalist' wing pushing for a ban on alcohol production and sale and for more decisive, if necessary criminal sanctions. Uglov, leader of this fundamentalist (and later secessionist) wing, complained that a 'powerful patriotic abstentionist movement' had been 'artificially' excluded from the sobriety society; others agreed that the society was 'full of drunks and hypocrites' and called for Uglov himself to be made chairman.[132] The Society's position was confused in any case by the development of a wide range of religious, charitable and other associations, which also sought to address the problem of alcoholism. A conference of eighteen societies of this kind which took place in 1991 found a clear division among them, some favouring a policy of total abstention but others unwilling to take so categoric a position.[133] Still more disturbingly, the sobriety society began to display a markedly Russophile and sometimes anti-Semitic tendency. Russophiles had always claimed that drunkenness was foisted on Russia by Jews and other hostile forces, and the fight against alcoholism became a dominant theme in magazines with Russophile sympathies.[134] Uglov himself drew attention to an obscure passage in which Marx and Engels had commented on the benefits that Jews derived from alcohol consumption, and he wrote elsewhere about the role of Jewish capital in the distilling industry.[135] Views of this kind were also reflected in the work of the temperance society and in its publications, which (for instance) took a particular interest in the state of Israel and in the 'cult of force' of its ruling circles.[136] In Novosibirsk, a local sobriety society went so far as to merge with the chauvinist association *Pamyat'*.[137]

Attitudes of this kind were reasonably widespread, if the correspondence that reached the temperance journal was any guide. Jews, wrote a thirty-year-old from Novosibirsk, were engaged in the 'deliberate promotion of alcohol among the *goyim* and the alcoholisation of other peoples'. For a lecturer in Irkutsk the alcoholisation of Russian society was the work of the 'American CIA, working through its fifth column – Masonic-Zionist agents'. There were even suggestions that the temperance society itself had been infiltrated, and that its journal incorporated 'Zionist-Masonic symbols, emblems and numbers' on its front cover.[138] The most remarkable manifestation of these views within the Society took the form of a lengthy 'open letter' circulated by one of its members, B. I. Iskakov. Iskakov, who claimed that his letter drew upon a 'great many meetings and rallies' of members of the Society, began by noting that the USSR had lost its second-ranking position in the world economy to Japan during the 1970s, and had at the same time become a society of advanced alcoholism. Who was answerable for this 'economic Tsushima'? Who was responsible for the 'besotting and weakening of the Soviet people with alcohol, the No. 1 narcotic?' And who had abolished the Leninist 'dry law' of 1919? None other, it appeared, than 'Trotsky-Bronshtein L. D., Kamenev-Rozenfel'd L. B., Zinoviev-Radomysl'skii-Apfel'baum G. E.', and other 'alcoholisers' of the Russian people.

Iskakov welcomed the measures taken in 1985, which had stopped the 'sinister process of the degradation of Soviet, socialist society' and averted an 'alcoholic apocalypse'. Already, however, at least 50–60 million of the population were alcoholics, and a further 110–110 million 'cultured drinkers' were alcohol-dependent. The mass media had been of no assistance, linked as they were to the 'alcohol mafia' and its clients. 'Real patriots' could accept nothing less than total abstinence, and only resolute measures in its defence would avoid another period of rule like the 'stagnating *Brezhnevshchina* and its zionocratic clan'. This would certainly require measures to ensure that all national groups were equally represented in the media and in propaganda work, and in the allocation of leading executive positions. The letter included a series of more detailed proposals, including the restitution of the dry law of 1919 and the 'removal from Red Square of the tomb of that Great Alcohol-Inquisitor of all times and peoples, L. I. Brezhnev, for reburial in some less honoured place'. Scientists were also urged to devise a programme of 'national renewal', including the 'speediest possible regeneration of the weakened gene-bank of the Soviet people'. Only in this way, the letter concluded, would the Soviet Union of peoples, headed by the Russians, defeat the 'bureaucracy, Eurocracy (Zionocracy) and plutocracy' and secure the wellbeing of the socialist motherland.[139]

The letter was followed by a commentary written by the journal's own staff, who asked how sobriety was going to be enhanced if alcohol addiction was replaced, for instance, by Zionomania which was, 'let's be completely frank about it, just a cover for the primeval narcotic of Judophobia'. And what kind of scientific strategy could it be that called down heavenly judgement on the 'heretics' who advocated cultured drinking (this would, they pointed out, consign the overwhelming majority of the adult population to perdition)?[140] In the event, the letter led to very little direct opposition in the journal, although responses were very varied in character. Indeed the editors' own commentary was criticised for failing to suggest an alternative to the policies advocated in the open letter. A Moscow branch chairman, for instance, agreed that drunken leaders had often been manipulated in the past by 'national minorities' (that is, Jews). To a reader in Dnepropetrovsk, 'zionocrats' had captured 70 per cent of leading positions in the media and other spheres, leaving Russians as 'white slaves' in their own country. Other commentaries suggested that the sobriety journal had itself been infiltrated by Zionists. Most characteristic of all were letters that began 'I'm not an educated person, and so I don't get into political arguments. However . . . ' The general tone of the correspondence, the journal's editor suggested, was reminiscent of nothing so much as the campaign against Zionism and 'cosmopolitanism' of the late 1940s.[141]

Approaches of this kind were sustained by a *failure to conceptualise alcoholism adequately*, and by a *neglect of international experience*. It had at least become clear that alcoholism was no longer a carry-over from the capitalist past, but a 'social phenomenon' that could 'only have resulted from social reasons and conditions'.[142] Rates of alcoholism, for instance, had increased most rapidly in the republics that had experienced the most rapid increase in urbanisation.[143] The breakup of traditional family life played a part, and the domestic burdens that many wives had to bear, which left them little time to share with their husbands.[144] Other research began to uncover the role that alcohol performed in interpersonal communication: lower levels of sociability, for instance, were among the 'main reasons for turning to alcohol as a means of self-expression'. But it was not only a lack of 'interior culture' that was responsible: the lack of cultural and recreational facilities, and of opportunities to interact with others outside the framework of official regulation, were also important. Substantial proportions, particularly of the young, drank simply 'out of boredom'; among other respondents alcohol had an 'intermediary' function, as a necessary part of celebrations or a means of paying for minor household work. No campaign would succeed that did not pay attention to these and the other 'sociocultural functions' that were performed by alcohol.[145] Nor could there be an adequate analysis, for other writers, without asking more fundamental questions; about the 'functions of alcohol in the maintenance and reproduction of power' and about the purposes that it served for the command-administrative system in particular.[146]

The Politburo's preparations, it emerged, had been entrusted to Mikhail Solomentsev, formerly the Russian prime minister and at this time chairman of the Committee of Party Control. Solomentsev, as Vitalii Vorotnikov recalled, had examined 'how these processes had taken place, in the historical sense – how they were dealt with under Lenin, how in the USA, how in other countries'. He 'got together all the literature about it, and periodically informed us about it, and gave us great tomes to read . . . he even brought up Peter the Great – they were fascinating conversations', Vorotnikov recalled with some amusement. Solomentsev himself had enjoyed a 'very good relationship with drink' in his earlier years; but when the campaign was launched he 'punished so many people, ruined so many people with terror if they dared to decline to carry out the decisions'.[147] The whole scheme, it emerged, had been put together in conditions of virtual secrecy, with responsible officials at the Ministry of Health left to gather the details from the daily press, and the key decisions made 'by instinct';[148] alternative proposals, such as an extension of the places in which alcohol was consumed in a more controlled manner, received no serious consideration, and no research was specially commissioned.[149] For some of the closest students of the alcoholism problem its shaky scientific foundation was one of the main reasons for its failure: it had led, for instance, to a crude identification of moderate drinking with genuine alcoholism.[150] And it had allowed unrealistic objectives to be put forward. The World Health Organisation suggested that, under the most favourable circumstances, a reduction in consumption of 1.5–2 per cent a year was possible; under the influence of militants like Uglov and Iskakov, there had been demands for total sobriety in five to ten years.[151]

The main emphasis, as the campaign developed, was in practice upon purely administrative methods. The May decrees, in fairness, had embraced other principles, and called for a 'complex programme' on alcohol abuse and its elimination. In the end more than seventy ministries, public bodies and organisations were involved in drafting a programme of this kind. It was 'worked out, agreed, worked out once

7.5 'Guess which side of the negotiating table the Russians will sit?' (*Izvestiya*, October 1994)

again, agreed once again . . . ' Four years or more after the adoption of the decree the programme that was to ensure its success was still languishing in government offices, and it was 'not known' when it would be adopted (in fact it never emerged). As for the commitment to provide the Soviet people with the facilities they needed by the year 2000, 'The programmes were drawn up, the amounts determined and the responsibilities allocated', Russian parliamentarians wanted to know, 'but where are the goods?'[152] A district party committee in Moscow undertook its own analysis, with more than 60 expert lawyers, doctors, sociologists and psychologists to advise it: the result, after a computer analysis, was a set of 269 'outcome measures'.[153] The sobriety society in Kazakhstan devised an even more elaborate 'anti-alcohol passport' for use throughout the republic, containing 440 separate questions.[154] This whole approach was not unreasonably described as 'reportomania' in the press;[155] it had more in common with the fulfilment of plan targets than a serious attempt to engage the energies of the society in dealing with a long-standing public issue.

The experience of other countries showed that there were, in fact, more discriminating and effective ways of approaching a problem that was of concern throughout the developed world. The idea of a 'campaign' for a start, was misconceived. It was generally more sensible to concentrate upon the use of existing laws and regulations, and to look for small changes at the margin rather than dramatic shifts in the behaviour patterns of whole societies. A policy on alcohol abuse, it was argued, should be part of a wider attempt to encourage an improvement in lifestyles, or a 'healthy public policy'. There should be a better understanding of the variety of interests, or of the 'policy network', that was involved. And there should be an emphasis upon local or more limited improvements, not necessarily a national programme.[156] In the case of specific problems like adolescent drinking, it was better seen as 'normal transitional behaviour' between the abstinence of childhood and the generally moderate drinking patterns of adult years. In turn the link with home life was a close one, according to research conducted in the West: and a 'warm, supportive family with firm guidance' was the single factor that was most likely to result in sensible drinking in adult years.[157] Research even suggested, a little tentatively, that moderate drinking of wine could help to reduce the incidence of heart attacks and strokes by producing higher levels of anti-clotting proteins in the blood, and might actually be 'good for you'.[158]

If the drive against alcohol abuse in late communist Russia was a classic campaign, its failure was an equally perfect illustration of the limitations of 'top-down' implementation even in a situation in which the authorities were unusually powerful in relation to the society over which they ruled. The strategy, in the first place, was based upon a narrow and inadequate understanding of the problem it was seeking to resolve, with alternative views and international experience excluded from the policy agenda. Those who were enforcing the strategy were divided in their views, and the 'street level bureaucrats' through which they worked were able to evade central directives and set their own priorities, overfulfilling as well as underfulfilling their original instructions. The mass public, initially favourable, became disillusioned by the manner in which the campaign was being conducted, and in the end they were drinking more than ever before (and more of it as spirits). The government, for its part, had less direct influence over production by the early 1990s than it had done before the campaign began (as more of it was in the private or illegal sectors), and it was less well informed because more consumption was outside the state system than ever before (and Russian drinkers were 'unduly modest' when it came to reporting their alcoholic behaviour).[159] Any larger attempt to encourage a healthy lifestyle, or even to provide social and medical support, had meanwhile become more difficult as a result of the budgetary deficit (to which the campaign had made a contribution), and the crisis into which all the social services had been plunged by the economic difficulties of the early 1990s. The failure of the anti-alcohol campaign was, in this sense, a paradigm: it showed not just the limitations of a policy that was determined without the direct participation of ordinary citizens, but more generally the limitations of a system of government that denied them a share in the management of the society in which they lived.

Notes

1 Russia, alcohol and politics

1 A. A. Shakhmatov, ed., *Povest' vremennykh let*, vol. 1 (Petrograd: Orlova, 1916), pp. 103–4.
2 V. N. Kudryavtsev, ed., *Sotsial'nye otkloneniya*, 2nd edn (Moscow: Yuridicheskaya literatura, 1989), p. 269.
3 R. E. F. Smith and David Christian, *Bread and Salt: A social and economic history of food and drink in Russia* (Cambridge: Cambridge University Press, 1984), p. 316; and (for the quotation) David Christian, *'Living Water': Vodka and Russian society on the eve of emancipation* (Oxford: Clarendon Press, 1990), p. 5.
4 Vera Dunham in Venedikt Erofeev, *Moscow to the End of the Line* (Evanston IL: Northwestern University Press, 1992), p. 10. Pushkin's 'Bacchic song' is in his *Sobranie sochinenii v desyati tomakh* (Moscow: Khudozhestvennaya literatura, 1974–78), vol. 2, p. 33. Tolstoy's most extended discussion of the subject, 'Dlya chego lyudi odurmanivayutsya?' (1890), is in his *Polnoe sobranie sochinenii*, vol. 27 (Moscow: Gosudarstvennoe izdatel'stvo khudozhestvennoi literatury, 1933), pp. 269–85. Mayakovsky is quoted in *Uchitel'skaya gazeta*, 25 May 1985, p. 2. On Erofeev, see Cynthia Simmons, 'An alcoholic narrative as "time out" and the double in *Moskva-Petushki*', *Canadian-American Slavic Studies*, vol. 24, no. 2 (Summer 1990), pp. 155–68.
5 V. Dal', *Poslovitsy russkogo naroda* (Moscow: Gosudarstvennoe izdatel'stvo khudozhestvennoi literatury, 1957; first published 1862), p. 794; and I. Kh. Ozerov, *Alkogolizm i bor'ba s nim* (Moscow 1909), pp. 31–2, cited in Patricia Herlihy, 'Joy of the Rus': Rites and rituals of Russian drinking', *Russian Review*, vol. 50, no. 2 (April 1991), pp. 131–47, at p. 134.
6 D. N. Borodin in *Itogi rabot pervogo vserossiiskogo s"ezda po bor'be s p'yanstvom* (St Petersburg: Vilenchik, 1910), as cited in Boris M. Segal, *The Drunken Society: Alcohol abuse and alcoholism in the Soviet Union* (New York: Hippocrene Books, 1990), p. xxi.
7 See especially Christian, *'Living Water'*, Part 3.

8 Ibid., pp. 5, 7. The share of national income is derived from the proportion of retail trade in 1913 reported in Paul R. Gregory, *Russian National Income, 1885–1913* (Cambridge: Cambridge University Press, 1982), p. 81.

9 The citation is drawn from the *Bol'shaya sovetskaya entsiklopediya*, 2nd edn, vol. 2 (Moscow: Sovetskaya entsiklopediya, 1950), p. 117.

10 E. Ch. Skrzhinskaya, ed., *Barbaro i Kontarini o Rossii* (Leningrad: Nauka, 1971), pp. 228–9. The fullest account of prerevolutionary practices is Boris Segal, *Russian Drinking: Use and abuse of alcohol in pre-revolutionary Russia* (New Brunswick NJ: Rutgers Center of Alcohol Studies, 1987), to which the following discussion is much indebted.

11 Richard Hakluyt, ed., *The Principal Navigations, Voyages, Traffiques and Discoveries of the English Nation*, 12 vols. (Glasgow: Maclehose, 1903-5), vol. 3, p. 124.

12 Giles Fletcher, *Of the Russe Commonwealth*, ed. Richard Pipes (Cambridge MA: Harvard University Press, 1966), pp. 44–44v, 112v.

13 Samuel H. Baron, ed., *The Travels of Olearius in Seventeenth-Century Russia* (Stanford CA: Stanford University Press, 1967), p. 144.

14 Baron, *Olearius*, p. 144; similarly Yurii Krizhanich, *Politika*, ed. M. N. Tikhomirov (Moscow: Nauka, 1965), p. 134 (Krizhanich, of Croatian origin, was in Russia from the late 1650s to the late 1670s).

15 Baron, *Olearius*, pp. 142, 143.

16 J. G. Kohl, *Petersburg in Bildern und Skizzen*, 2 vols. (Dresden: Arnoldische Buchhandlung, 1841), vol. 2, p. 84. Another traveller, Anatole Leroy-Beaulieu, took the view that Russian intemperance was 'greatly exaggerated' but also agreed that the 'taste for alcohol [was] as natural to the Russian peasant as temperance [was] to the Sicilian or Andalusian: it [was] not so much the man's vice as the climate's fault' (*L'Empire des tsars et les Russes*, 3 vols. (Paris: Hachette, 1881–9), vol. 1, p. 125).

17 Baron, *Olearius*, p. 144 (slightly adapted).

18 Hakluyt, *Principal Navigations*, vol. 2, pp. 423–4.

19 Baron, *Olearius*, p. 145.

20 See for instance ibid., p. 143.

21 John Perry, *The State of Russia, under the Present Czar* (London: Tooke, 1716; reprint edn, 1967), p. 228.

22 V. Ya. Kanel', *Alkogolizm i bor'ba s nim* (Moscow: Sytin, 1914), p. 89; and (for village weddings) O. P. Semenova-Tyan'-Shanskaya, *Zhizn' "Ivana". Ocherki iz byta krest'yan odnoi iz chernozemnykh gubernii* (St Petersburg: Zapiski Imperatorskogo russkogo geograficheskogo obshchestva po otdeleniyu etnografii, vol. 39, 1914), p. 48.

23 L. S. Minor in *Trudy tret'ego s"ezda otechestvennykh psikhiatrov* (St Petersburg: Tipografiya Pervoi trudovoi arteli, 1911), pp. 179–82; and (for comparative data) I. A. Sikirsky, *Alkogolizm i piteinoe delo* (Kiev: Kushnerev, 1897), p. 8 (there were however relatively fewer female deaths: Sikorsky, *O vliyanii spirtnykh napitkov na zdorov'e i nravstvennost' naseleniya Rossii*

(Kiev: Kushnerev, 1899), pp. 12–13). On female alcoholism during the prerevolutionary period see B. M. Guzikov and A. A. Meiroyan, *Alkogolizm u zhenshchin* (Leningrad: Meditsina, 1988), pp. 13–17.

24 Hakluyt, *Principal Navigations*, vol. 2, p. 267.

25 Jacques Margeret, *Un mousquetaire à Moscou: Mémoires sur la première revolution russe, 1604–1614* (Paris: La Découverte, 1983), p. 47.

26 Baron, *Olearius*, pp. 145–6.

27 Ibid., p. 146.

28 Perry, *State of Russia*, p. 227.

29 I. G. Pryzhov, *Istoriya kabakov v Rossii* (Moscow: Vol'f, 1868), pp. 278–9.

30 Segal, *Russian Drinking*, pp. 125–6.

31 See for instance I. Kh. Ozerov, *Gornye zavody Urala* (Moscow: Sytin, 1910), pp. 76–9; rather higher estimates are given in Kanel', *Alkogolizm*, pp. 124–9.

32 V. K. Dmitriev, *Kriticheskie issledovaniya o potreblenii alkogolya v Rossii* (Moscow: Ryabushinsky, 1911), p. 293.

33 R. Vlassak, ed., *Alkogolizm kak nauchnaya i butovaya problema* (Moscow–Leningrad: Gosizdat, 1928), p. 78.

34 A. I. Gertsen, *Sobranie sochinenii v tridtsati tomakh* (Moscow: Izdatel'stvo Akademii nauk SSSR, 1954–65), vol. 8, pp. 37–8 (slightly adapted).

35 V. M. Bekhterev, *Alkogolizm i bor'ba s nim* (Leningrad: Izd. Lengubprofsoveta, 1927), p. 9.

36 See for instance Sikorsky, *O vliyanii*, pp. 16–17 (variations in consumption ranged from 2.07 litres a head in Poland and 2.33 in the Far East to 9.07 in the area around St Petersburg).

37 Ibid., pp. 3–4; and Bekhterev, *Alkogolizm*, p. 9.

38 Sikorsky, *Alkogolizm*, pp. 18–19.

39 *Bol'shevik*, 1927, no. 19–20, p. 193.

40 *Trezvost' i kul'tura*, 1929, no. 11, p. 5.

41 N. I. Grigor'ev, *Alkogolizm kak obshchestvennoe zlo* (St Petersburg 1908), p. 2.

42 See S. S. Stupin, *Alkogolizm i bor'ba s nim v nekotorykh bol'shikh gorodakh Evropy* (Moscow: Mamontov, 1904), p. 255; and (on divorces) F. Ya. Nesmelov, *Alkogol'nyi tupik* (Khar'kov: Gosmedizat UkrSSR, 1931), p. 19.

43 See Dmitry Shlapentokh, 'Drunkenness and anarchy in Russia: A case of political culture', *Russian History*, vol. 18, no. 4 (Winter 1991), pp. 457–500, at pp. 465–75.

44 V. V. Pokhlebkin argues for the development of distilling 'somewhere between 1460 and 1550' (*Istoriya vodki* (Moscow: Inter-Verso, 1991), p. 154). M. Ya. Volkov argues similarly for a date at the end of the fifteenth or beginning of the sixteenth century (*Ocherki istorii promyslov v Rossii: vtoraya polovina XVII-pervaya polovina XVIII v. Vinokurennoe proizvodstvo* (Moscow: Nauka, 1979), p. 25).

45 Vlassak, ed., *Alkogolizm*, pp. 226–7.

46 Christian, *'Living Water'*, pp. 5, 6.
47 Volkov, *Ocherki istorii promyslov v Rossii*, pp. 25–6.
48 A. G. Man'kov, ed., *Akty Zemskikh soborov* (Moscow: Yuridicheskaya literatura, 1985), pp. 252-4.
49 Christian, *'Living Water'*, pp. 29, 31, 32.
50 Ibid., p. 32.
51 N. A. Paremskaya, comp., *Trezvyi byt* (Moscow: Fizkul'tura i sport, 1987), p. 8.
52 The poor quality of drink at this time is noted in D. N. Borodin, *Kabak i ego proshloe* (St Petersburg: Vilenchik, 1910), p. 59.
53 E. I. Deichman, *Alkogolizm i bor'ba s nim* (Moscow–Leningrad: Moskovskii rabochii, 1929), p. 75 (the monopoly, by 1914, had not yet been extended to the Caucasus, Central Asia and Far East).
54 August von Haxthausen, *Studien über die innern Zustände, das Volksleben, und insbesondere die ländlichen Einrichtungen Russlands*, 3 vols. (Hanover and Berlin: Hahn and Behr, 1847–52), vol. 2, p. 513.
55 T. S. Prot'ko, *V bor'be za trezvost'. Stranitsy istorii* (Minsk: Nauka i tekhnika, 1988), p. 20.
56 *Bor'ba*, 1914, no. 2, p. 8 (I owe this reference to Dr Ian Thatcher).
57 See Patricia Herlihy, *Strategies of Sobriety: temperance movements in Russia, 1880–1914* (Washington DC: Kennan Institute, Occasional Paper no. 238, 1990), pp. 16–17.
58 Quoted in Prot'ko, *V bor'be*, p. 5.
59 The first temperance society was established as early as 1854; by 1900 there were about 200, and by 1912 about 2,000 (Paremskaya, ed., *Trezvyi byt*, p. 9). On temperance more generally see Herlihy, *Strategies*, and George E. Snow, 'The temperance movement in Russia', *Modern Encyclopedia of Russian and Soviet History*, vol. 38 (Gulf Breeze FL: Academic International, 1984), pp. 226–33.
60 On the role of the medical profession see Prot'ko, *V bor'be*, pp. 66–82; John F. Hutchinson, 'Medicine, morality and the social policy in imperial Russia: the early years of the alcoholism commission', *Histoire social/Social History*, vol. 7 (November 1974), pp. 202–26; and Hutchinson, 'Science, politics and the alcohol problem in post-1905 Russia', *Slavonic and East European Review*, vol. 58, no. 2 (April 1980), pp. 231–54. The first temperance journal was *Narodnaya trezvost'*, published from 1898.
61 Pryzhkov, *Istoriya*, p. 122.
62 See David Christian, 'Vodka and corruption in Russia on the eve of emancipation', *Slavic Review*, vol. 44, nos. 3–4 (Fall-Winter 1987), pp. 471–88.
63 Prot'ko, *V bor'be*, p. 12.
64 Segal, *Russian Drinking*, pp. 95–6.
65 *Kommunist*, 1985, no. 12, p. 44; Prot'ko, *V bor'be*, p. 89. See also George E. Snow, 'Socialism, alcoholism, and the Russian working classes before 1917', in Susanna Barrows and Robin Room, eds., *Drinking: Behavior and*

belief in modern history (Berkeley: University of California Press, 1991), pp. 243–64. Translations of the Western classics of socialist temperance may have played a part: see for instance Emil' Vandervel'de, *Rabochaya partiya i alkogol'* (St Petersburg: Molot, 1906), and Emmanuil Vurm, *Alkogolizm i rabochie* (St Petersburg: Zhizn' i znanie, 1910). Yu. G. Marchenko et al., *Strategiya obnovleniya* (Novosibirsk: Novosibirskoe knizhnoe izdatel'stvo, 1990), note that the Soviet historiography of temperance is still 'in its infancy' (p. 7).

66 *Sobranie uzakonenii i rasporyazhenii rabochego-krest'yanskogo pravitel'stva* (title varies; hereafter *SU*), 1918, no. 82, art. 866; no. 99, art. 1026; and 1919, no. 3, art. 42. On the legislation of the period see A. V. Gapylov, 'K istorii razvitiya zakonodatel'stva o bor'be s alkogolizmom v SSSR', *Sovetskoe gosudarstvo i pravo*, 1989, no. 2, pp. 115-21.

67 *KPSS v rezolyutsiyakh i resheniyakh s"ezdov, konferentsii i plenumov TsK*, 9th edn, vol. 2 (Moscow: politizdat, 1983), p. 92.

68 V. I. Lenin, *Polnoe sobranie sochinenii*, 5th edn, 55 vols. (Moscow: Politizdat, 1958–65), vol. 43, p. 326.

69 Klara Tsetkin, *O Lenine. Sbornik statei i vospominanii* (Moscow: Partiinoe izdatel'stvo, 1933), p. 78.

70 Lenin, *Pol. sob. soch.*, vol. 45, p. 120.

71 John Reed, *Ten Days that Shook the World* (Harmondsworth: Penguin, 1977, first published 1926), pp. 112, 164.

72 The account that follows is based upon P. Ya. Kann, 'Bor'ba rabochikh Petrograda s p'yanymi pogromami (noyabr'–debakr' 1917 g.)', *Istoriya SSSR*, 1962, no. 3, pp. 133–6; Prot'ko, *V bor'be*, p. 97; and L. D. Miroshnichenko, 'Istoriya bor'by s p'yanstvom v 20–30-kh godakh', *Voprosy narkologii*, 1990, no. 3, pp. 54–9, at p. 55. Trotsky is as quoted in Anna Louise Strong, *The First Time in History* (London: Labour Publishing Company, 1924), p. 157.

73 Miroshnichenko, 'Istoriya', p. 55.

74 *Trezvost' i kul'tura*, 1988, no. 4, p. 9.

75 *SU*, 1918, no. 35, art 468.

76 Ibid., 1920, no. 1–2, art. 2.

77 Alfons Goldschmidt, *Moskau 1920* (Berlin: Rowohlt, 1920), p. 102.

78 E. Sylvia Pankhurst, *Soviet Russia as I Saw It* (London: Workers' Dreadnought, 1921), p. 184.

79 Strong, *First Time in History*, p. 154; and (for the 'American plan') Edwin W. Hullinger, *The Reforging of Russia* (London: Witherby, 1925), p. 277.

80 Hullinger, *Reforging of Russia*, p. 274.

81 *Russia. The Official Report of the British Trades Union Delegation to Russia in November and December 1924* (London: Trades Union Council, 1925), p. 107.

82 L. D. Trotsky, *Sochineniya*, vol. 21 (Moscow–Leningrad: Gosudarstvennoe izdatel'stvo, 1927), pp. 22–3.

83 E. Pinezhsky, *Krasnaya gvardiya*, 2nd edn (Moscow: Partizdat, 1933),

p. 129; *Novaya zhizn'*, 13 December 1917, and *Proletarskaya revolyutsiya*, vol. 40 (1925), p. 237, both cited in John L. H. Keep, *The Russian Revolution: A study of mass mobilization* (London: Weidenfeld and Nicolson, 1976), pp. 255–6. See also Shlapentokh, 'Drunkenness', pp. 485–98.

84 Louis de Robien, *Journal d'un diplomate en Russie 1917–1918* (Paris: Albin Michel, 1967), p. 193.

85 V. A. Antonov-Ovseenko, *Zapiski o grazhdanskoi voine*, vol. 1 (Moscow–Leningrad: Vysshii voennyi redaktsionnyi sovet, 1924), pp. 19–20. There is another account in Bessie Beatty, *The Red Heart of Russia* (New York: Century, 1918), pp. 329–34.

86 On illicit distilling see particularly Neil Weissman, 'Prohibition and alcohol control in the USSR: the 1920s campaign against illegal spirits', *Soviet Studies*, vol. 38, no. 3 (July 1986), pp. 349–68; Helena Stone, 'The Soviet government and moonshine 1917–1929', *Cahiers du monde russe et soviétique*, vol. 27, no. 3–4 (July–December 1986), pp. 359–80; and K. B. Litvak, 'Samogonovarenie i potreblenie alkogolya v rossiiskoi derevne 1920-kh godov', *Otechestvennaya istoriya*, 1992, no. 4, pp. 74–88. The experience of Leningrad during these years is considered in Christopher Williams, 'Old habits die hard: alcoholism in Leningrad under NEP and some lessons for the Gorbachev administration', *Irish Slavonic Studies*, no. 12 (1991), pp. 69–96.

87 *Statisticheskoe obozrenie*, 1929, no. 2, p. 101 (a figure of 34.6 per cent was suggested); *Pravda*, 16 June 1992, p. 4, and (for 'lemonade') 13 October 1922, p. 5.

88 Strong, *First Time in History*, p. 160.

89 Deichman, *Alkogolizm*, p. 108; for the arrests see M. N. Gernet, *Prestupnost' za granitsei i v SSSR* (Moscow: Sovetskoe zakonodatel'stvo, 1931), p. 76.

90 For the reimposition of the state monopoly see *SU*, 1925, art. 426, 28 August 1925. The law as revised in January 1924 is in *Ugolovnyi kodeks RSFSR* (Moscow: Yuridicheskoe izdatel'stvo, 1925), art. 140, pp. 35–6. According to official sources excise duties rose from 10.5 per cent of all revenues in 1924/5 to 18.9 per cent in 1926/7 (*Tyazhest' oblozheniya v SSSR* (Moscow: Finansovoe izdatel'stvo Soyuza SSSR, 1929), p. 39). On the 'inactive' police see for instance Gosudarstvennyi arkhiv Rossiiskoi Federatsii (GARF), *fond* 395, *opis'* 2, *delo* 236.

91 Bekhterev, *Alkogolizm*, p. 5.

92 *Alkogolizm v sovremennoi derevne* (Moscow: TsSU RSFSR, 1929), p. 16; Yu. Larin, *Alkogolizm i sotsializm* (Moscow: Gosudarstvennoe izdatel'stvo, 1929) estimated that consumption of vodka and samogon together exceeded pre-war levels by 25 per cent (p. 48). A somewhat different view is given in *Statisticheskoe obozrenie*, 1929, no. 2, which suggests that urban consumption was still lower than pre-war levels but that rural consumption was higher (p. 103).

93 *Bol'shevik*, 1927, no. 19–20, p. 131; *Sotsial'naya gigiena*, 1928, no. 4, p. 22.

94 *Trezvost' i kul'tura*, 1929, no. 11, p. 5.

95 Deichman, *Alkogolizm*, p. 108.

96 According to Larin, Tver' textile workers spent about 11 per cent of their income on alcohol and Moscow workers and white-collar staff 13.7 per cent (*Alkogolizm i sotsializm*, pp. 20, 95). Deichman suggested a figure of 8 per cent of family income (*Alkogolizm*, p. 99). Bukharin, speaking to the Komsomol, opted for 14–15 per cent (*VIII Vsesoyuznyi s"ezd VLKSM 5–16 maya 1928 goda: Stenograficheskii otchet* (Moscow: Molodaya gvardiya, 1928), p. 24).

97 Deichman, *Alkogolizm*, p. 143.

98 Yu. Larin, *Alkogolizm. Prichiny, zadachi i sposoby bor'by* (Khar'kov: Nauchnaya mysl', 1930), pp. 26–7.

99 Yu. Larin, *Novye zakony protiv alkogolizma i protivoalkogol'noe dvizhenie*, 2nd edn (Moscow: Gosudarstvennoe meditsinskoe izdatel'stvo, 1929), p. 6; and (for drinking parties) Merle Fainsod, *Smolensk under Soviet Rule* (Cambridge MA: Harvard University Press, 1959), p. 49.

100 Larin, *Alkogolizm i sotsializm*, pp. 47–8; for the 80 per cent estimate see Stone, 'The Soviet government', p. 373.

101 See, for instance, Prime Minister Rykov's acknowledgement that repressive methods had simply encouraged *samogon* and deprived the state of much-needed revenue: *Pravda*, 16 January 1925, pp. 6–7 (government-issue alcohol became known as 'Rykovka' in tribute).

102 *XIV s"ezd Vsesoyuznoi Kommunisticheskoi partii (b) 18–31 dekabrya 1925 g. Stenograficheskii otchet* (Moscow–Leningrad: Gosudarstvennoe izdatel'stvo, 1926), pp. 49–50.

103 I. V. Stalin, *Sochineniya*, 13 vols. (Moscow: Ogiz, 1946–51), vol. 9, pp. 191–2.

104 Ibid., vol. 10, pp. 232–3.

105 *XV s"ezd Kommunisticheskoi partii (b). Stenograficheskii otchet* (Moscow–Leningrad: Gosudarstvennoe izdatel'stvo, 1928), p. 60.

106 *VIII Vsesoyuznyi s"ezd VLKSM*, p. 25.

107 G. G. Zaigraev, *Obshchestvo i alkogol'* (Moscow: Ministerstvo vnutrennykh del Rossiiskoi Federatsii, 1992), p. 37 (article 102 of the 1926 Criminal Code referred only to sale or *sbyt*: *Ugolovnyi kodeks RSFSR: redaktsiya 1926 goda* (Moscow: Yuridicheskoe izdatel'stvo NKYust RSFSR, 1926), p. 31); possession became a criminal offence under an amendment of 1927 (*SU*, 1928, no. 10, art. 92).

108 T. P. Korzhikhina, 'Bor'ba s alkogolizmom v 1920-e-nachale 1930-kh godov', *Voprosy istorii*, 1985, no. 9, p. 24.

109 See Susan Gross Solomon, 'David and Goliath in Soviet public health: the rivalry of social hygienists and psychiatrists for authority over the *bytovoi* alcoholic', *Soviet Studies*, vol. 41, no. 2 (April 1989), pp. 254–75; also Solomon, 'Social hygiene in Soviet public health, 1920–1930', in Solomon and John F. Hutchinson, eds., *Health and Society in Revolutionary Russia* (Bloomington IN: Indiana University Press, 1990).

110 *SU*, 1926, no. 57, art. 447.

111 *Voprosy istorii*, 1994, no. 2, p. 41.

112 *SU*, 1928, no. 2, art. 14, 27 December 1927.

113 Ibid., 1929, no. 20, art. 224.

114 Gosudarstvennyi arkhiv Rossiiskoi Federatsii, *fond* 5465, *opis'* 10, *delo* 189; see also Korzhina, 'Bor'ba', and Prot'ko, *V bor'be*, pp. 114–23. The Society's archives were lost during World War II.

115 *Za novyi byt*, 1928, no. 7–8, p. 22.

116 Larin, *Alkogolizm i sotsializm*, pp. 34, 37.

117 *Trezvost' i kul'tura*, 1928, no. 1, p. 4 (editorial). A Ukrainian counterpart, *Za trezvost'*, was published from 1929.

118 *Trezvost' i kul'tura*, 1929, no. 12, p. 5.

119 Ibid., no. 13–14, p. 15.

120 On children's demonstrations see for instance Deichman, *Alkogolizm*, pp. 165–6; *Trezvost' i kul'tura*, 1928, no. 5, p. 1, 1929, no. 1, p. 13, and no. 2, p. 9; and Larin, *Alkogolizm i sotsializm*, pp. 139-42. For brief discussions see *Agitator*, 1987, no. 20, pp. 57–8, and *Trezvost' i kul'tura*, 1988, no. 2, pp. 18–20.

121 Larin, *Alkogolizm i sotsializm*, p. 80.

122 Paremskaya, ed., *Trezvyi byt*, pp. 67, 85.

123 *Trezvost' i kul'tura*, 1928, no. 5, p. 6. Did a member of the Society have to abstain entirely, Leningrad workers wanted to know? The answer was those who were unable to break the habit but who wished to support the Society could become candidate members (ibid., no. 3, p. 7).

124 *Kul'tura i byt*, 1930, no. 1, p. 4.

125 Ibid., no. 9, p. 18.

126 Ibid., no. 1, inside cover.

127 Ibid., 1931, no. 22, p. 2; from January 1932 the journal merged with *Kul'turnaya revolyutsiya* as a trade union journal.

128 Solomon, 'David and Goliath', p. 267 (on the hygienists) and Prot'ko, *V bor'be*, pp. 126–7.

129 Larin, *Alkogolizm i sotsializm*, pp. 35, 54.

130 *Kul'tura i byt*, 1930, no. 8, p. 4.

131 See V. P. Lazovsky, *Administrativno-pravovye mery bor'by s p'yanstvom i alkogolizmom* (avtoreferat kand. diss., Moscow: Institut gosudarstva i prava AN SSSR, 1990), p. 15.

132 *Kul'tura i byt*, 1930, no. 1, p. 4.

133 *Narodnoe khozyaistvo SSSR v 1959 godu. Statisticheskii ezhegodnik* (Moscow: Gosudarstvennoe statisticheskoe izdatel'stvo, 1959), p. 686. Levels of consumption were about 2.24 litres of absolute alcohol per person in 1940, excluding cognac, fruit and berry wines, champagne and imports, for which no data are available (Prot'ko, *V bor'be*, p. 129). Output rose from 36.5 million decalitres in 1932 to 94.5 million in 1939: V. G. Pykhov, *Ekonomika, organizatsiya i planirovanie spirtnogo proizvodstva* (Moscow: Pishchevaya promyshlennost', 1966), p. 12.

2 A drunken society

1 The historical background is considered in Raymond Hutchings, *Soviet Secrecy and Non-Secrecy* (London: Macmillan, 1987).

2 Zdeněk Mlynář, *Night Frost in Prague* (London: Hurst, 1980), p. 239.

3 On the 1937 census see Yu. A. Polyakov, ed., *Vsesoyuznaya perepis' naseleniya 1939 goda: Osnovnye itogi* (Moscow: Nauka, 1992), pp. 4–8; and also M. A. Tol'ts in A. G. Vishnevsky, ed., *V chelovecheskom izmerenii* (Moscow: Progress, 1989), pp. 327–31. The results appeared in *Sotsiologicheskie issledovaniya*, 1990, nos. 6 and 7. On more general issues see Ralph Clem, ed., *Research Guide to the Russian and Soviet Censuses* (Ithaca NY: Cornell University Press, 1986).

4 *Chislennost' i sostav naseleniya SSSR. Po dannym Vsesoyuznoi perepisi naseleniya 1979 goda* (Moscow: Finansy i statistika, 1984).

5 These deficiencies were noted by the sociologist Tat'yana Zaslavskaya in *Pravda*, 6 February 1987, pp. 2–3, and in *Sotsiologicheskie issledovaniya*, 1987, no. 2, pp. 3–15. Developments in Soviet statistical practice are considered in Vladimir Treml, 'Perestroika and Soviet statistics', *Soviet Economy*, vol. 4, no. 1 (1988), pp. 64–94, and Tim Heleniak and Albert Motivans, 'A note on *glasnost'* and the Soviet statistical system', *Soviet Studies*, vol. 43, no. 3 (1991), pp. 473–90. For a discussion of statistical practices in the late 1980s see M. G. Nazarov, ed., *Sotsial'naya statistika* (Moscow: Finansy i statistika, 1988).

6 Vladimir Treml, *Alcohol in the USSR: A statistical study* (Durham NC: Duke University Press, 1982), p. 4.

7 Ibid., pp. 18–19, 27, 20.

8 For these estimates of homebrew production see for instance *EKO*, 1974, no. 4, p. 37, and (for the 1980s) G. G. Zaigraev, *Bor'ba s alkogolizmom: problemy, puti resheniya* (Moscow Mysl', 1986), p. 12.

9 A. Krasikov, 'Tovar nomer odin', *Dvadtsatyi vek*, no. 2 (London 1977), pp. 105–50, at pp. 114–15.

10 B. S. Beisenov, *Alkogolizm: ugolovno-pravovye i kriminologicheskie problemy* (Moscow: Yuridicheskaya literatura, 1981), pp. 5–6.

11 A. Krasikov in Roy Medvedev, ed., *Samizdat Register*, vol. 1 (London: Merlin Press, 1971), p. 111.

12 Gur Ofer and Aaron Vinokur, *The Soviet Household under the Old Regime* (Cambridge: Cambridge University Press, 1992), p. 15.

13 Treml, *Alcohol in the USSR*, p. 15.

14 Ibid. See also Treml, 'Alcohol in the USSR: a fiscal dilemma', *Soviet Studies*, vol. 27, no. 2 (April 1975), pp. 161–77; Treml, 'Production and consumption of alcoholic beverages in the USSR: a statistical study', *Journal of Alcohol Studies*, vol. 36, no. 3 (March 1975), pp. 285–320; and Treml, 'Death from alcoholic poisoning in the USSR', *Soviet Studies*, vol. 34, no. 4 (October 1982), pp. 487–505.

15 Treml, *Alcohol in the USSR*, p. 68.

16 Ibid., p. 67.
17 Ibid.
18 Ibid.
19 Ibid., p. 70.
20 Ibid.
21 Ibid.
22 I. G. Urakov and K. A. Khotinyani, *Regional'nye osobennosti alkogolizma* (Kishinev: Shtiintsa, 1989), pp. 13, 9.
23 Treml, *Alcohol in the USRR*, pp. 74–5; similarly Z. V. Korobkina, *U opasnoi cherty* (Moscow: Mysl', 1991), pp. 24–5. Variations in alcohol consumption between republics are also noted in *Sotsiologicheskie issledovaniya*, 1983, no. 4, p. 102.
24 *Znamya*, 1993, no. 3, p. 186.
25 See G. V. Morozov et al., eds. *Voprosy kliniki, diagnostiki i profilaktiki alkogolizma i narkomanii* (Moscow: Ministerstvo zdravokhraneniya SSSR, 1983), p. 122 (which focuses on alcohol-related illness), and Urakov and Khotinyanu, *Regional'nye osobennosti*, p. 12.
26 Goskomstat Rossii, *Pokazateli sotsial'nogo razvitiya Rossiiskoi Federatsii i ee regionov* (Moscow: Respublikanskii informatsionno-izdatel'skii tsentr, 1993), pp. 257–9.
27 Treml, *Alcohol in the USSR*, p. 75.
28 Ibid.
29 Ibid.
30 *Pravda*, 29 July 1978, p. 3. The same figure (6.7 per cent) is reported in L. T. Mashkova, *Eshche raz ob alkogolizme* (Krasnodar: Krasnodarskoe knizhnoe izdatel'stvo, 1985), p. 34.
31 Treml, *Alcohol in the USSR*, p. 75 (slightly modified).
32 Treml in *Radio Liberty Research Bulletin* RL 317/87, 3 August 1987, p. 1.
33 Treml, *Alcohol in the USSR*, p. 79.
34 Ibid., p. 80. Korobkina, *U opasnoi cherty*, suggests an average of 15 per cent of family spending and 12–14 per cent of budgetary income (p. 25).
35 Treml, *Alcohol in the USSR*, p. 80.
36 Ibid., p. 79.
37 Ibid., p. 21.
38 See James R. Millar, ed., *Politics, Work, and Daily Life in the USSR* (Cambridge: Cambridge University Press, 1987), pp. 249, 265.
39 On Krasikov see Roy Medvedev, ed., *Samizdat Register*, vol. 2 (London: Merlin Press, 1981), pp. 208–9. Krasikov's paper exists in two parts, and in two languages. The first part appeared as 'Commodity number one (Part I)' in ibid., vol. 1, pp. 93–115, and the second part as 'Commodity number one (Part II)' in ibid., vol. 2, pp. 163–204. The second part only appeared as 'Tovar nomer odin' in *Dvadtsatyi vek*, 1977, no. 2, pp. 105–50; the original manuscript appears to be lost (Zhores Medvedev, personal communication). A translation of Part I also appeared in *Dissent*, vol. 24 (Fall 1977), pp. 364–78.

40 Krasikov, 'Commodity number one (Part I)', pp. 94–5.

41 Ibid., pp. 95–6.

42 Ibid., p. 96.

43 Ibid., pp. 96–7.

44 Ibid., pp. 97–9.

45 Ibid., p. 99.

46 Ibid., p. 101 ('clothing and underwear' was No. 2, and 'meat and sausages' the suggested No. 3).

47 Ibid., pp. 101–2.

48 'Vinnaya monopoliya', in the *Bol'shaya Sovetskaya Entsiklopediya*, 2nd edn, vol. 8 (Moscow: Sovetskaya entsiklopediya, 1951), p. 94.

49 Krasikov, 'Commodity number one (Part I)', pp. 103, 106.

50 Ibid., p. 108.

51 Treml, 'Production and consumption', p. 302.

52 *Pravda*, 9 August 1987, p. 3; the new head, M. A. Korolev, was interviewed in ibid., 11 August 1987, p. 2 (he had headed the Central Statistical Administration since 1985).

53 *Pravda*, 3 April 1987, p. 1.

54 For a discussion see Treml, 'Perestroika and Soviet statistics', and Heleniak and Movians, 'A note'.

55 *Narodnoe khozyaistvo SSSR v 1985 godu* (Moscow: Finansy i statistika, 1986), pp. 254, 471, 469.

56 *Narodnoe khozyaistvo SSSR za 70 let. Yubileinyi statisticheskii ezhegodnik* (Moscow: Finansy i statistika, 1987), p. 433; *Narodnoe khozyaistvo SSSR v 1988 godu* (Moscow: Finansy i statistika, 1989), p. 141.

57 Korobkina, *U opasnoi cherty*, p. 23.

58 See Table 2.1; calculated on the basis of state sales.

59 *Literaturnaya gazeta*, 3 September 1980, p. 12 (his remarks related particularly to the rate of increase).

60 G. G. Zaigraev, *Obraz zhizni i alkogol'noe potreblenie* (Moscow: Znanie, 1991), p. 21.

61 This was noted in *Sovetskaya Rossiya*, 13 March 1984, p. 2; similarly *EKO*, 1985, no. 9, p. 112.

62 L. N. Anisimov, *Profilaktika p'yanstva, alkogolizma i narkomanii sredi molodezhi* (Moscow: Yuridicheskaya literatura, 1988), p. 25.

63 *Molodoi kommunist*, 1980, no. 2, p. 69.

64 G. G. Zaigraev, *Obshchestvo i alkogol'* (Moscow: Ministerstvo vnutrennykh del Rossiiskoi Federatsii, 1992), p. 52.

65 B. M. Levin and M. V. Levin, *Demograficheskie shtrikhi k portretu p'yanitsy* (Moscow: Institut sotsiologii AN SSSR, 1988), p. 4.

66 *Trezvost' i kul'tura*, 1988, no. 5, pp. 31–2.

67 Ibid., and ibid., 1987, no. 5, p. 11. For the term 'alcoholic emancipation' see B. M. and M. V. Levin, *Mnimye potrebnosti* (Moscow: Izdatel'stvo politicheskoi literatury, 1986), p. 62. On female alcoholism more generally see Korobkina, *U opasnoi cherty*, pp. 83–102; N. G. Shumsky, *Alkogolizm u*

zhenshchin (Moscow: Meditsina, 1983); B. M. Guzikov and A. A. Meioryan, *Alkogolizm u zhenshchin* (Leningrad: Meditsina, 1988); and Yu. N. Ikonnikova in B. M. Levin, ed., *Za zdorovyi obraz zhizni*, 2 vols. (Moscow: Institut sotsiologii AN SSSR, 1991), vol. 2, pp. 168–76.

68 V. T. Kondrashchenko, *P'yanstvo i alkogolizm u podrostkov* (Minsk: Vysheishaya shkola, 1986), p. 5; see similarly Kondrashchenko and A. F. Skugarevsky, *Alkogolizm* (Minsk: Melarus', 1983), p. 14. Young people themselves regarded alcoholism as their main social problem, according to a survey conducted by *Komsomol'skaya pravda* (see B. A. Grushin and V. V. Chikin, *Ispoved' pokoleniya* (Moscow: Molodaya gvardiya, 1962), p. 154).

69 G. G. Zaigraev, *Bor'ba s alkogolizmom: problemy, puti resheniya* (Moscow: Mysl', 1986), pp. 14–15.

70 *Molodoi kommunist*, 1980, no. 2, p. 64.

71 *Istoricheskii arkhiv*, 1994, no. 1, p. 193.

72 *Literaturnaya gazeta*, 21 December 1983, p. 15; similarly ibid., 16 May 1984, p. 11; On 'infantile alcoholism' see *Izvestiya*, 4 July 1983, p. 3.

73 See for instance Ye. V. Borisov and L. P. Vasilevskaya, *Alkogol' i deti*, 2nd edn (Moscow: Meditsina, 1983), p. 27 (attendance), and I. V. Galina, *Alkogolizm i deti* (Moscow: Znanie, 1985), pp. 35 (progress), 33, 77 (attendance).

74 A. G. Kharchev, *Stanovlenie lichnosti* (Leningrad: Znanie, 1972), p. 26.

75 Krasikov, 'Commodity number one (Part I)', p. 111.

76 These figures are from the *United Nations Demographic Yearbook 1981* (New York: United Nations, 1983), pp. 461–3.

77 Yu. A. Korolev, *Brak i razvod. Sovremennye tendentsii* (Moscow: Yuridicheskaya literatura, 1978), pp. 136–7.

78 L. V. Chuiko, *Braky i razvody* (Moscow: Statistika, 1975), p. 162.

79 Ibid., p. 163.

80 Ibid., p. 162. Similar social differences are noted in *Sotsiologicheskie issledovaniya*, 1982, no. 2, p. 101.

81 *Sotsiologicheskie issledovaniya*, 1981, no. 2, pp. 115–18.

82 Chuiko, *Braky i razvody*, pp. 163–4.

83 *Sotsiologicheskie issledovaniya*, 1982, no. 2, p. 101.

84 Chuiko, *Braky i razvody*, pp. 163, 170.

85 D. M. Chechot, *Sotsiologiya braka i razvoda* (Leningrad: Znanie, 1973), p. 16.

86 N. Ya. Solov'ev, ed., *Problemy byta, braka i semi'i* (Vilnius: Mintis, 1970), p. 123.

87 Korolev, ed., *Brak i razvod*, p. 145.

88 T. E. Chumakova, *Sem'ya, moral', pravo* (Minsk: Nauka i tekhnika, 1974), pp. 133–4.

89 A. D. Ursul, ed., *K obshchestvu bez alkogolya* (Kishinev: Shtiintsa, 1989), p. 215.

90 Mashkova, *Eshche raz ob alkogolizme*, p. 3; G. G. Zaigraev notes that this

represented up to 400,000 divorces a year associated with alcohol (*Sotsiologicheskie issledovaniya*, 1983, no. 4, p. 98).

91 Michael Ryan, *Contemporary Soviet Society: A statistical handbook* (Aldershot: Gower, 1990), p. 202.

92 Average life expectations were last reported in *Narodnoe khozyaistvo SSSR v 1979 godu. Statisticheskii ezhegodnik* (Moscow: Statistika, 1980), p. 436.

93 See for instance Barbara A. Anderson and Brian D. Silver, 'Trends in mortality of the Soviet people', *Soviet Economy*, vol. 6, no. 3 (September 1990), pp. 191–251, and Alain Blum, 'Mortality patterns in the USSR and causes of death: Political unity and regional differentials', in Walter Joyce, ed., *Social Change and Social Issues in the Former USSR* (London: Macmillan, 1992), pp. 80–94.

94 V. N. Kudryavtsev, ed., *Sotsial'nye otkloneniya*, 2nd edn (Moscow: Yuridicheskaya literatura, 1989), p. 272.

95 *Naselenie SSSR 1988* (Moscow: Finansy i statistika, 1989), p. 494.

96 Goskomstat Rossii, *Statisticheskii press-byulleten'*, 1994, no. 1, p. 85; and (for the rural figure) *Naselenie SSSR 1988*, p. 495.

97 *Statisticheskii press-byulleten'*, 1994, no. 1, p. 85. For the comparison, see Ryan, *Contemporary Soviet Society*, p. 203.

98 *Naselenie SSSR 1988*, pp. 496–8.

99 *Izvestiya*, 30 October 1989, p. 1.

100 I. P. Lanovenko et al., *P'yanstvo i prestupnost': istoriya, problemy* (Kiev: Naukova dumka, 1989), pp. 6–7. V. P. Lazovsky, *Administrativno-pravovye mery bor'by s p'yanstvom i alkogolizmom* (avtoreferat kand. diss., Moscow: Institut gosudarstva i prava AN SSSR, 1990), suggests the more moderate figure of 17–18 million by 1990 if deaths from alcoholism had remained at their 1960 level (p. 9).

101 V. I. Bartel's, *Alkogol' – sputnik avarii* (Moscow: DOSAAF, 1987), p. 4. Similar figures were reported in *Pravda*, 31 August 1983, p. 6. According to *Sotsialisticheskaya industriya* alcohol was associated with between 50 and 60 per cent of such incidents (8 June 1972, p. 3); *Zdravookhranenie Rossiiskoi Federatsii* suggested a figure in excess of 60 per cent (1984, no. 2, pp. 43–4). For the deaths figure (of 88.7 per cent) see I. I. Alekperov and I. E. Loseva, *Alkogol' i proizvoditel'nost' truda* (Moscow: Ministerstvo zdravookhraneniya SSSR, 1987), p. 14.

102 Korobkina, *U opasnoi cherty*, p. 19.

103 I. N. Pyatnitskaya, *Zloupotreblenie alkogolem i nachal'naya stadiya alkogolizma* (Moscow: Meditsina, 1988), p. 9; on the increasing incidence see Kudryavtsev, ed., *Sotsial'nye otkloneniya*, p. 273.

104 See *Agitator*, 1985, no. 17, p. 29 (accidents), and *Pravda*, 3 March 1969, p. 3 (drownings in Moscow region).

105 See Boris Segal, *The Drunken Society* (New York: Hippocrene Books, 1990), p. 329.

106 Borisov and Vasilevskaya, *Alkogol' i deti*, 2nd edn, p. 13; similarly Lanovenko et al., *P'yanstvo i prestupnost'*, p. 6.

107 See respectively Mashkova, *Eshche raz ob alkogolizme*, p. 17 (underweight babies); G. G. Zaigraev and V. A. Konstantinovsky, *P'yanstvo: mery bor'by i profilaktiki* (Moscow: Znanie, 1985), p. 11 (infant mortality); Yu. P. Lisitsyn and N. Ya. Kopyt, *Alkogolizm. Sotsial'no-gigienicheskie aspekty*, 2nd edn (Moscow: Meditsina, 1983), p. 138, and Kondrashchenko and Skugarevsky, *Alkogolizm*, p. 16 (abortions); G. Kutsenko and Yu. Novikov, *Podarite sebe zdorov'e* (Moscow: Moskovskii rabochii, 1988), p. 41 (premature births); *Literaturnaya gazeta*, 26 December 1979, p. 12 (retarded children); and Borisov and Vasilevskaya, *Alkogol' i deti*, 2nd edn, p. 18 (earlier infertility).

108 See respectively N. Ya. Kopyt and P. I. Sidorov, *Profilaktika alkogolizma* (Moscow: Meditsina, 1986), p. 211 (impotence) and Mashkova, *Eshche raz ob alkogolizme*, pp. 31-2 (sex drive and infertility). Kondrashchenko and Skugarevsky cite data showing sexual malfunction in about 30 per cent of male drinkers (*Alkogolizm*, p. 53).

109 *Pravda*, 1 November 1984, p. 6.

110 *Izvestiya*, 17 June 1965, p. 3 (an earlier but celebrated case that led to an extended correspondence).

111 *Chelovek i zakon*, 1985, no. 9, pp. 34–5.

112 *Ogonek*, 1976, no. 2, pp. 28–9.

113 *Sovetskaya yustitsiya*, 1985, no. 22, p. 12; similarly A. V. Yastrebov, *Alkogol' i pravonarusheniya* (Moscow: Vysshaya shkola, 1987), p. 22.

114 B. M. Levin, intr., *Mnenie neravnodushnykh*, 2nd edn (Moscow: Politizdat, 1972), p. 72.

115 E. Boldyrev et al., *Alkogolizm – put' k prestupleniyu* (Moscow: Yuridicheskaya literatura, 1966), pp. 9, 77. According to *Trud*, as much as 88 per cent of all juvenile crime was committed under the influence of alcohol (15 April 1978, p. 4).

116 *Byulleten' Verkhovnogo Suda SSSR*, 1969, no. 2, p. 40.

117 Yastrebov, *Alkogol' i pravonarusheniya*, p. 23.

118 V. I. Kononenko and V. T. Kalyarenko, *P'yanstvo i prestupnost'* (Kiev: Izdatel'stvo politicheskoi literatury Ukrainy, 1988), pp. 14, 31.

119 L. N. Anisimov, *Profilaktika p'yanstva, alkogolizma i narkomanii sredi molodezhi* (Moscow: Yuricheskaya literatura, 1988), p. 21 (43 per cent).

120 B. S. Beisenov, *Alkogolizm: ugolovno-pravovye i kriminologicheskie problemy* (Moscow: Yuridicheskaya literatura, 1981), p. 33.

121 Levin, intr., *Mnenie neravnodushnykh*, pp. 85–6; similarly Beisenov, *Alkogolizm*, pp. 33–4 (the 'peak' for drinking in Kazakhstan was Fridays and Saturdays, with a corresponding 'peak' for crime on Saturdays and Sundays).

122 Levin and Levin, *Mnimye potrebnosti*, p. 44; similarly *Literaturnaya gazeta*, 4 July 1979, p. 13.

123 *Izvestiya*, 13 February 1982, p. 6.

124 *Sovetskaya Rossiya*, 18 May 1979, p. 4.

125 *Izvestiya*, 11 April 1980, p. 6.
126 Kononenko and Malyarenko, *P'yanstvo i prestupnost'*, p. 32.
127 G. M. Blinov, *Samoobman* (Moscow: Moskovskii rabochii, 1986), p. 175; and *Literaturnaya gazeta*, 26 November 1980, p. 13. In Valentin Rasputin's 'The fire', published in 1985, Siberian villagers immediately formed a human chain to pass out 'crates of the most popular item – vodka' (Rasputin, *Siberia on Fire*, tr. and ed. Gerald Mikkelson and Margaret Winchell (DeKalb IL: Northern Illinois University Press, 1989), p. 128).
128 Zaigraev, *Alkogol' i obshchestvo*, p. 51.
129 Beisenov, *Alkogolizm*, p. 36.
130 Radio Moscow, 17 January 1983, in FBIS-SOV 20 January 1983, pp. R7–10.
131 *Trud*, 22 October 1981, cited in Elizabeth Teague, *Solidarity and the Soviet Worker* (London: Croom Helm, 1988), p. 228.
132 *Pravda*, 11 December 1982, p. 3.
133 Lisitsyn and Kopyt, *Alkogolizm. Sotsial'no-gigienicheskie aspekty*, p. 106.
134 Zaigraev and Konstantinovsky, *P'yanstvo: mery bor'by i profilaktiki*, p. 9; for the higher figure see *Voprosy teorii i metodov ideologicheskoi raboty*, vyp. 6 (1976), p. 129.
135 *EKO*, 1985, no. 9, p. 96, and (for the 'reasons') *Sotsiologicheskie issledovaniya*, 1976, no. 4, p. 76.
136 Yu. M. Tkachevsky, *Pravovye aspekty bor'by s narkomaniei i alkogolizmom* (Moscow: Profizdat, 1990), pp. 31–2.
137 *Literaturnaya gazeta*, 4 July 1979, p. 13.
138 Levin, intr., *Mnenie neravnodushnykh*, p. 74; similarly Tkachevsky, *Pravovye aspekty*, p. 32.
139 T. S. Prot'ko, *V bor'be za trezvost'. Stranitsy istorii* (Minsk: Nauka i tekhnika, 1988), p. 143. See similarly S. I. Kramarenko et al., *Profsoyuzy v bor'be za trezvyi obraz zhizni* (Moscow: Profizdat, 1987), p. 123 (on Mondays after an alcoholic weekend productivity went down by 10–13 per cent, or after a major celebration by 25–30 per cent).
140 See Kondrashenko and Skugarevsky, *Alkogolizm*, p. 16, and Alekperov and Loseva, *Alkogol' i proizvoditel'nost' truda*, p. 14.
141 *Pravda*, 28 October 1974, p. 1.
142 Segal, *The Drunken Society*, p. 349.
143 A figure of 81.1 per cent was cited in *Sotsialisticheskii trud*, 1969, no. 1, p. 135, and a figure of 65.6 per cent in *Voprosy teorii i metodov ideologicheskoi raboty*, vyp. 6 (1976), p. 129.
144 *Sotsialisticheskaya industriya*, 8 June 1972, p. 3.
145 *Zdravokhranenie Rossiiskoi Federatsii*, 1984, no. 2, pp. 43–4.
146 *Sotsiologicheskie issledovaniya*, 1987, no. 3, p. 86.
147 *Literaturnaya gazeta*, 6 June 1984, p. 11.
148 According to N. Ya. Kopyt, *Alkogol' i zdorov'e* (Moscow: Znanie, 1982), illness rates were almost twice as high as among the population as a whole (p. 12.)

149 I. N. Pyatnitskaya, *Zloupotreblenie alkogolem i nachal'naya stadiya alkogolizma* (Moscow: Meditsina, 1988), p. 11.
150 Lisitsyn and Kopyt, *Alkogolizm*, p. 139.
151 Zaigraev and Konstantinovsky, *P'yanstvo*, p. 9.
152 Kondrashenko and Skugarevsky, *Alkogolizm*, p. 16.
153 Kutsenko and Nivokov, *Podarite sebe zdorov'e*, pp. 39, 41.
154 *Argumenty i fakty*, 1990, no. 31, p. 7.
155 *Novoe russkoe slovo*, 18 April 1985, p. 3.
156 Segal, *Drunken Society*, p. 350.
157 *Novoe russkoe slovo*, 18 April 1985, p. 3.
158 Segal, *The Drunken Society*, p. 352.
159 *Izvestiya*, 2 May 1985, p. 3.
160 Michael Ryan, *The Organization of Soviet Medical Care* (Oxford and London: Blackwell and Martin Robertson, 1978), pp. 118–19.
161 Segal, *The Drunken Society*, p. 353.
162 Ibid., pp. 353, 354.
163 Ibid., pp. 356–66.
164 *EKO*, 1974, no. 4, p. 38.
165 *New York Times*, 17 May 1985, p. A1.
166 Korobkina, *U opasnoi cherty*, p. 19.
167 *EKO*, 1987, no. 1, p. 117.
168 Ibid., 1985, no. 9, p. 115.
169 *Sotsialisticheskaya zakonnost'*, 1980, no. 1, p. 49; similarly *Literaturnaya gazeta*, 21 June 1978, p. 9.
170 Segal, *Drunken Society*, pp. 368, 369. Levin and Levin, *Mnimye potrebnosti*, estimate direct alcohol-related losses at 60–80 billion rubles a year as compared with an income from such sources of 50 billion (p. 18).
171 Ellen Jones, *Red Army and Society. A sociology of the Soviet military* (Boston: Allen and Unwin, 1985), p. 137.
172 *Sovetskaya Rossiya*, 3 December 1989, p. 6.
173 Jones, *Red Army and Society*, p. 137 (change); Andrew Cockburn, *The Threat: Inside the Soviet military machine* (London: Hutchinson, 1983), p. 38.
174 *Guardian* (London), 5 August 1985, p. 6.
175 John Barron, *MiG Pilot* (New York: McGraw Hill, 1980), p. 97.
176 *Sovetskaya Rossiya*, 3 December 1989, p. 6.
177 Robert B. Davis, 'Alcohol abuse and the Soviet military', *Armed Forces and Society*, vol. 11 no. 3 (Spring 1985), pp. 399–412, at p. 404; similarly *Posev*, 1982, no. 6, p. 63 (a letter from a former officer).
178 Richard A. Gabriel, *The New Red Legions. An attitudinal portrait of the Soviet soldier* (Westport CT: Greenwood Press, 1980), pp. 154–5.
179 Ibid., p. 153; similarly Davis, 'Alcohol abuse', p. 402.
180 Davis, 'Alcohol abuse', p. 403.
181 Gabriel, *New Red Legions*, p. 153.

182 Based upon the *New York Times*, 13 January 1974, p. 1; ibid., 10 September 1974, p. 24; and Barron, *MiG Pilot*, p. 81.
183 Based upon Svetlana Alexievich, *Zinky Boys. Soviet voices from a forgotten war* (London: Chatto and Windus, 1992), p. 80 (customs) and Alexander Alexiev, *Inside the Soviet Army in Afghanistan* (Santa Monica CA: Rand Corporation, 1988), p. 52.
184 *Sovetskaya Rossiya*, 3 December 1989, p. 6.
185 O. P. Kolupaev and L. L. Galin, *Kovarnyi vrag* (Moscow: Voennoe izdatel'stvo, 1987), p. 19.
186 *Posev*, 1982, no. 6, p. 63.
187 Jones, *Red Army and Society*, p. 138.
188 Davis, 'Alcohol abuse', p. 403; Alexiev, *Inside the Soviet Army in Afghanistan*, p. 52.
189 E. S. Williams, *The Soviet Military: Political education, training and morale* (London: Macmillan, 1987), p. 94.
190 Gabriel, *New Red Legions*, p. 154, and (for the 'epidemic') Cockburn, *The Threat*, p. 40.

3 The campaign is launched

1 *Spravochnik partiinogo rabotnika*, vyp. 2 (Moscow: Izdatel'stvo politicheskoi literatury, 1959), pp. 404–8. A resolution on labour discipline of 1956 had already made passing reference to alcoholism: *KPSS v rezolyutsiyakh i resheniyakh s"ezdov, konferentsii i plenumov TsK*, 9th edn, 15 vols. (Moscow: Izdatel'stvo politicheskoi literatury, 1983–9), vol. 9, pp. 98–104.
2 *Sbornik zakonov SSSR i ukazov Prezidiuma Verkhovnogo Soveta SSSR (1938 g.-noyabr' 1958 g.)* (Moscow: Izvestiya sovetskikh deputatov trudyashchikhsya, 1959), p. 547. For the 1960 measures see *Vedomosti Verkhovnogo Soveta RSFSR*, 1960, no. 5, art. 32; for 1961 see ibid., no. 18, art. 274.
3 See *Ugolovnyi kodeks RSFSR* (Moscow: Gosudarstvennoe izdatel'stvo yuridicheskoi literatury, 1960), arts. 39 and 62.
4 *Vedomosti Verkhovnogo Soveta SSSR*, 1966, no. 30, art. 595 (points 12 and 13).
5 See *Vedomosti Verkhovnogo Soveta RSFSR*, 1967, no. 15, art. 333; for the extensions see ibid., 1972, no. 35, art. 870, and 1974, no. 10, art. 287. Legislation had provided for LTPs in the Ukraine from 1961 (E. Boldyrev et al., *Alkogolizm – put' k prestupleniyu* (Moscow: Yuridicheskaya literatura, 1966), p. 54); the first prototype had been established in Kazakhstan in 1964 (E. A. Babayan and M. Kh. Gonopol'sky, *Uchebnoe posobie po narkologii* (Moscow: Meditsina, 1981), p. 33) and in Moscow in the same year (*Novaya ezhednevnaya gazeta*, 5 July 1994, p. 1). For a discussion of the early stages see Walter Connor, *Deviance in Soviet Society* (New York: Columbia University Press, 1972), pp. 65–8.

6 *Spravochnik partiinogo rabotnika,* vyp. 13 (Moscow: Izdatel'stvo politicheskoi literatury, 1973), pp. 182–3.

7 *Sobranie postanovlenii Pravitel'stva Soyuza SSR* (hereafter *SP SSSR*), 1972, no. 11, art. 61.

8 *Vedomosti Verkhovnogo Soveta RSFSR,* 1972, no. 25, art. 639.

9 Ibid., no. 34, art. 845 (commissions); for the service see T. S. Prot'ko, *V bor'be za trezvost'* (Minsk: Nauka i tekhnika, 1988), p. 140.

10 *Spravochnik partiinogo rabotnika,* vyp. 20 (Moscow: Izdatel'stvo politicheskoi literatury, 1980), p. 414.

11 Prot'ko, *V bor'be,* pp. 141–2 (increased output); G. G. Zaigraev, *Obshchestvo i alkogol'* (Moscow: Ministerstvo vnutrennykh del Rossiiskoi Federatsii, 1992), p. 51 (violations increased from 7.3 million in 1973 to 13.6 in 1983); and (for the opinion of the Khabarovsk first secretary) *Pravda,* 26 August 1978, p. 3. The Ministry of the Interior reported on fulfilment of the 1972 decree in Centre for the Preservation of Contemporary Documentation (TsKhSD), *fond* 5, *opis'* 64, *delo* 45.

12 *Izvestiya,* 9 September 1994, p. 3.

13 Armand Hammer with Neil Lyndon, *Hammer: Witness to History* (London: Coronet, 1988), p. 553. Brezhnev used to take vodka as a nightcap, a double dose if it was insufficient (*Trud,* 25 September 1992, p. 3). There was however no truth in newspaper reports that he had got his bodyguard drunk (Yurii Churbanov, *Ya rasskazhu vse, kak bylo . . . ,* 2nd edn (Moscow: Nezavisimaya gazeta, 1993), pp. 72–3).

14 I. S. Klemashev, *Fenomen Andropova. Vospominaniya i razmyshleniya lechashchego vracha* (Moscow: TsNIIatominform, 1992), pp. 14-16.

15 *Materialy XXVI s"ezda KPSS* (Moscow: Izdatel'stvo politicheskoi literatury, 1981), p. 64.

16 For the background to this campaign see for instance Stephen White, *After Gorbachev* (Cambridge: Cambridge University Press, 1993), pp. 10–13, and John W. Parker, *Kremlin in Transition,* 2 vols. (Boston: Unwin Hyman, 1991), vol. 1, pp. 200–4.

17 V. T. Syzrantsev et al., *Kratkii slovar'-spravochnik agitatora i politinformatora* (Moscow: Politizdat, 1977), p. 71.

18 I. F. Il'ichev et al., eds., *Filosofskii entsiklopedicheskii slovar'* (Moscow: Sovetskaya entsiklopediya, 1983), p. 488, and for 'liquidation', see B. V. Petrovsky, ed., *Populyarnaya meditsinskaya entsiklopediya* (Moscow: Sovetskaya entsiklopediya, 1979), p. 17.

19 Prot'ko, *V bor'be,* p. 7; for falling consumption, see *Bol'shaya Sovetskaya Entsiklopediya,* 2nd edn, vol. 2 (Moscow: Sovetskaya Entsiklopediya, 1950), p. 119.

20 *Materialy XXVI s"ezda KPSS,* p. 64.

21 Yu. V. Andropov, *Izbrannye rechi i stat'i,* 2nd edn (Moscow: Politizdat, 1983), pp. 245–6.

22 K. U. Chernenko, *Narod i partiya ediny: Izbrannye rechi i stat'i* (Moscow: Politizdat, 1984), p. 246. Chernenko expressed similar sentiments in *Kommunist*, 1984, no. 18, pp. 3–21.

23 See particularly Anatolii Butenko in *Voprosy filosofii*, 1982, no. 10, pp. 16–29, and 1984, no. 2, pp. 116–23.

24 M. S. Gorbachev, *Izbrannye rechi i stat'i*, 7 vols. (Moscow: Politizdat, 1987–90), vol. 3, p. 269. For a further discussion see Stephen White and Alex Pravda, eds., *Ideology and Soviet Politics* (London: Macmillan, 1988), chs. 1 and 5.

25 See White, *After Gorbachev*, pp. 10–11.

26 *Trud*, 29 December 1982, p. 2.

27 *Pravda*, 28 December 1982, p. 3.

28 Klemashev, *Fenomen Andropova*, p. 4.

29 Andropov, *Izbrannye rechi i stat'i*, pp. 239, 174. There was a reference to 'drunks' in February 1980 (ibid., p. 185).

30 *Plenum Tsentral'nogo komiteta KPSS 14–15 iyunya 1983 goda. Stenograficheskii otchet* (Moscow: Izdatel'stvo politicheskoi literatury, 1983), pp. 16–17.

31 *Spravochnik partiinogo rabotnika*, vyp. 24, part 2 (Moscow: Izdatel'stvo politicheskoi literatury, 1984), pp. 95–9. Other legislative measures included changes in the labour law (*Vedomosti Verkhovnogo Soveta SSSR*, 1983, no. 33, art. 507), and a relevant section in the law on labour collectives (ibid., no. 25, art. 382). Andropov did however introduce a cheaper vodka, dubbed 'Andropovka' by grateful Russians: Viktor Afanas'ev, *4-ya vlast' i 4 Genseka* (Moscow: Kedr, 1994), p. 51; similarly Roy Medvedev, *Gensek s Lubyanki* (Nizhnii Novgorod: Leta, 1993), p. 132.

32 Chernenko, *Narod i partiya ediny*, pp. 243, 353.

33 K. U. Chernenko, *Po puti sovershenstvovaniya razvitogo sotsializma* (Moscow: Izdatel'stvo politicheskoi literatury, 1985), p. 264.

34 Parker, *Kremlin in Transition*, vol. 2, p. 26.

35 *Izvestiya*, 17 May 1984, p. 3.

36 *Trezvost' i kul'tura*, 1987, no. 5, pp. 6–11, and no. 6, pp. 8–13.

37 *Molodoi kommunist*, 1981, no. 11, p. 69.

38 See for instance *Pravda*, 18 October 1978, p. 3, and 3 March 1969, p. 3 (a national temperance society).

39 On the fall in crime in particular see *Literaturnaya gazeta*, 29 August 1984, p. 10. There had also been a fall in the incidence of severe alcoholism and of new cases: Moscow domestic service, 5 April 1985, in *FBIS: Soviet Union*, SOV-85-067. Other evidence suggested a fall of a third in the consumption of fruit and berry wines; and in the previous ten years the number of shops selling alcohol had fallen by a quarter (*Pravda*, 17 July 1982, p. 3). This apparent fall is queried by Zaigraev: there was an unexpected rise in sugar consumption, and *samogon* accounted at this time for about a quarter of alcohol consumption (*Obshchestvo i alkogol'*, p. 45).

40 E. K. Ligachev, *Zagadka Gorbacheva* (Novosibirsk: Interbuk, 1992), p. 286. A 'significant increase' in letters on the subject at this time was noted by (for instance) *Moskovskaya pravda*, 15 May 1985, p. 3, and *Pravda*, 13 May 1986, p. 6.
41 *Pravda*, 23 March 1985, p. 3. The paper reported that a 'large place' in its postbag had been taken by letters on alcoholism, and that there had been a 'broad response' to the Saratov worker's letter; most favoured a 'decisive struggle' (ibid., 13 May 1986, p. 6; there were further responses in ibid., 14 May 1985, p. 3).
42 *Materialy vneocherednogo Plenuma TsK KPSS 11 marta 1985 goda* (Moscow: Politizdat, 1985), p. 9.
43 Gorbachev, *Izbrannye rechi i stat'i*, vol. 2, pp. 152–73, esp. pp. 153–67. The speech as delivered was reported to have contained references to the economic costs of heavy drinking: *Guardian* (London), 30 April 1985, p. 7.
44 Ibid., vol. 1, p. 39.
45 Ibid., p. 104 (similarly p. 110).
46 Ibid., pp. 131–2.
47 Ibid., p. 168. Gorbachev made clear at the same time that the problem would not be resolved simply by administrative measures.
48 Ibid., p. 396, and vol. 2, p. 17 (election address).
49 Ibid., vol. 2, pp. 96–7; Gorbachev referred, in particular, to 'hidden forms of distribution of income and benefits' (p. 97).
50 Ibid., p. 130.
51 Ibid., p. 224. The speech, delivered on the date the Central Committee resolution was published, went on to promise there would be 'no compromises'.
52 Ibid., pp. 394–5.
53 Ibid., p. 429.
54 Raisa Gorbachev, *Ya nadeyus'* (Moscow: Novosti, 1991), p. 38.
55 See Urda Jurgens, *Raisa* (London: Weidenfeld and Nicolson, 1990), p. 134. The head of Gorbachev's personal staff, however, noted that Raisa had declared it 'utterly absurd to prohibit the consumption of wine' (Valery Boldin, *Ten Years that Shook the World* (New York: Basic Books, 1994), p. 105).
56 Angus Roxburgh, *The Second Russian Revolution* (London: BBC, 1991), p. 27.
57 *Pravda*, 4 March 1991, p. 4. For Gorbachev's concern about 'moral atmosphere' see Nikolai Ryzhkov, *Perestroika: Istoriya predatel'stv* (Moscow: Novosti, 1992), p. 95.
58 *Moskovskaya pravda: Vzglyad i drugie*, 1992, no. 8, p. 3.
59 *La Repubblica*, 7 October 1986, p. 13, in *FBIS: Soviet Union*, SOV-86-196. Gaidar Aliev later identified the campaign with Gorbachev as well as Ligachev and Solomentsev: *Nashe delo*, 1990, no. 4 (7), p. 10.

60 *Pravda*, 2 July 1988, p. 11.
61 E. K. Ligachev, *Izbrannye rechi i stat'i* (Moscow: Izdatel'stvo politicheskoi literatury, 1989), p. 36.
62 Ibid., p. 57.
63 Roxburgh, *Second Russian Revolution*, p. 27.
64 Ligachev, *Izbrannye rechi i stat'i*, p. 86.
65 Ligachev, *Zagadka Gorbacheva*, pp. 286–7.
66 According to Vorotnikov, Solomentsev had been responsible for the preparation of the policy at Politburo level; he produced 'great tomes' for them to read, with accounts of anti-alcoholism policy under Lenin, in the USA, and so forth (interview, 26 June 1990). Solomentsev himself recalled finding the documents, including Lenin's decree of 19 October 1919, in the archives. He had taken over the commission that was responsible for preparing the resolution from Arvid Pel'she, at Andropov's initiative; he recalled that his early draft of the resolution had the General Secretary's full support (interview, May 1993).
67 Ryzhkov, *Perestroika*, p. 96. A similar view is presented in Boldin, *Ten Years* (p. 102), and in Vadim Medvedev, *V komande Gorbacheva. Vzglyad izvnutri* (Moscow: Bylina, 1994), p. 40.
68 Boris Yel'tsin, *Ispoved' na zadannuyu temu* (Leningrad: Chas pik, 1990), pp. 97–8. He told the press that the campaign had been 'the idea of Ligachev and Solomentsev': why had Gorbachev not overruled them? (*Argumenty i fakty*, 1990, no. 9, p. 4).
69 *Pravda*, 9 June 1993, p. 1. Aliev recalled no direct opposition on Yel'tsin's part, but thought he might have made his feelings apparent to Gorbachev in personal discussions (*Nashe delo*, 1990, no. 4 (7), p. 11). The Politburo, in May 1987, noted that 'considerable efforts' had been made in Moscow to 'affirm the sober way of life' (*Pravda*, 23 May 1987, p. 1).
70 *Nashe delo*, 1990, no. 4 (7), p. 10.
71 Valentin Pavlov in *Izvestiya*, 15 June 1991, p. 2, and 18 June 1991, pp. 1–2.
72 Eduard Shevardnadze, *Moi vybor* (Moscow: Novosti, 1991), p. 32.
73 Roxburgh, *Second Russian Revolution*, pp. 27–8. Ryzhkov nonetheless called for an 'uncompromising struggle with drunkenness and alcoholism' at the 27th Party Congress in 1986; he provided his own account in his *Perestroika*, pp. 94–6, 242–3.
74 *Pravda*, 5 April 1985, p. 1.
75 Ibid., 18 May 1985, p. 1; *Izvestiya*, 18 May 1985, p. 1.
76 *Krasnaya zvezda*, 21 May 1985, p. 1; *Literaturnaya gazeta*, 1985, no. 21, p. 1.
77 *Pravda* and *Izvestiya*, 17 May 1985, p. 1. The resolution and related documentation is reprinted in B. A. Stolbov, ed., *Zakonodatel'stvo o bor'be s p'yanstvom i alkogolizmom* (Moscow: Yuridicheskaya literatura, 1985), and in *Trezvost' - zakon nashei zhizni* (Moscow: Politizdat, 1985).

78 Boldin, *Ten Years*, p. 103.
79 Ryzhkov, *Perestroika*, p. 95.
80 *SP SSSR* 1985, no. 17, art. 82; also in *Pravda* and *Izvestiya*, 17 May 1985, pp. 1–2.
81 *Vedomosti Verkhovnogo Soveta RSFSR*, 1985, no. 21, art. 738. For the decree adopted by the Presidium of the USSR Supreme Soviet see *Vedomosti Verkhovnogo Soveta SSSR*, 1985, no. 21, art. 369.
82 The regulations appeared in *Vedomosti Verkhovnogo Soveta RSFSR*, 1985, no. 40, art. 1399, 1 October 1985.
83 Stolbov, ed., *Zakonodatel'stvo*, p. 10.
84 *Pravda*, 2 August 1985, p. 3.
85 Ibid., 29 August 1985, p. 6.
86 Ibid., 26 September 1985, p. 3. A full report appeared in *Materialy uchreditel'noi konferentsii Vsesoyuznogo dobrovol'nogo obshchestva bor'by za trezvost' (25 sentyabrya 1985 g.)* (Moscow: Profizdat, 1985).
87 For Ovchinnikov's address see *Trezvost' i kul'tura*, 1986, no. 1, pp. 7–9, and also *Materialy*, pp. 18–37. The Society's statute is in *Trezvost' i kul'tura*, 1986, no. 1, pp. 10–11, and in *Materialy*, pp. 131–9; the membership of its Central Council is listed in *Trezvost' i kul'tury*, 1986, no. 1, pp. 13, 15, 17–28, and in *Materialy*, pp. 108–21. For the resolution to establish the Society see ibid., pp. 129–31.
88 Ibid., 1986, no. 7, p. 2.
89 *Agitator*, 1987, no. 14, p. 38; for workplaces see *Trezvost' i kul'tura*, 1987, no. 2, p. 2.
90 *Trezvost' i kul'tura*, 1986, no. 5, p. 7.
91 *Pravda*, 27 April 1986, p. 6.
92 *Trezvost' i kul'tura*, 1986, no. 5, p. 7.
93 Ibid., 1987, no. 1, pp. 2–3.
94 *Moskovskaya pravda*, 28 December 1985, p. 2.
95 *Pravda*, 29 January 1986, p. 3; for the early contents see for instance *Trezvost' i kul'tura*, 1986, no. 11, and 1987, no. 1.
96 *Trezvost' i kul'tura*, 1986, no. 4, pp. 30–1.
97 Ibid., no. 7, p. 20.
98 Ibid., no. 10, pp. 33–4 (cf. *Macbeth* III.1.28).
99 Ibid., 1988, no. 12, pp. 47–9.
100 *Komsomol'skaya pravda*, 22 May 1985, p. 4.
101 *Trezvost' i kul'tura*, 1988, no. 7, p. 30.
102 Ibid., 1986, no. 4, p. 41.
103 *Pravda*, 7 January 1986, p. 3.
104 *Trezvost' i kul'tura*, 1986, no. 4, p. 41.
105 *Pravda*, 30 October 1985, p. 3.
106 *Zhurnalist*, 1985, no. 11, p. 49. Other academics to be attacked for their support of 'cultured drinking' included G. G. Zaigraev (see the review of his *Bor'ba s alkogolizmom: problemy, puti resheniya* (Moscow: Mysl', 1986) that appeared in *Trezvost' i kul'tura*, 1987, no. 1, pp. 18–19).

4 The campaign advances

1 The term 'treadmill of reform' was popularised by Gertrude Schroeder in this connection: see Schroeder, 'The Soviet economy on a treadmill of "reforms"', in US Congress Joint Economic Committee, *Soviet Economy in a Time of Change*, vol. 1 (Washington DC: US Government Printing Office, 1979), pp. 312–40. For a further discussion, see chapter 7.

2 To adapt the title of L. N. Kritsman, *Geroicheskii period velikoi russkoi revolyutsii* (Moscow: Gosudarstvennoe izdatel'stvo, 1925).

3 There are particularly close parallels with Chinese experience, and the notion of the advancing 'high tide': see Ronald E. Rice and William J. Paisley, eds., *Public Communication Campaigns* (Beverly Hills: Sage, 1987), Chapter 10.

4 *Pravda*, 10 April 1985, p. 6.

5 *Izvestiya*, 27 June 1985, p. 3.

6 *Pravda*, 3 November 1985, p. 6.

7 Moscow radio, 20 May 1985, in *FBIS: Soviet Union*, SOV-85-097.

8 *Izvestiya*, 4 July 1985, p. 3.

9 *Pravda*, 29 May 1985, p. 3.

10 *Kommunist*, 1985, no. 12, pp. 77–8 (slightly adapted).

11 Moscow radio, 14 September 1985, in *FBIS: Soviet Union*, SOV-85-179.

12 Agence France Presse, 25 August 1986, in ibid., SOV-86-165; and for 'show trials', Moscow television, 18 June 1985, ibid., SOV-85-117.

13 *Pravda*, 19 November 1985, p. 3 (rubber tie), and *Izvestiya*, 11 January 1986, p. 3 (cognac).

14 *Pravda*, 15 July 1985, p. 7.

15 Ibid., 30 October 1985, p. 3.

16 *Trud*, 15 September 1985, p. 2.

17 *Izvestiya*, 27 September 1986, p. 2.

18 *Pravda*, 15 August 1985, p. 3.

19 Ibid., 1 August 1986, p. 2.

20 *Pyataya sessiya Verkhovnogo Soveta SSSR (odinnadtsatyi sozyv) 18–19 iyunya 1986 g. Stenograficheskii otchet* (Moscow: Izdanie Verkhovnogo Soveta SSSR, 1986), p. 39. Ryzhkov noted that the policy to reduce alcohol output was being pursued 'undeviatingly' (ibid.).

21 *Sbornik postanovlenii VTsSPS, aprel'-iyun' 1985 g.* (Moscow: Profizdat, 1985), pp. 140–3. The trade union rules were altered subsequently to include a requirement that members promote (among other things) a 'healthy, sober way of life' (*XXVIII s"ezd professional'nykh soyuzov SSSR 24-28 fevralya 1987 goda. Stenograficheskii otchet* (Moscow: Profizdat, 1987), p. 507). See also S. I. Kramarenko et al., *Profsoyuzy v bor'be za trezvyi obraz zhizni* (Moscow: Profizdat, 1987), p. 8, and Yu. M. Tkachevsky, *Pravovye aspekty bor'by s narkomaniei i alkogolizmom* (Moscow: Profizdat, 1990), p. 8.

22 *Dokumenty TsK VLKSM, 1985* (Moscow: Molodaya gvardiya, 1986), pp. 63–5; and (for the change in its statute) *XX s"ezd VLKSM 15–18 aprelya*

1987 g. Stenograficheskii otchet, 2 vols. (Moscow: Molodaya gvardiya, 1987), vol. 1, p. 171.

23 ORF (Vienna), 24 November 1985, in *FBIS: Soviet Union*, SOV-85-227. For Pushkin and Omar Khayyam see B. M. Levin, ed., *Za zdorovyi obraz zhizni* (Moscow: Institut sotsiologii RAN, 1993), p. 88.

24 *Literaturnaya gazeta*, 1988, no. 11, p. 13.

25 *Trezvost' i kul'tura*, 1990, no. 2, pp. 23, 27.

26 *Molodoi kommunist*, 1975, no. 9, pp. 98–101.

27 *Kommunist*, 1985, no. 17, p. 79.

28 For the Party Rules see *Materialy XXVII s"ezda KPSS* (Moscow: Izdatel'stvo politicheskoi literatury, 1986), p. 220 (Rule 58), and for the programme, ibid., p. 160.

29 Ibid., p. 165 (the draft was identical).

30 Ibid., p. 106. The chairman of the Committee of Party Control told the Congress that it had prepared briefings for the Politburo and Secretariat on the alcohol problem (ibid., p. 209).

31 Ibid., p. 50.

32 Ibid., p. 263.

33 Ibid., p. 314. For the draft see *Pravda*, 9 November 1985, pp. 1–6.

34 *XXVII S"ezd Kommunisticheskoi partii Sovetskogo Soyuza 25 fevralya– 6 marta 1986 goda. Stenograficheskii otchet*, 3 vols. (Moscow: Izdatel'stvo politicheskoi literatury, 1986), vol. 2, p. 180 (Kostenko); vol. 1, p. 420 (Shatalov); vol. 1, p. 421 (farm worker); vol. 1, p. 465 (Zhelnina).

35 Ibid., vol. 1, p. 167 (Patiashvili); vol. 1, pp. 292–3 (Solomentsev); vol. 1, p. 494 (Kolbin); vol. 1, p. 279 (Bagirov); vol. 1, p. 393 (Grossu); vol. 1, pp. 209 (Usmankhodzhaev). Kolbin's experiences in Ul'yanovsk were given considerable prominence in the party press: see for instance *Pravda*, 31 May 1985, p. 2, and 4 September 1985, p. 2; also *Partiinaya zhizn'*, 1986, no. 15, pp. 64–8, and *Trezvost' i kul'tura*, 1986, no. 1, pp. 19–21. He became a member of the Central Council of the Sobriety Society on its inception.

36 *Pravda*, 14 March 1986, p. 2.

37 *Partiinaya zhizn'*, 1985, no. 22–3, p. 122.

38 *Pravda*, 6 August 1985, p. 2.

39 Ibid., 24 September 1985, p. 3.

40 Yu. A. Manaenkov et al., *Utverzhdat' trezvost'!* (Moscow: Politizdat, 1986), p. 55 (Belgorod); *Trezvost' i kul'tura*, 1989, no. 8, p. 14 (Tambov).

41 *Kommunist*, 1987, no. 11, p. 34.

42 *Pravda*, 13 September 1985, p. 1.

43 Ibid., 19 September 1985, p. 1.

44 *Kommunist*, 1985, no. 16, p. 87.

45 *Partiinaya zhizn'*, 1985, no. 18, p. 13.

46 *Pravda*, 11 June 1986, p. 2.

47 Moscow radio, 10 November 1986, in *FBIS; Soviet Union*, SOV-86-219.

48 E. K. Ligachev, *Izbrannye rechi i stat'i* (Moscow: Izdatel'stvo politicheskoi literatury, 1989), pp. 156–7.

49 *Pravda*, 15 March 1986, p. 1.
50 M. S. Gorbachev, *Izbrannye rechi i stat'i*, 7 vols. (Moscow: Izdatel'stvo politicheskoi literatury, 1987–90), vol. 3, p. 454.
51 Ibid., 27 July 1986, pp. 1–2.
52 Quoted in *Agitator*, 1986, no. 24, p. 29.
53 *Sovetskaya Rossiya*, 18 September 1985, p. 2.
54 *Pravda*, 15 February 1986, p. 2. For the Presidium's resolution of 14 February 1986 see *Vedomosti Verkhovnogo Soveta SSSR*, 1986, no. 8, item 141.
55 *Sovetskaya Rossiya*, 13 December 1985, p. 2. Other discouraging reports on the Chuvash republic appeared in *Trud*, 22 December 1985, p. 4, and on Novgorod in *Pravda*, 31 January 1986, p. 1.
56 Moscow radio, 24 November 1985, in *FBIS: Soviet Union*, SOV-85-227.
57 *Pravda*, 22 November 1986, p. 3.
58 *Izvestiya*, 5 February 1986, p. 1.
59 *Pravda*, 20 March 1986, p. 6.
60 Moscow radio, 3 May 1986, in *FBIS: Soviet Union*, SOV-86-088; see also *Sovetskaya Rossiya*, 27 March 1986, p. 2.
61 Moscow television, 21 March 1986, in *FBIS: Soviet Union*, SOV-86-057S.
62 *Chelovek i zakon*, 1985, no. 10, p. 43.
63 Moscow television, 5 April 1985, in *FBIS: Soviet Union*, SOV-85-067.
64 *Agitator*, 1986, no. 14, p. 39.
65 *Ogonek*, 1986, no. 20, p. 26.
66 *Soviet Weekly*, 28 March 1987, p. 7.
67 *Partiinaya zhizn'*, 1986, no. 3, pp. 75–6.
68 Ibid., 1985, no. 11, pp. 64–5 (slightly adapted).
69 *Pravda*, 3 June 1985, p. 3.
70 *Izvestiya*, 29 October 1985, p. 3. Other cases of the surrender of home-brew equipment were reported in *Pravda*, 15 June 1986, p. 3, and in L. I. Blinova and P. V. Grishanin, *Otvetstvennost' za samogonovarenie i spekulyatsiya spirtnimi napitkami* (Moscow: Yuridicheskaya literatura, 1986), p. 41.
71 Moscow radio, 11 December 1985, in *FBIS: Soviet Union*, SOV-85-239.
72 *Trezvost' i kul'tura*, 1987, no. 3, p. 13.
73 Ibid., 1986, no. 8, p. 21.
74 Ibid., 1987, no. 4, p. 11.
75 Ibid., 1988, no. 4, p. 53.
76 Ibid., 1986, no. 2, p. 61. Kasparov was interviewed again in ibid., 1989, no. 10, pp. 20–3.
77 *Sovetskaya kul'tura*, 11 February 1986, p. 3.
78 *Trezvost' i kul'tura*, 1990, no. 5, p. 3.
79 See respectively ibid., 1986, no. 2, pp. 30–1 (Pikul'); no. 1, p. 27 (Voznesensky); and 1987, no. 7, pp. 42–4 (Aitmatov).
80 Ibid., 1990, no. 1, pp. 14–15.
81 Ibid., no. 3, p. 38 (Pugacheva); 1992, no. 5–6, pp. 14–15 (Elton John). The

journal also carried the sad but instructive story of Judy Garland (1986, no. 5, pp. 59–61).

82 Ibid., 1988, no. 9, pp, 8–10.
83 *Pravda*, 24 February 1986, p. 4.
84 *Trezvost' i kul'tura*, 1988, no. 12, pp. 6–7.
85 See for instance Phil Davies and Dermot Walsh, *Alcohol Problems and Alcohol Control in Europe* (London: Croom Helm, 1983), Chapter 2.
86 *Izvestiya*, 27 August 1985, p. 2.
87 Ibid., 12 October 1986, p. 2.
88 *Narodnoe khozyaistvo SSSR v 1988 g.* (Moscow: Finansy i statistika, 1989), p. 466.
89 Ibid., p. 504.
90 Ibid., p. 109.
91 *Vestnik statistiki*, 1989, no. 6, p. 54; and (for second last) *Izvestiya*, 12 May 1987, p. 3.
92 See respectively *Narodnoe khozyaistvo SSSR v 1988 g.*, p. 115; *Vestnik statistiki*, 1989, no. 6, p. 55 (share in retail sales); *Narodnoe khozyaistvo SSSR v 1988 g.*, p. 91.
93 *Narodnoe khozyaistvo SSSR v 1988 g.*, p. 336.
94 *Izvestiya*, 10 September 1986, p. 6.
95 *The Independent* (London), 27 September 1986, p. 6; and (for the Russian figures) *Soviet Weekly*, 6 August 1988, p. 7.
96 *Sovetskoe gosudarstvo i pravo*, 1986, no. 4, p. 58.
97 *Vestnik statistiki*, 1989, no. 6, pp. 55–6.
98 Ibid., p. 58.
99 *Soviet Weekly*, 21 February 1987, p. 7.
100 *Ekonomicheskaya gazeta*, 1987, no. 43, p. 23.
101 *Trezvost' i kul'tura*, 1988, no. 1, p. 29.
102 *Pravda*, 20 January 1987, p. 3 (birth rate up from 19.4 per 1,000 in 1985 to 19.9 in 1986); *Izvestiya*, 12 May 1987, p. 3 (an 8 per cent improvement in the proportion of healthy births); Goskomstat Rossii, *Statisticheskii press-byulleten'*, 1994, no. 1, p. 88 (infant mortality rate).
103 Gorbachev in *Pravda*, 27 July 1986, p. 2.
104 *Statisticheskii press-byulleten'*, 1994, no. 1, p. 85.
105 See for instance *Ekonomicheskaya gazeta*, 1987, no. 43, p. 23; similarly *Vestnik statistiki*, 1989, no. 6, p. 54.
106 For the commissions see *Trud*, 30 February 1986, p. 2; the increased number of divorces is in *Vestnik statistiki*, 1987, no. 1, p. 68.
107 *Trud*, 14 August 1986, p. 2 (falsification of the causes of disciplinary offences); *Vozdushnyi transport*, 8 April 1986, p. 4.
108 For the estimate see Vladimir Treml in Maurice Friedburg and Hayward Isham, eds., *Soviet Society under Gorbachev* (Armonk NY: Sharpe, 1987), p. 65; and Treml in Anthony Jones, Walter D. Connor and David E. Powell, eds., *Soviet Social Problems* (Boulder CO: Westview, 1991), p. 129.

109 *Sotsiologicheskie issledovaniya*, 1983, no. 4, p. 104 ('overwhelming majorities'); B. M. Levin, intr., *Mnenie neravnodushnykh*, 2nd edn (Moscow: Politizdat, 1972), p. 132 (similarly *Literaturnaya gazeta*, 28 November 1979, p. 13).

110 *Chelovek i zakon*, 1986, no. 4, p. 38.

111 *Sovetskaya torgovlya*, 1986, no. 8, p. 13.

112 *Izvestiya*, 22 June 1986, p. 3. See also *Sotsiologicheskie issledovaniya*, 1986, no. 1, pp. 42–9, for a June 1985 survey; as many as 88 per cent claimed to have studied the legislation itself (p. 43). According to data cited in M. K. Gorshkov, *Obshchestvennoe mnenie: istoriya i sovremennost'* (Moscow: Politizdat, 1988) as many as 80.5 per cent welcomed and supported the new measures, with only 8.8 per cent doubtful (p. 233). Yet another survey, in January 1986, found an 'overwhelming majority' in favour of the measures; a third believed they should be strengthened, and only 15 per cent thought they should be relaxed (*Sovetskoe zdravokhranenie*, 1987, no. 5, p. 38).

113 *Izvestiya*, 9 December 1985, p. 3.

114 V. V. Andrianov et al., eds., *Formirovanie zdorovogo obraza zhizni: Obshchestvennoe mnenie* (Sverdlovsk: Institut ekonomiki UO AN SSSR, 1988), p. 8.

115 *Sibirskie ogni*, 1988, no. 6, pp. 133–4.

116 Yu. G. Marchenko et al., *Strategiya obnovleniya* (Novosibirsk: Novosibirskie knizhnoe izdatal'stvo, 1990), p. 78.

117 *Sotsiologicheskie izzledovaniya*, 1988, no. 4, pp. 8405.

118 A. G. Safonov, deputy USSR health minister, in *Sovetskoe zdravokhranenie*, 1985, no. 10, p. 3.

119 Moscow radio, 31 January 1986, ibid., SOV-86-022S.

120 See for instance *Izvestiya*, 26 November 1985, p. 3.

121 *The Economist* (London), 14 December 1985, p. 51.

122 *Kommunist*, 1985, no. 16, p. 87.

123 Agence France Presse, 27 May 1986, in *FBIS: Soviet Union*, SOV-86-102; and *The Times*, 30 August 1985, p. 30.

124 *The Economist* (London), 14 December 1985, p. 51.

125 Fedor Uglov as cited in *Sovetskaya kul'tura*, 25 July 1987, p. 6; for the Ukrainian health minister speaking in Atlanta, Georgia, see UPI, 30 April 1986.

5 The campaign retreats

1 For the text see *Pravda*, 2 June 1987, pp. 1 and 3, and *Izvestiya*, 2 June 1987, pp. 1–2. The Politburo's discussion is reported in *Pravda*, 23 May 1987, p. 1. The Politburo subsequently approved a Secretariat recommendation that the legislation on homebrewing be applied more stringently: Centre for the Preservation of Contemporary Documentation (TsKsSD), *fond* 89, *perechen'* 12, document 6, 17 October 1987.

2 *Pravda*, 13 September 1987, p. 2; and (for home delivery) B. M. Levin, ed., *Aktual'nye voprosy antialkogol'noi propagandy i puti povysheniya ee effektivnosti* (Moscow: Znanie, 1987), p. 55.
3 *Pravda*, 6 August 1986, p. 2.
4 Ibid., 22 February 1987, p. 3.
5 *Nedelya*, 1987, no. 23, p. 9 (alcoholics obtaining coupons); *Sovetskaya Rossiya*, 5 February 1988, p. 2 (Petrozavodsk); letter to *Ogonek* (not published) in Christopher Cerf and Marina Albee, eds., *Voices of Glasnost* (London: Kyle Cathie, 1990), p. 93; and *Guardian* (London), 16 September 1991, p. 22.
6 *Kommunist*, 1986, no. 12, p. 70.
7 *Izvestiya*, 28 August 1991, p. 2.
8 *Pravda Ukrainy*, 17 April 1987, p. 4.
9 *Trezvost' i kul'tura*, 1990, no. 2, pp. 30, 32.
10 *Moskovskie novosti*, 1990, no. 24, p. 9 (the 28th Congress made no changes of this kind).
11 *Trezvost' i kul'tura*, 1989, no. 3, p. 11.
12 Ibid., 1990, no. 8, pp. 3–4.
13 *Izvestiya TsK KPSS*, 1989, no. 9, p. 22.
14 *Izvestiya*, 11 March 1987, p. 3, and ibid., 3 March 1988, p. 6.
15 *Meditsinskaya gazeta*, 1 March 1989, p. 1.
16 *Khimicheskaya promyshlennost'*, 1988, no. 7, pp. 60–1.
17 *Izvestiya*, 10 March 1988, p. 1.
18 Moscow radio, 27 April 1988, in *FBIS: Soviet Union*, SOV-88-083.
19 *Pravda*, 7 March 1988, p. 3.
20 Ibid., 31 October 1987, p. 2.
21 Ibid., 15 November 1987, pp. 3, 6.
22 TsKhSD, *fond* 89, *perechen'* 11, document 129, Secretariat meeting of 8 January 1987.
23 G. G. Zaigraev and A. V. Murashev, *Aktual'nye voprosy bor'by s samogonovareniem* (Moscow: Znanie, 1990), p. 58.
24 *Pravda*, 20 March 1986, p. 6.
25 Ibid.
26 Ibid.
27 *Nedelya*, 1987, no. 23, p. 9.
28 *Izvestiya*, 3 October 1987, p. 3.
29 Ibid.
30 *Pravda*, 27 April 1986, p. 6.
31 *Moskovskie novosti*, 1988, no. 30, p. 2.
32 *Izvestiya*, 3 December 1987, p. 3 (police raids); *Ogonek*, 1988, no. 39, p. 22 (*kefir*); *Trezvost' i kul'tura*, 1986, no. 6, p. 24 (liqueur chocolates).
33 *Nedelya*, 1987, no. 35, p. 17 (isolation); *Pravda*, 30 March 1988, p. 6 (exile); *Voprosy ekonomiki*, 1988, no. 12, p. 116 (prison); *Trezvost' i kul'tura*, 1989, no. 7, p. 2 (enemies of the people).
34 *Sovetskaya Rossiya*, 27 September 1987, p. 3. For 'voluntary' approaches

see Dmitrii Chechot as reported in Anatolii Sobchak, *Khozhdenie vo vlast'* (Moscow: Novosti, 1991), pp. 20–1. Chechot, a Leningrad professor, himself argued that drinkers be 'categorically advised' not to have children because of the risk of congenital defects, and that voluntary sterilisation be encouraged in suitable cases (D. M. Chechot and A. A. Shestakov, *Sotsial'noe zlo – alkogolizm* (Leningrad: Izdatel'stvo Leningradskogo universiteta, 1988), pp. 55, 60).

35 *Pravda*, 27 April 1986, p. 6.

36 *Ogonek*, 1988, no. 39, p. 22 (alcohol-free weddings) and *Pravda*, 30 March 1988, p. 6 (occasional confusion).

37 *Ogonek*, 1986, no. 20, p. 27 (Fanta or Borzhomi); *Trezvost' i kul'tura*, 1987, no. 12, p. 7 (sales reporting); *Izvestiya*, 10 January 1986, p. 3 (the concealment of 400 bottles by a shop in the Kuibyshev region).

38 *Sovetskaya Rossiya*, 24 September 1988, p. 2.

39 *Ogonek*, 1986, no. 20, p. 27 (pensioners) and 1987, no. 8, pp. 12–13 (vagrants).

40 *Izvestiya*, 3 October 1987, p. 3.

41 *Financial Times*, 18 January 1986, p. 6.

42 *Trezvost' i kul'tura*, 1989, no. 5, p. 32.

43 *Izvestiya*, 30 October 1989, p. 1.

44 *Sotsialisticheskaya industriya*, 14 June 1988, p. 3.

45 V. V. Men'shikov et al., *Otchet o naucho-issledovatel'skoi rabote 'Trezvost' i kul'tura'* (Daugavpils: Daugavpilsskii pedagogicheskii institut, typescript, 1988), p. 80.

46 *Trezvost' i kul'tura*, 1988, no. 4, p. 4.

47 *Sovetskaya Rossiya*, 5 February 1988, p. 2.

48 Cited in Ron McKay, ed., *Letters to Gorbachev* (London: Michael Joseph, 1991), p. 28.

49 *Trezvost' i kul'tura*, 1989, no. 1, p. 11.

50 *Sovetskaya Rossiya*, 31 December 1989, p. 6.

51 *Izvestiya*, 3 December 1987, p. 6.

52 Ibid., 3 October 1987, p. 3.

53 Ibid.

54 Ibid.

55 Cited in G. G. Zaigraev, *Obraz zhizni i alkogol'noe potreblenie* (Moscow: Znanie, 1991), p. 31; and (for the grim sequence) *Pravda*, 30 March 1988, p. 6.

56 McKay, ed., *Letters to Gorbachev*, p. 40.

57 *Literaturnaya gazeta*, 25 January 1989, p. 13.

58 *Izvestiya*, 3 October 1987, p. 3.

59 *Trezvost' i kul'tura*, 1987, no. 8, p. 22.

60 Ibid., 1989, no. 5, pp. 31–2.

61 *Izvestiya*, 16 June 1987, p. 2.

62 Ibid., 21 June 1986, p. 3; similarly Men'shikov et al., *Otchet*, p. 52.

63 See Z. V. Korobkina, *U opasnoi cherty* (Moscow: Mysl', 1991), p. 39.

64 *Pravda*, 15 November 1987, pp. 3, 6
65 *Izvestiya*, 3 October 1987, p. 3, and for 'taking turns', *Pravda*, 23 August 1987, p. 3.
66 *Trezvost' i kul'tura*, 1989, no. 5, pp. 31–3.
67 Men'shikov et al., *Otchet*, p. 47.
68 For the estimate, see Strumilin and Sonin in *EKO*, 1974, no. 4, p. 37; on the publication of data see Vladimir Treml, *Alcohol in the USSR: A statistical study* (Durham NC: Duke University Press, 1982), p. 48.
69 For tomato paste in particular see *Trezvost' i kul'tura*, 1988, no. 2, p. 7.
70 Ibid.
71 *Izvestiya*, 11 March 1987, p. 3.
72 Zaigraev, *Obraz zhizni*, p. 32.
73 The American Prohibition experience is particularly instructive: see for instance David E. Kyvig, *Repealing National Prohibition* (Chicago: University of Chicago Press, 1979); Sean Cashman, *Prohibition: The lie of the land* (New York: Free Press, 1981); and two older and more popular accounts, Andrew Sinclair, *Prohibition: the era of excess* (Boston: Little, Brown, 1962), and Kenneth Allsop, *The Bootleggers* (London: Hutchinson, 1961).
74 *Izvestiya*, 29 October 1985, p. 3.
75 *Trud*, 19 May 1988, p. 4.
76 Tass, 29 February 1988, in *FBIS: Soviet Union*, SOV-88-050, and (for the views of others) *Kommunist*, 1987, no. 11, p. 37.
77 *Sovetskaya Rossiya*, 30 October 1988, p. 1; and (for the 'dangerous spurt') *Pravda*, 15 November 1987, pp. 3, 6.
78 *Izvestiya TsK KPSS*, 1989, no. 1, p. 50.
79 *Pravda*, 15 November 1987, pp. 3, 6
80 *Sovetskaya Rossiya*, 30 October 1988, p. 1.
81 *Trezvost' i kul'tura*, 1988, no. 2, p. 6.
82 Ibid.; and for the Pioneer camp, *Izvestiya*, 3 March 1988, p. 6.
83 *Trezvost' i kul'tura*, 1988, no. 2, p. 6.
84 Moscow TV, 21 September 1987, FBIS-SOV-184, p. 52.
85 *Izvestiya*, 3 December 1987, p. 6.
86 Ibid., 11 March 1987, p. 3; slightly different figures are presented in ibid., 3 March 1988, p. 6. For women's greater concern see for instance Men'shikov et al., *Otchet*, pp. 28, 79.
87 *Sotsialisticheskaya zakonnost'*, 1989, no. 11, pp. 27–8.
88 *Izvestiya*, 11 March 1987, p. 3.
89 *Sotsiologicheskie isslevodaniya*, 1988, no. 4, p. 85.
90 *Ogonek*, 1988, no. 39, p. 21.
91 *Pravda*, 12 September 1988, p. 4.
92 *Izvestiya*, 8 April 1988, p. 2.
93 *Trezvost' i kul'tura*, 1988, no. 2, p. 7.
94 Ibid., 1987, no. 9, p. 2.
95 Ibid., 1988, no. 2, p. 7.

96 *Izvestiya*, 11 March 1987, no. 3.
97 *Moskovskie novosti*, 1988, no. 21, p. 13.
98 Ibid., 1987, no. 44, p. 12.
99 *Izvestiya*, 11 March 1987, p. 3.
100 *Trezvost' i kul'tura*, 1988, no. 2, p. 7.
101 *Sovetskaya Rossiya*, 25 April 1989, p. 4.
102 Ibid.
103 *Pravda*, 15 November 1987, pp. 3, 6.
104 *Observer* (London), 12 July 1987, p. 13, and (for car sales) *Aktual'nye voprosy antialkogol'noi propagandy*, p. 52.
105 *Pravda*, 15 November 1987, pp. 3, 6.
106 *Izvestiya*, 3 March 1988, p. 6.
107 Ibid., 23 June 1988, p. 2 (slightly adapted).
108 *Pravda*, 24 July 1989, p. 4.
109 *Sotsialisticheskaya zakonnost'*, 1989, no. 11, pp. 27–8.
110 *Trezvost' i kul'tura*, 1988, no. 2, p. 7 (use of ruins) and *Izvestiya*, 11 March 1987, p. 3.
111 *Ogonek*, 1988, no. 39, p. 21.
112 *Kommunist Sovetskoi Latvii*, 1989, no. 5, p. 58.
113 *Izvestiya*, 21 February 1987, p. 2.
114 *Financial Times*, 18 January 1986, p. 6.
115 Quoted in Dusko Doder and Louise Branson, *Gorbachev: Heretic in the Kremlin* (New York: Viking, 1990), p. 168.
116 Ibid.
117 *Ogonek*, 1988, no. 39, p. 21 (only consultants were allowed to use a spirit compress, according to *Pravda*, 30 March 1988, p. 6).
118 *Pravda*, 11 March 1987, p. 3.
119 *Trezvost' i kul'tura*, 1988, no. 2, p. 7.
120 *Aktual'nye voprosy antialkogol'noi propagandy*, p. 55.
121 *Izvestiya*, 9 December 1985, p. 4, and (for Voronezh) *Aktual'nye voprosy antialkogol'noi propagandy*, pp. 55–6.
122 Moscow radio, 20 June 1988, in *FBIS: Soviet Union*, SOV-88-119.
123 *Ogonek*, 1988, no. 39, pp. 21; similar figures were reported in *Izvestiya TsK KPSS*, 1989, no. 1, p. 50.
124 *Izvestiya TsK KPSS*, 1989, no. 9, p. 22; on the membership composition see *Trezvost' i kul'tura*, 1989, no. 6, p. 5 (mid-1989 data).
125 *Pravda*, 28 January 1986, p. 2.
126 *Izvestiya TsK KPSS*, 1989, no. 9, p. 22.
127 Ibid.
128 *Trezvost' i kul'tura*, 1989, no. 3, p. 1.
129 For his election see ibid., no. 4, p. 5; an interview appeared in *Pravda*, 15 March 1989, p. 6.
130 *Trezvost' i kul'tura*, 1990, no. 5, p. 11.
131 Ibid., 1988, no. 9, pp. 1–2.
132 Yevtushenko's views appeared in *Literaturnaya gazeta*, 11 May 1988, p. 13;

the views of K. Karpov were in *Sovetskie profsoyuzy*, 1988, no. 7, pp. 10–11, and no. 14, pp. 28–9.

133 *Trezvost' i kul'tura* quoted, among others, Nikolai Shmelev in *Novyi mir*, 1988, no. 4, and G. G. Zaigraev in *Sotsialisticheskaya industriya*, 14 June 1988 (1988, no. 9, p. 2).

134 *Trezvost' i kul'tura*, 1990, no. 2, p. 32.

135 Ibid., 1989, no. 5, p. 23.

136 Laptev in *Meditsinskaya gazeta*, 10 February 1989, p. 1.

137 See for instance *Nedelya*, 1988, no. 8, p. 10; similarly V. Nadein in *Izvestiya*, 7 May 1988, p. 1.

138 *Trezvost' i kul'tura*, 1988, no. 1, p. 35.

139 Ibid., 1987, no. 11, p. 30.

140 Ibid.

141 Ibid., 1988, no. 4, p. 34.

142 Ibid., 1989, no. 5, p. 23.

143 *Meditsinskaya gazeta*, 10 February 1989, p. 1; the establishment of the Society is also reported in *Trezvost' i kul'tura*, 1989, no. 11, p. 1, and *Nash sovremennik*, 1989, no. 1, p. 192 (a letter from Uglov). On divisions within the Society see below, Chapter 7.

144 *Pravda*, 12 September 1987, p. 3; similarly ibid., 23 August 1987, p. 2. There were even 'plans' for increased membership: *Izvestiya*, 11 May 1987, p. 1. In Smolensk the State Bank enrolled its members without discrimination and told them there would be no embarrassment if they had a drink on a holiday, or on their birthday, or for any other 'valid' reason (*Pravda*, 27 April 1986, p. 6). The members of a 'Vivat Bacchus Order for the Struggle against Sobriety' reported that all had been enrolled, and that one had even become chairman of a branch of the Society (*Trezvost' i kul'tura*, 1986, no. 9, p. 10).

145 *Pravda*, 15 October 1987, p. 3.

146 *Trezvost' i kul'tura*, 1988, no. 4, p. 46.

147 Cited in B. M. Levin et al., *Effektivnost' alkogol'noi reformy: nekotorye sotsiologicheskie aspekty* (Moscow: Institut sotsiologii AN SSSR, 1988), p. 44.

148 *Pravda*, 30 March 1988, p. 6 (a third still drinking); in the Ukraine, for instance, 13,000 members of the Society were expelled (*Izvestiya*, 11 August 1987, p. 1).

149 *Sovetskaya kul'tura*, 25 June 1988, p. 6.

150 *Trezvost' i kul'tura*, 1988, no. 11, p. 5.

151 Ibid., 1989, no. 5, p. 24.

152 Ibid., 1988, no. 8, pp. 6–8.

153 *Sovetskoe zdravokhranenie*, 1987, no. 5, p. 39.

154 *Trezvost' i kul'tura*, 1988, no. 5, p. 27.

155 *Moskovskii avtozavodets*, 9 February 1988, p. 2.

156 *Trezvost' i kul'tura*, 1988, no. 1, p. 21.

157 *Ogonek*, 1988, no. 39, p. 22.

158 *Izvestiya TsK KPSS*, 1989, no. 9, pp. 21–2.
159 Ibid., p. 24.
160 An obituary appeared in *Trezvost' i kul'tura*, 1988, no. 3, p. 5; for Laptev's election see ibid., no. 12, p. 15.
161 Ibid., 1989, no. 4, p. 1.
162 Ibid., 1991, no. 1, p. 6; the new Statute appeared on pp. 40–1. Later still, at a third conference in 1991, the Society became part of an International League for Sobriety and Health with a confederal rather than individual membership structure (ibid., 1992, no. 1, p. 5).
163 *Izvestiya TsK KPSS*, 1989, no. 9, pp. 23–4. For the winding up of branches see *Trezvost' i kul'tura*, 1991, no. 1, p. 4, and no. 3, p. 1; for a financial appeal see for instance ibid., 1991, no. 2, p. 1.

6 The impact of the campaign

1 *Sovetskaya Rossiya* and *Pravda*, 26 October 1988, p. 1.
2 *Pravda*, 1 October 1988, p. 1.
3 Angus Roxburgh, *The Second Russian Revolution* (London: BBC, 1991), p. 115.
4 Ibid., pp. 116–17.
5 *XXVIII s"ezd Kommunisticheskoi partii Sovetskogo Soyuza 2–13 iyulya 1990 goda. Stenograficheskii otchet*, 2 vols. (Moscow: Izdatel'stvo politicheskoi literatury, 1991), vol. 1, p. 174.
6 *Pervyi s"ezd narodnykh deputatov RSFSR 16 maya-22 iyunya 1990 goda*, 5 vols. (Moscow: Respublika, 1992–3), vol. 2, pp. 152–3. For the consultation with Gorbachev see Vorotnikov, interview transcript, 26 June 1990.
7 *Izvestiya TsK KPSS*, 1989, no. 1, pp. 48–51.
8 Ibid., p. 50.
9 *Trud*, 6 October 1988, p. 2.
10 *XXVIII s"ezd*, vol. 1, pp. 154–5; see also his interview in *Pravda*, 30 June 1990, p. 2.
11 *XXVIII s"ezd*, vol. 2, p. 246. Gorbachev went on to point out that the decision to launch the campaign had been taken by the Politburo as a whole (ibid.).
12 *Pervyi s"ezd narodnykh deputatov SSSR 25 maya–9 iyunya 1989 g. Stenograficheskii otchet*, 6 vols. (Moscow: Izdatel'stvo Verkhovnogo Soveta SSSR, 1989), vol. 2, p. 157.
13 See for instance *Pravda*, 10 November 1990, p. 2 (trial) and *Trezvost' i kul'tura*, 1989, no. 1, p. 10 ('stab in the back'). I. A. Nazarov, a *raikom* secretary from the Omsk region, told the First Congress of People's Deputies of his constituents' concern that the campaign was being wound down: *Pervyi s"ezd*, vol. 3, p. 68.
14 Nikolai Shmelev as quoted in *Trezvost' i kul'tura*, 1990, no. 3, p. 69. The reference appears to be to the Laws of Hammurabi, of Babylonian rather

than Sumerian origin, under which the sale of drink was closely regulated but not restricted (G. R. Driver and John C. Miles, eds., *The Babylonian Laws*, 2 vols. (Oxford: Clarendon Press, 1952–5), vol. 1, pp. 202–7).

15 *Novyi mir*, 1988, no. 4, p. 162. There was a passing reference to alcoholism in an article Shmelev had published the previous year: ibid., 1987, no. 6, p. 149.

16 *Pervyi s"ezd*, vol. 3, pp. 51, 53; and *Znamya*, 1988, no. 1, p. 144 ('second Afghanistan').

17 *Izvestiya*, 15 June 1991, p. 2.

18 Vorotnikov, interview transcript, 26 June 1990.

19 *XIX Vsesoyuznaya konferentsiya Kommunisticheskoi partii Sovetskogo Soyuza 28 iyuna–1 iyulya 1988 goda. Stenograficheskii otchet*, 2 vols. (Moscow: Izdatel'stvo politicheskoi literatury, 1988), vol. 1, p. 269.

20 See for instance N. S. Sazonov in *Tret'ya sessiya Verkhovnogo Soveta SSSR. Stenograficheskii otchet*, part 1 (Moscow: Izdanie Verkhovnogo Soveta SSSR, 1990), p. 33 (he believed the whole Politburo should answer for this attack on 'honest toilers'); and *Pravda*, 5 May 1990, p. 5 ('bacchanalia'). The former interior minister, A. V. Vlasov, was asked in the Russian parliament what he had done to resist the 'mindless anti-alcoholic policy of the union government' (*Pervyi s"ezd narodnykh deputatov RSFSR*, vol. 1, p. 531).

21 *Vestnik statistiki*, 1989, no. 6, p. 55; and B. M. Levin and M. B. Levin, *Alkogol'naya situatiya – 1988* (Moscow: Institut sotsiologii AN SSSR, 1988), p. 30 (New Year's Eve queue).

22 Vorotnikov, interview transcript, 26 June 1990.

23 *Nashe delo*, 1990, no. 4 (7), p. 11.

24 *Izvestiya*, 3 October 1988, p. 1 (on Moscow); Levin and Levin, *Alkogol'naya situatsiya*, p. 30 (on Chelyabinsk); *Moskovskie novosti*, 1988, no. 45, p. 14 (for the restriction on Sunday trading).

25 *Moskovskie novosti*, 1988, no. 37, p. 14.

26 *Narodnoe khozyaistvo SSSR v 1990 g.* (Moscow: Finansy i statistika, 1991), p. 113 (share of spending), 132 (sales), 523 (output).

27 *Sovetskaya Rossiya*, 4 February 1990, p. 2.

28 *Trezvost' i kul'tura*, 1990, no. 3, pp. 68–9.

29 Ibid., 1989, no. 5, p. 33 (referring to 1988).

30 *Izvestiya*, 28 January 1990, p. 2.

31 *Trezvost' i kul'tura*, 1989, no. 11, pp. 12–15.

32 *Sovetskaya Rossiya*, 1 September 1989, p. 6.

33 *Ekonomika i zhizn'*, 1991, no. 5, p. 11.

34 G. G. Zaigraev, *Obraz zhizni i alkogol'noe potreblenie* (Moscow: Znanie, 1991), p. 27.

35 *Izvestiya*, 24 July 1990, p. 2.

36 *Zhenshchiny v SSSR 1990* (Moscow: Finansy i statistika, 1990), p. 18.

37 *Trud*, 19 August 1989, p. 2.

38 *Skhola i sem'ya*, 1990, no. 3, pp. 7–9.

39 Ibid.
40 *Izvestiya*, 1 June 1990, p. 3.
41 *Trezvost' i kul'tura*, 1989, no. 8, pp. 13–15.
42 *Nedelya*, 1987, no. 23, p. 9.
43 *Trezvost' i kul'tura*, 1989, no. 1, p. 10.
44 Ibid., no. 4, pp. 8–10.
45 Ibid., no. 5, pp. 10–12; see also ibid., no. 6, pp. 28–30 (a further report), and 1990, no. 2, pp. 33–4 (readers' comments).
46 *Narodnoe khozyaistvo SSSR v 1990 g.*, pp. 250 (diagnoses and patient numbers), 88 (birth and death rates); *Narodnoe khozyaistvo Rossiiskoi Federatsii 1992* (Moscow: Respublikanskii informatsionno-izdatel'skii tsentr, 1992), p. 108, and *Ekonomika i zhizn'*, 1992, no. 30, p. 5 (Russian data).
47 *Izvestiya*, 30 October 1989, p. 1.
48 *Narodnoe khozyaistvo Rossiiskoi Federatsii 1992*, p. 116 (alcohol-related deaths), 118 (life expectancy).
49 *Sovetskaya Rossiya*, 26 December 1990, p. 6.
50 *Trezvost' i kul'tura*, 1989, no. 6, p. 16.
51 Ibid., pp. 16–19.
52 *Sovetskaya Rossiya*, 29 January 1989, p. 1 (Taganrog appeal); *Trezvost' i kul'tura*, 1990, no. 10, p. 3 (Chelyabinsk deputies); and ibid., 1990, no. 7, pp. 3–4.
53 *Izvestiya*, 30 October 1989, p. 1, and *Trezvost' i kul'tura*, 1991, no. 1, p. 2 (for the end 1989 figure).
54 *Izvestiya TsK KPSS*, 1989, no. 1, p. 49.
55 Anders Aslund, *Gorbachev's Struggle for Economic Reform*, 2nd edn (London: Pinter, 1991), p. 191.
56 *Chetvertaya sessiya Verkhovnogo Soveta SSSR (odinnadtsatyi sozyv) 26–27 noyabrya 1985 g. Stenograficheskii otchet* (Moscow: Izdanie Verkhovnogo Soveta SSSR, 1985), pp. 28, 36.
57 *Shestaya sessiya Verkhovnogo Soveta SSSR (odinnadtsatyi sozyv) 17–19 noyabrya 1986 g. Stenograficheskii otchet* (Moscow: Izdanie Verkhovnogo Soveta SSSR, 1986), p. 26.
58 *Vos'maya sessiya Verkhovnogo Soveta SSSR (odinnadtsatyi sozyv) 19–20 oktyabrya 1987 g. Stenograficheskii otchet* (Moscow: Izdanie Verkhognogo Soveta SSSR, 1987), p. 28.
59 *Odinnadtsataya sessiya Verkhovnogo Soveta SSSR (odinnadtsatyi sozyv) 27–28 oktyabrya 1988 g. Stenograficheskii otchet* (Moscow: Izdanie Verkhovnogo Soveta SSSR, 1988), p. 43.
60 *Politicheskoe obrazovanie*, 1989, no. 1, pp. 54–7. Shmelev later dated the collapse of the economy itself to the 'mindless, idiotic anti-alcoholic campaign': *Pravda*, 31 October 1992, p. 2.
61 For the loss see for instance Abel Aganbegyan in *Pravda*, 6 February 1989, p. 3; total losses were put at 40 billion rubles (*Argumenty i fakty*, 1990, no. 35, p. 5) or $25 billion (*The Guardian* (London), 16 May 1989, p. 8).

The Moldavian first secretary G. I. Eremei told the Central Committee that the losses in his republic alone had been 6 billion rubles: *Pravda*, 27 July 1991, p. 3. For the proposal to cut prices see Zaigraev, *Obraz zhizni*, p. 56.

62 *Politicheskoe obrazovanie*, 1989, no. 17, pp. 94–6.

63 *Voprosy ekonomiki*, 1988, no. 12, pp. 121–2, 126; for export losses see *Argumenty i fakty*, 1990, no. 31, pp. 6–7.

64 *Voprosy ekonomiki*, 1988, no. 12, p. 112.

65 *Narodnoe khozyaistvo Rossiiskoi Federatsii 1992*, pp. 458 (the reduction for the USSR as a whole was less marked), 460 (output) and 160 (wine).

66 *Izvestiya*, 20 October 1990, p. 2.

67 Nikolai Shmelev and Vladimir Popov, *Na perelome: perestroika ekonomiki v SSSR* (Moscow: Novosti, 1989), pp. 380–2.

68 Ibid., p. 383.

69 Ibid., pp. 383–4.

70 *Trezvost' i kul'tura*, 1988, no. 11, p. 5.

71 *Trezvost' i kul'tura*, 1988, no. 6, pp. 40–1; *Pravda*, 23 December 1990, p. 4 (persistent critics).

72 *Trezvost' i kul'tura*, 1988, no. 6, p. 41.

73 *Izvestiya*, 27 October 1990, p. 1.

74 See below, p. 159.

75 *Moskovskie novosti*, 1988, no. 30, p. 2.

76 *Sovetskoe gosudarstvo i pravo*, 1987, no. 7, p. 72. Attempts were made in subsequent legislation to define these terms more precisely: see *Vedomosti Verkhovnogo Soveta SSSR*, 1985, no. 41, item 777 (definitions of 'strong spirits' and 'public drunkenness').

77 *Izvestiya*, 26 November 1985, p. 3.

78 *Trezvost' i kul'tura*, 1988, no. 7, pp. 23–5.

79 Ibid.

80 *Sovetskoe gosudarstvo i pravo*, 1990, no. 3, p. 71. There were recommendations for changes in the law in *Sotsialisticheskaya zakonnost'*, 1989, no. 2, pp. 16–17, and in *Sovetskoe gosudarstvo i pravo*, 1990, no. 3, pp. 68–74, and 1991, no. 7, pp. 125–8.

81 *Pravda*, 18 March 1987, p. 6.

82 On the development of the LTP system see above, Chapter 2.

83 *Izvestiya*, 31 July 1988, p. 3.

84 *Trezvost' i kul'tura*, 1988, no. 1, p. 24.

85 *Pravda*, 23 December 1990, p. 4.

86 *Sovetskaya Rossiya*, 2 October 1990, p. 4.

87 Ibid.

88 *Sotsialisticheskaya zakonnost'*, 1989, no. 11, pp. 54–5.

89 *Trezvost' i kul'tura*, 1988, no. 9, p. 26.

90 *Sovetskaya Rossiya*, 2 October 1990, p. 4. For 'plans' see *Trezvost' i kul'tura*, 1988, no. 9, p. 26, and (for the period of the 1980 Olympic Games) *Izvestiya*, 22 July 1990, p. 4.

91 *Izvestiya*, 31 July 1988, p. 3.

92 Ibid., 9 September 1989, p. 6.
93 Ibid., 19 July 1990, p. 2.
94 *Izvestiya*, 23 November 1988, p. 3.
95 Ibid.
96 *Trezvost' i kul'tura*, 1988, no. 1, p. 24.
97 *Pravda*, 18 March 1987, p. 6.
98 *Trezvost' i kul'tura*, 1988, no. 12, pp. 39–41.
99 Moscow television, 28 December 1988, FBIS-SOV-88-249.
100 *Sotsialisticheskaya zakonnost'*, 1989, no. 11, p. 28.
101 Ibid.
102 *Izvestiya*, 9 September 1989, p. 6.
103 *Trezvost' i kul'tura*, 1988, no. 1, p. 25.
104 *Sovetskaya Rossiya*, 2 October 1990, p. 4.
105 *Trezvost' i kul'tura*, 1988, no. 1, p. 25.
106 For the text, dated 28 February 1991, see *Vedomosti S"ezda narodnykh deputatov RSFSR i Verkhovnogo Soveta RSFSR*, 1991, no. 9, art. 262.
107 *Trezvost' i kul'tura*, 1991, no. 7, p. 25 (numbers); *Novaya ezhednevnaya gazeta*, 5 July 1991, p. 1 (wives). A system of compulsory treatment of alcoholics had existed in some form since the eighteenth century: *Moskovskie novosti*, 1993, no. 38, p. 2A.

7 Russia, alcohol and the policy process

1 *Argumenty i fakty*, 1993, no. 16, p. 3.
2 Yeltsin commented on the incident very briefly in his memoir *Ispoved' na zadannuyu temu* (Leningrad: Chas pik, 1990), pp. 187–8.
3 See for instance *Den'*, 1992, no. 27, p. 5.
4 *The Guardian* (London), 29 March 1993, p. 18.
5 Ibid., 9 September 1994, p. 12.
6 *Der Spiegel*, 7 October 1991, p. 205; also in *Izvestiya*, 10 October 1991, p. 7.
7 *Wall Street Journal*, 29 August 1991, p. A6.
8 Irina Boeva and Viacheslav Shironin, *Russians between State and Market* (Glasgow: University of Strathclyde Centre for the Study of Public Policy, SPP 205, 1992), p. 41.
9 See for instance Peter Rutland, *The Politics of Economic Stagnation in the Soviet Union* (Cambridge: Cambridge University Press, 1993), pp. 65–72; see also below, pp. 179–82.
10 For some recent overviews see Robert Nakamura and Frank Smallwood, eds., *The Politics of Policy Implementation* (New York: St Martin's, 1980); Paul A. Sabatier, 'Top-down and bottom-up approaches to implementation research', *Journal of Public Policy*, vol. 6, no. 1 (1986), pp. 21–48; Dennis J. Palumbo, 'Introduction', and James P. Lester et al., 'Public policy implementation: evolution of the field and agenda for future research',

Policy Studies Review, vol. 7, no. 1 (August 1987), pp. 91–102 and 200–16; Talib Younis, ed., *Implementation in Public Policy* (Aldershot: Dartmouth, 1990); and Christopher Ham and Michael Hill, *The Policy Process in the Modern Capitalist State*, 2nd edn (Hemel Hempstead: Harvester Wheatsheaf, 1993). Palumbo notes the predominance of case studies and the lack of a 'coherent, systematic body of knowledge' ('Introduction', p. 91).

11 In what follows I have drawn upon David Marsh and R. A. W. Rhodes, 'Implementing Thatcherism: policy change in the 1980s', *Parliamentary Affairs*, vol. 45 no. 1 (January 1992), p. 33. See also Marsh and Rhodes, eds., *Implementing Thatcherite Policies* (Milton Keynes: Open University Press, 1992), Ch. 1.

12 Marsh and Rhodes, 'Implementing Thatcherism', p. 49.

13 Ibid.

14 *Izvestiya*, 4 September 1992, p. 15.

15 Ibid., 28 September 1993, p. 5; *Krasnoe znamya* (Syktyvkar), 29 July 1994, p. 3 (bottles per day).

16 *Moskovskie novosti*, 1994, no. 14, p. A14.

17 *Pravda*, 10 November 1990, p. 2.

18 *Argumenty i fakty*, 1994, no. 23, Moscow supplement, p. 3 (younger drinkers); *Literaturnaya gazeta*, 1994, no. 32, p. 12 (girls compared with boys).

19 *Izvestiya*, 13 October 1992, no. 1.

20 *The Guardian* (London), 16 April 1994, p. 2.

21 *Izvestiya*, 18 February 1992, p. 1 (in Uzbekistan).

22 Ibid., 18 June 1992, p. 1 (the vodka was their own production).

23 *Nezavisimaya gazeta*, 23 September 1993, p. 6 (there was a similar report in ibid., 16 July 1994, pp. 1, 4).

24 Ibid., 7 October 1992, p. 6.

25 *The Guardian* (London), 6 April 1994, p. 9.

26 *Izvestiya*, 13 November 1992, p. 2; similarly *Moskovskaya pravda*, 6 May 1994, p. 10 (between 10 and 30 per cent). *Rabochaya tribuna* suggested over 50 million were alcoholics (1 July 1994, p. 7).

27 *Izvestiya*, 23 February 1994, p. 1, and 2 February 1994, p. 7 (deaths in sobering-up stations).

28 *Moskovskie novosti*, 1994, no. 14, p. A14.

29 *The Guardian* (London), 4 April 1994, p. 10.

30 *Izvestiya*, 10 February 1993, p. 1.

31 *Komsomol'skaya pravda*, 25 September 1992, p. 1.

32 *The Guardian* (London), 18 October 1993, p. 9.

33 *Trud*, 11 January 1992, p. 2.

34 G. G. Zaigraev, *Obraz zhizni i alkogol'noe potreblenie* (Moscow: Znanie, 1991), p. 28.

35 *Izvestiya*, 14 August 1993, p. 8.

36 *Sotsiologicheskie issledovaniya*, 1992, no. 2, p. 43 (1989 data).

37 *Izvestiya*, 14 September 1993, p. 5.

38 Ibid., 15 December 1992, p. 8. An earlier case involving the sale of an infant for 4 rubles was reported in *Nash sovremennik*, 1987, no. 7, p. 148.

39 *Pravda*, 16 November 1991, p. 2 (Chelyabinsk); *Izvestiya*, 30 September 1991, p. 2 (Perm').

40 *Pravda*, 18 October 1991, p. 3.

41 *Izvestiya*, 4 November 1991, p. 1 (counterfeiting), and 9 April 1990, p. 6 (theft and resale).

42 *Sovetskaya Rossiya*, 1 January 1990, p. 4.

43 *Trezvost' i kul'tura*, 1990, no. 6, p. 58.

44 *Moskovskaya pravda*, 6 May 1994, p. 10 (the figure referred to the proportion of fatal accidents).

45 *Trezvost' i kul'tura*, 1991, no. 5, p. 6.

46 *Izvestiya*, 12 November 1992, p. 7; see also ibid., 29 November 1992, p. 8.

47 *Pravda*, 1 January 1992, p. 3.

48 *Izvestiya*, 7 May 1992, p. 1 (prices of drink were freed on 1 June: ibid., 30 May 1992, p. 1).

49 Ibid., 6 January 1992, p. 3.

50 Ibid., 22 November 1991, p. 8.

51 *Argumenty i fakty*, 1994, no. 13, p. 16 ('Gorbachev' vodka was in fact derived from the name of a Russian family that had emigrated to Germany after 1917: *Izvestiya*, 28 October 1991, p. 3).

52 *Nezavisimaya gazeta*, 5 February 1994, p. 2.

53 For the discussion see *Argumenty i fakty*, 1993, no. 9, p. 2. Yeltsin's decree of 11 June 1993 is in *Sobranie aktov Prezidenta i pravitel'stva Rossiiskoi Federatsii*, 1993, no. 24, art. 2235. Its implementation, after some delay, was reported in *Izvestiya*, 26 April 1994, p. 1.

54 *Komsomol'skaya pravda*, 9 October 1992, p. 1.

55 The entire north-western liquor industry had closed down, and it was 'goodbye to vodka': *Nezavisimaya gazeta*, 5 February 1994, p. 2; the figures were queried in *Izvestiya*, 24 February 1994, p. 2. The largest factory of all, Kristall, was declared technically bankrupt in 1994: *Sovershenno sekretno*, 1994, no. 9, p. 3; *Kommersant'*, 1994, no. 35, p. 21.

56 *Moskovskie novosti*, 1993, no. 27, p. 9B, and no. 31, p. 2A; for the evasion of customs see *Izvestiya*, 16 September 1994, p. 5.

57 The cases of Sakha (Yakutia), St Petersburg and Moscow were reported in *Izvestiya*, 27 August 1992, p. 1; on Moscow again see ibid., 4 September 1992, p. 1; on St Petersburg again ibid., 1 September 1992, p. 8.

58 *Izvestiya*, 21 February 1995, p. 1.

59 *Moskovskaya pravda*, 6 May 1994, p. 10; similarly Uglov in *Rabochaya tribuna*, 26 July 1994, p. 3, and the Russian Security Council as reported on 'Ekho Moskvy', Radio Moscow, 30 September 1994. An advisory group had already been established under the Russian presidency: *Moskovskie novosti*, 1994, no. 14, p. A14.

60 *Izvestiya TsK KPSS*, 1991, no. 2, p. 101; for the text of the letter see *Trezvost' i kul'tura*, 1990, no. 7, pp. 3–4.

61 *Izvestiya TsK KPSS*, 1991, no. 2, p. 100.

62 *Trezvost' i kul'tura*, 1990, no. 2, p. 13.

63 Ibid., 1991, no. 9, p. 4.

64 *Partiinaya zhizn'*, 1991, no. 12, p. 56.

65 F. G. Uglov, *Iz plena illyuzii*, 2nd edn (Moscow: Molodaya gvardiya, 1986), p. 5.

66 F. G. Uglov, *Lomekhuzy* (Leningrad: the author, 1991), p. 123; Uglov put forward similar views in *Kuban'*, 1991, no. 7, pp. 89–94.

67 *Partiinaya zhizn'*, 1991, no. 12, p. 57.

68 Uglov, *Lomekhuzy*, p. 121.

69 *Pravda*, 9 June 1993, p. 3. Uglov related his early life in *Serdtse khirurga*, 3rd edn (Leningrad: Detskaya literatura, 1987).

70 Yu. G. Marchenko et al., *Strategiya obnovleniya* (Novosibirsk: Novosibirskoe knizhnoe izdatel'stvo, 1990), p. 57.

71 *Trezvost' i kul'tura*, 1990, no. 1, pp. 10–13. Bestuzhev-Lada contributed a related series of articles to *Nedelya*, 1987, no. 32, p. 12; no. 33, pp. 21–3; no. 34, pp. 6–7; and no. 35, pp. 17–18.

72 *Pravda*, 10 November 1990, p. 2.

73 *Trezvost' i kul'tura*, 1988, no. 1, pp. 16–19.

74 Ibid., 1988, no. 8, pp. 4–6 (slightly adapted).

75 Ibid., 1990, no. 2, pp. 4–9.

76 *Sovetskaya Rossiya*, 29 January 1989, p. 1.

77 *Moskovskaya pravda*, 14 September 1988, p. 3.

78 *Sovetskaya Rossiya*, 30 October 1988, p. 1.

79 *Moskovskaya pravda*, 14 September 1988, p. 3.

80 *Trezvost' i kul'tura*, 1990, no. 8, p. 3; and *Voprosy narkologii*, 1990, no. 2, p. 57.

81 *Trezvost' i kul'tura*, 1990, no. 8, p. 2.

82 The foregoing is based on *Izvestiya*, 19 June 1990, p. 6, and *Voprosy narkologii*, 1990, no. 2, p. 57.

83 *Izvestiya*, 22 September 1990, p. 2.

84 In Tula: *Soviet Weekly*, 25 October 1990, p. 10.

85 *Soyuz*, 1990, no. 6, p. 24; see also *Trezvost' i kul'tura*, 1988, no. 7, pp. 44–9.

86 See for instance *Izvestiya*, 22 July 1990, p. 4. For a recent overview of forms of treatment see P. M. Fleming et al., 'Alcohol treatment in Russia: a worsening crisis', *Alcohol and Alcoholism*, vol. 29, no. 4 (1994), pp. 357–62.

87 *Trezvost' i kul'tura*, 1991, no. 6, pp. 4–7. For 'several thousand', see Yu. S. Borodkin and T. I. Grekova, *Alkogolizm: prichiny, sledstviya, profilaktika* (Leningrad: Nauka, 1987), p. 187; the estimate of a 90 per cent success rate is based upon I. G. Astaf'ev, interview, September 1992.

88 For Dovzhenko's own account see A. R. Dovzhenko, *Vozvrashchayu vas k zhizni* (Kiev: Molod', 1986). The approach generated a large literature: see for instance *Trezvost' i kul'tura*, 1989, no. 6, pp. 12–14, and no. 12, pp. 2–3; *EKO*, 1986, no. 1, pp. 164–76; and *Nedelya*, 3–9 January 1983, pp. 16–17.

89 Borodkin and Grekova, *Alkogolizm*, pp. 107–8.

90 *Nedelya*, 25 February–3 March 1985, p. 14.

91 *Izvestiya*, 17 June 1992, p. 7.

92 See for instance *Nash sovremennik*, 1986, no. 2, pp. 140–65; *Sovetskaya Rossiya*, 24 October 1989, p. 4; *Trezvost' i kul'tura*, 1989, no. 10, pp. 15–16, 1990, no. 1, pp. 17–22, and 1990, no. 2, pp. 15–22. There were also cases in which Shichko's methods were misused: see for instance ibid., 1989, no. 12, pp. 13–14.

93 *Trud*, 12 May 1985, p. 4.

94 See for instance *Izvestiya*, 9 September 1986, p. 3.

95 Ibid., 24 July 1986, p. 6.

96 Ibid., 22 July 1990, p. 4.

97 *Sovetskaya Rossiya*, 29 January 1909, p. 1.

98 *Sovetskoe gosudarstvo i pravo*, 1987, no. 7, p. 70; similarly *Moskovskaya pravda*, 14 September 1988, p. 3.

99 See for instance Ham and Hill, *Policy Process*, and their reference to implementation as a '"missing link" between the concern with policy-making and the evaluation of policy outcomes' (p. 97).

100 Younis, ed., *Implementation*, pp. 3–4.

101 Jeffrey L. Pressman and Aaron Wildavsky, *Implementation* (Berkeley: University of California Press, 1973), p. xv.

102 Susan Barrett and Colin Fudge, eds., *Policy and Action* (London: Methuen, 1981), p. 12.

103 Based upon Christopher Hood, *The Limits of Administration* (London: Wiley, 1976), pp. 6–7.

104 Ham and Hill, *Policy Process*, p. 101.

105 Paul A. Sabatier, 'What can we learn from implementation research?', in Franz-Xaver Kaufman et al., *Guidance, Control and Evaluation in the Public Sector* (Berlin: de Gruyter, 1986), p. 320.

106 Ibid., p. 316.

107 See M. Lipsky, *Street-Level Bureaucracy* (New York: Russell Sage, 1980), p. xii. For the study see R. Weatherley and Lipsky, 'Street-level bureaucrats and institutional innovation: implementing Special Educational Reform', *Harvard Educational Review*, vol. 47, no. 2 (1977), pp. 171–97.

108 Younis, ed., *Implementation*, p. 12. The term 'implementation as evolution' is taken from G. Majone and A. Wildavsky in *Policy Studies Annual Review* (Beverly Hills: Sage, 1978).

109 For an overview of such studies see for instance John Lowenhardt, *Decision Making in Soviet Politics* (London: Macmillan, 1981).

110 Kenneth Lieberthal and Michel Oksenberg, *Policy Making in China: Leaders, structures and processes* (Princeton NJ: Princeton University Press, 1988), p. 27.

111 *Pravda*, 16 August 1986, p. 1.

112 For the discussion law see *Vedomosti Verkhovnogo Soveta SSSR*, 1987, no. 26, item 387; for the referendum law of 27 December 1990 see *Vedo-*

mosti S"ezda narodnykh deputatov SSSR i Verkhovnogo Soveta SSSR, 1991, no. 1, item 10.

113 See for instance Donald Filtzer, *Soviet Workers and the Collapse of Perestroika* (Cambridge: Cambridge University Press, 1994), pp. 94–122.

114 See for instance Rutland, *Politics of Economic Stagnation*, pp. 65–72.

115 See for instance William Odom, *Soviet Volunteers: Modernization and bureaucracy in a public mass organization* (Princeton NJ: Princeton University Press, 1974).

116 S. L. Ronin, *K istorii razrabotki, utverzhdeniya i razvitiya stalinskoi konstitutsii* (Moscow: Izdatel'stvo Akademii nauk SSSR, 1951), p. 63. On the discussion see Ellen Wimberg, 'Socialism, democratism and criticism: the Soviet press and the national discussion of the 1936 draft Constitution', *Soviet Studies*, vol. 44, no. 2 (1992), pp. 312–32.

117 L. I. Brezhnev, *Leninskim kursom*, vol. 6 (Moscow: Izdatel'stvo politicheskoi literatury, 1978), p. 518.

118 For the '25,000ers' see Lynne Viola, *The Best Sons of the Fatherland* (New York: Oxford University Press, 1987); for the Stakhanovite movement see Lewis Siegelbaum, *Stakhanovism and the Politics of Productivity in the USSR, 1935–1941* (Cambridge: Cambridge University Press, 1988); for the 'experiments' of the 1970s and 1980s see Rutland, *Politics of Economic Stagnation*, pp. 65–72.

119 *Pravda*, 13 May 1985, p. 6; there was further correspondence in ibid., 14 May 1985, p. 3.

120 There were 3,650 responses to an article in *Izvestiya* in May 1984 on a sobriety club, for instance (ibid., 19 March 1985, p. 3); and there were over 2,000 responses to a similar article in *Komsomol'skaya pravda* in December 1984 (ibid., 22 May 1985, p. 4). Solomentsev later recalled the 'heart-rending letters' he had received through the Central Committee and Committee of Party Control, most of them from women, before the campaign was launched (interview, May 1993).

121 See Stephen White, 'Political communications in the USSR: letters to party, state and press', *Political Studies*, vol. 31, no. 1 (January 1983), p. 60.

122 For trade union chairman Stepan Shalaev it was not 'one more campaign' (Moscow television, 23 May 1985, FBIS SOV-85-101); Ligachev insisted it was 'not a shortlived campaign', *Partiinaya zhizn'*, 1985, no. 18, p. 13; Gromyko expressed similar sentiments in *Pravda*, 14 November 1985, p. 3.

123 This distinction is drawn in Don Van Atta, '"Full scale, like collectivization, but without collectivization's excesses": the campaign to introduce the family and lease contract in Soviet agriculture', *Comparative Economic Studies*, vol. 32, no. 2 (Summer 1990), pp. 109–43.

124 *Trezvost' i kul'tura*, 1986, no. 1, pp. 19–21.

125 For the comparison see for instance Z. V. Korobkina, *U opasnoi cherty* (Moscow: Mysl', 1991), p. 66.

126 For 'treadmill of reform' see Gertrude Schroeder in US Congress Joint Economic Committee, *Soviet Economy in a Time of Change*, vol. 1

(Washington DC: US Government Printing Office, 1979), pp. 312–40; for the 'cycle' see David Lampton, ed., *Policy Implementation in Post-Mao China* (Berkeley: University of California Press, 1987), p. 8.

127 *Pravda*, 17 October 1992, p. 4 (the references to wine were in Ligachev's oral testimony as relayed on television).

128 *Den'*, 1992, no. 27, p. 5.

129 *XXVIII s"ezd Kommunisticheskoi partii Sovetskogo Soyuza 2–13 iyulya 1990 goda. Stenograficheskii otchet*, 2 vols. (Moscow: Izdatel'stvo politicheskoi literatury, 1990), vol. 2, p. 246; similarly in *La Repubblica*, 7 October 1986, p. 13, in *FBIS: Soviet Union*, SOV-86-116.

130 Gorbachev to a Moscow city party conference in January 1989, cited in *Trezvost' i kul'tura*, 1989, no. 4, p. 3 (the version of his speech that was printed omitted this passage). Vladimir Dolgikh later recalled that Gorbachev had identified more closely with the campaign than any other member of the leadership, and described him as 'in reality its initiator' (interview, 1993).

131 *Moskovskaya pravda: Vzglyad i drugie*, 1992, no. 8, p. 3.

132 *Nash sovremennik*, 1987, no. 7, p. 156 (Uglov); ibid., 1988, no. 3, p. 144.

133 *Trezvost' i kul'tura*, 1991, no. 9, pp. 1–4.

134 See for instance *Nash sovremennik*, 1987, no. 7, pp. 144–50, and 1988, no. 3, pp. 130–45.

135 Uglov quoted *Arkhiv Marska i Engel'sa*, vol. 5 (Moscow, 1938), p. 348, in his *Lomekhuzy*, p. 127; see also *Ogonek*, 1988, no. 11, p. 3.

136 *Trezvost' i kul'tura*, 1986, no. 3, pp. 52–4.

137 *Soyuz*, 1990, no. 6, p. 24.

138 *Trezvost' i kul'tura*, 1988, no. 5, p. 8.

139 Ibid., 1989, no. 3, pp. 24–8 (the letter appeared in a somewhat abbreviated form).

140 Ibid., p. 29.

141 Ibid., 1989, no. 7, p. 5.

142 *Sovetskaya Rossiya*, 30 October 1988, p. 1.

143 *Sotsiologicheskie issledodaniya*, 1983, no. 4, p. 97.

144 *EKO*, 1985, no. 9, pp. 95–128; similarly Korobkina, *U opasnoi cherty*, pp. 30–2.

145 *Sotsiologicheskie issledovaniya*, 1988, no. 2, pp. 81–3.

146 *Trezvost' i kul'tura*, 1990, no. 2, p. 32.

147 V. I. Vorotnikov, interview transcript, 26 May 1990.

148 *Sovetskaya Rossiya*, 5 April 1990, p. 1.

149 G. G. Zaigraev, 'Proschety lyuboi ataky', *Vestnik Akademii nauk SSSR*, 1991, no. 8, pp. 34, 28.

150 Ibid., p. 28.

151 Ibid., pp. 32–3 (Zaigraev referred mistakenly to B. I. Iskhakov).

152 *Izvestiya*, 30 October 1989, p. 1.

153 *Partiinaya zhizn'*, 1990, no. 4, p. 67.

154 *Kommunist*, 1986, no. 12, p. 68.

155 *Pravda*, 30 March 1988, p. 6.

156 See Alan Maynard and David Robinson, 'Preventing alcohol and tobacco problems', in Christine Godfrey and Robinson, eds., *Preventing Alcohol and Tobacco Problems*, vol. 2 (Aldershot: Avebury, 1990), pp. 166, 167, 178, 181.

157 See David Foxcroft in Geoff Lowe et al., *Adolescent Drinking and Family Life* (London: Harwood Academic, 1993).

158 See for instance Eric B. Rimm et al., 'Prospective study of alcohol consumption and risk of coronary disease in men', *The Lancet*, vol. 338 (24 August 1991), pp. 464–8; H. F. J. Hendriks et al., 'Effects of moderate dose of alcohol with evening meal on fibrinolytic factors', *British Medical Journal*, vol. 308, no. 6935 (16 April 1994), pp. 1003–6; and Richard Doll et al., 'Mortality in relation to consumption of alcohol: 13 years' observations on British male doctors', ibid., vol. 309, no. 6959 (8 October 1994), pp. 911–18. For a recent review of these and other findings prepared for the WHO see Griffith Edwards et al., *Alcohol Policy and the Public Good* (Oxford: Oxford University Press, 1994).

159 *Sotsiologicheskie issledovaniya*, 1988, no. 2, p. 81.

Select bibliography

A note on sources

This study is based in the first instance upon the Soviet and Russian press, particularly the monthly temperance journal *Trezvost' i kul'tura* (1928–32, and then from January 1986 to date). A wider range of other public health journals and newspapers was important, including *Meditsinskaya gazeta*, *Voprosy narkologii* and *Sovetskoe zdravookhranenie*; and a range of legal, sociological and other journals including *Sotsialisticheskaya zakonnost'*, *Sovetskaya yustitsiya* and *Sotsiologicheskie issledovaniya*. The daily papers most frequently cited include *Izvestiya*, *Moskovskaya Pravda*, *Pravda*, *Sovetskaya Rossiya* and *Trud*; among the journals, *Literaturnaya gazeta*, *Nash sovremennik*, *Ogonek* and *Nedelya*. Some use has been made of the main translating and abstracting services, particularly the *Current Digest of the Soviet Press*, the *BBC Summary of World Broadcasts* and the *Foreign Broadcast Information Service* (which cover radio and television as well as printed sources). Several bibliographies were useful, among them L. P. Borovetskaya, comp., *Aktual'nye voprosy alkogolizma. Ukazatel' literatury za 1983–1986 gody* (Kishinev, 1986), M. Yu. Chuchumasheva, comp., *Bor'ba s p'yanstvom i alkogolizmom. Sotsial'no-pravovye aspeky, 1985–1986 gg.*, typescript (Moscow, 1987), and V. A. Nasedkina and G. V. Shandurenko, comps., *Za zdorovyi obraz zhizni* (Moscow, 1986).

An important contribution was made by unpublished material of various kinds, including the archives of the CPSU Central Committee held at the Centre for the Preservation of Contemporary Documentation in Moscow. For their willingness to grant interviews I am grateful to Dr A. A. Glazov, Chief Narcologist of the Directorate of Specialist Medical Care, USSR Ministry of Health, and to Dr Vadim Pelipas and his colleagues at the All-Union Narcological Research Centre in Moscow. I am also grateful to Igor' Astaf'ev, first deputy chairman of the International League for Sobriety and Health and editor of the temperance society's journal *Trezvost' i kul'tura*. Access to an unpublished survey conducted in Daugavpils was made possible through the good offices of Dr Aadne Aasland. Interview material gathered in connection with the BBC series 'The Second Russian Revolution' was made available to me at the British Library of Political and Economic Science; I am grateful to Angus Roxburgh for calling my attention to it. I have also used the interviews of the Brezhnev era Central Committee that were conducted for the Soviet Elites Project at the University of Glasgow, particularly the interviews with Vladimir Dolgikh and Mikhail Solomentsev.

Among published works a place of particular importance is occupied by memoirs of various kinds, including those of Leonid Abalkin, Vladimir Afanas'ev, Valery Boldin, Anatolii Chernyaev, Yegor Ligachev, Vadim Medvedev, Nikolai Ryzhkov, Eduard Shevardnadze, and Anatolii Sobchak, as well as (in various forms) Gorbachev himself. The published secondary literature is immense, and mostly ephemeral in character; it can nonetheless help to provide a non-metropolitan point of view, and a wide range of telling examples and illustrations. I have consulted this literature as fully as possible: published in all corners of the former USSR, it could be examined adequately only in the largest copyright libraries of Moscow and what is now St Petersburg. These libraries could also make available unpublished dissertations, and a range of small-circulation publications intended for a limited audience (for instance, those that appeared under the auspices of the Ministry of Internal Affairs). The Institute of Scientific Information in the Social Sciences, within the Academy of Sciences framework, holds a number of deposited manuscripts that were also consulted. Items to which only passing reference is made, particularly in earlier chapters, have for the most part been excluded from the list that follows.

Published works

Abalkin, L., *Neispol'zovannyi shans. Poltora goda v pravitel'stve* (Moscow: Izdatel'stvo politicheskoi literatury, 1991)

Afanas'ev, V. G., *4-ya vlast' i 4 Genseka* (Moscow: Kedr, 1994)

Agrenkova, G. T. et al., *Pravovye mery bor'by s p'yanstvom, alkogolizmom i samogonovareniem* (Moscow: Vsesoyuznyi yuridicheskii zaochnyi institut, 1987)

Aktual'nye voprosy antialkogol'noi propagandy i puti povysheniya ee effektivnosti, eds. B. M. Levin et al., 2 vols. (Moscow: Znanie, 1987–8)

Aktual'nye voprosy utverzhdeniya zdorovogo obraza zhizni, preodoleniya p'yanstva i alkogolizma (Moscow: Profizdat, 1987)

Alekperov, I. I. and Loseva, I. E., *Alkogol' i proizvoditel'nost'* (Moscow: Ministerstvo zdravokhraneniya SSSR, 1987)

Alexiev, Alexander, *Inside the Soviet Army in Afghanistan* (Santa Monica CA: Rand, 1988)

Alexievich, Svetlana, *Zinky Boys. Soviet voices from a forgotten war* (London: Chatto and Windus, 1992)

Alkogolizm i bor'ba s nim, ed. M. N. Nizhegorodtsev (St Petersburg: Tipografiya P. P. Soikina, 1909)

Alkogolizm v sovremennoi derevne, intr. N. Cherlyunchakevich (Moscow: TsSU RSFSR, 1929)

Andrianov, V. V. et al., eds., *Formirovanie zdorovogo obraza zhizni: obshchestvennoe mnenie* (Sverdlovsk: Institut ekonomiki UO AN SSSR, 1988)

Anisimov, L. N., *Profilaktika p'yanstva, alkogolizma i narkomanii sredi molodezhi* (Moscow: Yuridicheskaya literatura, 1988)

Antonov-Ovseenko, V. A., *Zapiski o grazhdanskoi voine*, vol. 1 (Moscow-Leningrad: Vysshii voennyi redaktsionnyi sovet, 1924)

Antonov-Romanovsky, G. V., *P'yanstvo pod zapretom zakona* (Moscow: Yuricheskaya literatura, 1985)

Aronov, D. M., *Tvoi i nash dolg* (Moscow: Fizkul'tura i sport, 1986)

Aslund, Anders, *Gorbachev's Struggle for Economic Reform*, 2nd edn (London: Pinter, 1991)

Babayan, E. A., *Vnimanie – yad!*, 2nd edn (Moscow: Sovetskaya Rossiya, 1980)

Babayan, E. A. and M. Kh. Gonopol'sky, *Uchebnoe posobie po narkologii* (Moscow: Meditsina, 1981)

Babayan, E. A. and M. D. Pyatov, *Profilaktika alkogolizma*, 2nd edn (Moscow: Meditsina, 1982)

Babii, N. A., *Ugolovnaya otvetstvennost' za spaivanie nesovershennoletnykh* (Minsk: Universitetskoe, 1986)

Baggott, Rob, *Alcohol, Politics and Social Policy* (Aldershot, Hants: Avebury, 1990)

Bakhrakh, D. N., *Administrativno-pravovye mery bor'by s p'yanstvom* (Moscow: Yuridicheskaya literatura, 1986)

Bakhrakh, D. N. and A. Telegin, *Alkogolizm i pravonarusheniya* (Perm': Permskoe knizhnoe izdatel'stvo, 1987)

Baranovsky, N. A., *Bor'ba s p'yanstvom kak antisotsial'nym yavleniem* (Minsk: Nauka i tekhnika, 1987)

Barbaro i Kontarini v Rossii, ed. E. Ch. Skrzhinskaya (Leningrad: Nauka, 1971)

Barrow, John, *MiG Pilot* (New York: McGraw-Hill, 1980)

Barrows, Susanna and Robin Room, eds., *Drinking: Behaviour and belief in modern history* (Berkeley: University of California Press, 1991)

Bartel's, V. I., *Alkogol' – sputnik avarii* (Moscow: DOSAAF, 1987)

Beisenov, B. S., *Alkogolizm: ugolovno-pravovye i kriminologicheskie problemy* (Moscow: Yuridicheskaya literatura, 1981)

Bekhterev, V. M., *Alkogolizm i bor'ba s nim* (Leningrad: Izdanie Lengubprofsoveta, 1927)

Berlyand, A. S., *Alkogolizm i bor'ba s nim*, 2nd edn (Moscow: Gosudarstvennoe meditsinskoe izdatel'stvo, 1929)

Bernshtein, V. M., *Mozhem i dolzhny?* (Petrozavodsk: Kareliya, 1986)

Besedy o trezvosti, comp. V. A. Ryazanstev (Kiev: Vishcha shkola, 1987)

Beylakov, V. A. and M. E. Skryabin, *Sniskhozhdeniya ne budet* (Leningrad: Lenizdat, 1986)

Blankov, A. S. et al., *Organizatsiya izucheniya obshchestvennogo mneniya po voprosam bor'by s p'yanstvom i alkogolizmom* (Moscow: Ministerstvo vnutrennykh del SSSR, 1991)

Blinov, G. M., *Samoobman* (Moscow: Moskovskii rabochii, 1986)
Blinova, L. I. and P. F. Grishanin, *Otvetstvennost' za samogonovarenie i
spekulyatsiya spirtnimi napitkami* (Moscow: Yuridicheskaya literatura, 1986)
Boenko, I. E. et al., *Zhizn' bez alkogolya* (Voronezh: Tsentral'no-chernozemnoe
knizhnoe izdatel'stvo, 1986)
Bogdanovich, L. A. and G. T. Bogdanov, *Dlya chego lyudi odurmanivayutsya?*
(Moscow: Moskovskii rabochii, 1988)
Boiko, V. V., *V otvete za kazhdogo* (Leningrad: Lenizdat, 1986)
Boldin, Valery, *Ten Years that Shook the World* (New York: Basic Books,
1994)
Boldyrev, E. et al., *Alkogolizm: put' k prestupleniyu* (Moscow: Yuridicheskaya
literatura, 1966)
*Bor'ba s alkogolizmom v SSSR. Pervyi plenum Vsesoyuznogo Soveta protivo-
alkogol'nykh obshchestv v SSSR* (Moscow: Gosudarstvennoe meditsinskoe
izdatel'stvo, 1929)
Borisov, Ye. V. and L. P. Vasilevskaya, *Alkogol' i deti* (Moscow: Meditsina,
1981; 2nd edn, 1983)
Borodin, D. N., *Kabak i ego proshloe* (St Petersburg: Vilenchik, 1910)
Lechebnitsy dlya p'yanits (St Petersburg: Vilenchik, 1893)
P'yanstvo sredi detei (St Petersburg: Vilenchik, 1910)
Znachenie chainykh v bor'be s alkogolizmom (St Petersburg: Sankt-
Peterburgskaya elektropechatka, 1903)
Borodin, Yu. S. and T. I. Grekova, *Alkogolizm: prichiny, sledstviya, profilaktika*
(Leningrad: Nauka, 1987)
Borovikov, V. B. et al., *Ugolovno-pravovaya bor'ba organov vnutrennykh del s
p'yanstvom i alkogolizmom* (Moscow: Ministerstvo vnutrennykh del SSSR,
1988)
Brandt, B. F., *Bor'ba s p'yanstvom zagranitsei i v Rossii* (Kiev: Tipografiya Petra
Barskogo, 1897)
Chechot, D. M., *Sotsiologiya braka i razvoda* (Leningrad: Znanie, 1973)
Chechot, D. M. and A. A. Shestakov, *Sotsial'noe zlo-alkogolizm* (Leningrad:
Izdatel'stvo Leningradskogo gosudarstvennogo universiteta, 1988)
Chernyaev, A. S., *Shest' let s Gorbachevym* (Moscow: Progress, 1993)
Christian, David, *'Living Water'. Vodka and Russian society on the eve of
emancipation* (Oxford: Clarendon Press, 1990)
Chuiko, L. V., *Braki i razvody* (Moscow: Statistika, 1975)
Chumakova, T. E., *Sem'ya, moral', pravo* (Minsk: Nauka i tekhnika, 1974)
Connor, Walter D., *Deviance in Soviet Society: Crime, delinquency and alcoholism*
(New York: Columbia University Press, 1972)
Davies, Phil and Dermot Walsh, *Alcohol Problems and Alcohol Control in Europe*
(London: Croom Helm, 1983)
Deichman, E. I., *Alkogolizm i bor'ba s nim* (Moscow-Leningrad: Moskovskii
rabochii, 1929)
Dmitriev, V. K., *Kriticheskie issledovaniya o potreblenii alkogolya v Rossii*
(Moscow: Izdanie V. P. Ryabushinskogo, 1911)

Doder, Dusko and Louise Branson, *Gorbachev: Heretic in the Kremlin* (New York: Viking, 1990)

Dorogikh, N. M., *Administrativno-pravovye mery po preodoleniyu p'yanstva i alkogolizma* (Kiev: Vishcha shkola, 1988)

Douglas, Mary, *Constructive Drinking. Perspectives on drink from anthropology* (Cambridge: Cambridge University Press, 1987)

Dovzhenko, A. R., *Vozvrashchayu vas k zhizni* (Kiev: Molod', 1986)

Drozdov, E. S. and E. I. Zenchenko, *Alkogolizm: 100 voprosov i otvetov* (Moscow: Sovetskaya Rossiya, 1986; 2nd edn, 1988)

Edwards, Griffith, *Alcohol Policy and the Public Good* (Oxford: Oxford University Press, 1994)

El'tsin, B. N., *Ispoved' na zadannuyu temu* (Leningrad: Chas pik, 1990)

Entin, G. M., *Lechenie alkogolizma i organizatsiya narkologicheskoi pomoshchi* (Moscow: Meditsina, 1979)

Filimonov, G. A., *P'yanstvo, prestuplenie, prigovor* (Rostov on Don: Knizhnoe izdatel'stvo, 1986)

Fletcher, Giles, *Of the Russe Commonwealth*, ed. Richard Pipes (Cambridge MA: Harvard University Press, 1966)

Gabriel, Richard A., *The New Red Legions. An attitudinal portrait of the Soviet soldier* (Westport CT: Greenwood Press, 1980)

Galina, I. V., *Alkogolizm i deti* (Moscow: Znanie, 1985)

Chto gubit nas (Leningrad: Lenizdat, 1990)

Gertsenzon, A. A., *Prestupnost' i alkogolizm v RSFSR* (Moscow: Izdanie Moskoblispolkoma, 1930)

Sovetskoe zakonodatel'stvo po bor'be s alkogolizmom (Moscow: Znanie, 1966)

Godfrey, Christine and David Robinson, eds., *Preventing Alcohol and Tobacco Problems*, vol. 2 (Aldershot: Avebury, 1990)

Golubega, L. M., *Pravovye osnovy bor'by s p'yanstvom i alkogolizmom* (Frunze: Kyrgyzstan, 1987)

Gorbachev, M. A., *Izbrannye rechi i stat'i*, 7 vols. (Moscow: Izdatel'stvo politicheskoi literatury, 1987–90)

Gorbacheva, Raisa, *Ya nadeyus'* (Moscow: Novosti, 1991)

Gordin, V. E. and E. P. Murav'ev, *Sotsial'no-ekonomicheskie aspekty bor'by za trezvost'* (Leningrad: Znanie, 1987)

Gorshkov, M. K., *Obshchestvennoe mnenie: istoriya i sovremennost'* (Moscow: Politizdat, 1988)

Grigor'ev, N. I., *Alkogolizm kak obshchestvennoe zlo* (St Petersburg: no publisher, 1908)

Grushin, B. A. and V. V. Chikin, *Ispoved' pokoleniya* (Moscow: Molodaya gvardiya, 1962)

Guzikov, B. M. and A. A. Meiroyan, *Alkogolizm u zhenshchin* (Leningrad: Meditsina, 1988)

Preodolenie alkogolizma (Leningrad: Lenizdat, 1986)

Ham, Christopher and Michael Hill, *The Policy Process in the Modern Capitalist State*, 2nd edn (Hemel Hempstead: Harvester Wheatsheaf, 1993)

Hammer, Armand and Neil Lyndon, *Hammer: Witness to History* (London: Coronet, 1988)

Hutchinson, John F., *Politics and Public Health in Revolutionary Russia, 1890–1918* (Baltimore MD: Johns Hopkins University Press, 1990)

Illarionov, N. A., *Novoe kachestvo sotsializma: ozdorovlenie, gumanizatsiya, demokratizatsiya* (Kishinev: Shtiintsa, 1990)

Illarionova, N. V. and N. S. Illarionov, *Razum protiv spirtnogo* (Kishinev: Karta Moldavenska, 1986)

Ivanets, N. N. and Yu. V. Valentik, *Alkogolizm* (Moscow: Nauka, 1988)

Iz istorii bor'by s p'yanstvom, alkogolizmom, samogonovareniem v Sovetskom gosudarstve (1917–1985 gg.), comp. T. I. Zheludkova (Moscow: Akademiya Ministerstva vnutrennykh del SSSR, 1988)

Izmailova, F. Sh. and O. N. Kondrashkova, *Profilaktika pravonarushenii v trudovom kollektive* (Moscow: Moskovskii rabochii, 1987)

Jones, Anthony, Walter D. Connor and David E. Powell, eds., *Soviet Social Problems* (Boulder CO: Westview, 1991)

Jones, Ellen, *Red Army and Society: A sociology of the Soviet military* (Boston: Allen and Unwin, 1985)

Joyce, Walter, ed., *Social Change and Social Issues in the Former USSR* (London: Macmillan, 1992)

Kanel', V. Ya., *Alkogolizm i bor'ba s nim* (Moscow: Sytin, 1914)

Kharchev, A. G., *Stanovlenie lichnosti* (Leningrad: Znanie, 1972)

Klemashev, I. S., *Fenomen Andropova. Vospominaniya i razmyshleniya lechashchego vracha* (Moscow: TsNIIatominform, 1992)

Koklyukin, V. V. ed., *Za zdorovyi obraz zhizni. Bor'ba so sotsial'nymi boleznyami*, 3 vols. (Moscow and Brest: Sovetskaya sotsiologicheskaya assotsiatsiya, 1987)

Molesova, D. V., ed., *Preodolenie alkogolizma u podrostkov i yunoshei* (Moscow: Pedagogika, 1987)

Kolupaev, G. P. and L. L. Galin, *Kovarnyi vrag* (Moscow: Voennoe izdatel'stvo, 1987)

Kondrashenko, V. T., *P'yanstvo i alkogolizm u podrostkov* (Minsk: Vysheishaya shkola, 1986)

Kondrashenko, V. T. and A. F. Skugarevsky, *Alkogolizm* (Minsk: Belarus', 1983)

Kononenko, V. I. and V. T. Malyarenko, *P'yanstvo i prestupnost'* (Kiev: Izdatel'stvo politicheskoi literatury Ukrainy, 1988)

Konstantinovsky, V. A., *Sotsial'nye problemy preodoleniya p'yanstva i alkogolizma* (avtoreferat kandidatskoi dissertatsii, Moscow: Moskovskii gosudarstvennyi universitet, 1989)

Konyaev, N., et al., *Trezvost' – norma zhizni* (Kuibyshev: Kuibyshevskoe knizhnoe izdatel'stvo, 1987)

Kopyt, N. Ya., *Alkogol' i zdorov'e* (Moscow: Znanie, 1982)

Kopyt, N. Ya. and P. I. Sidorov, *Profilaktika alkogolizma* (Moscow: Meditsina, 1986)

Korobkina, Z. V., *U opasnoi cherty* (Moscow: Mysl', 1991)

Korolenko, Ts. P., ed., *Meditsinskie i sotsial'no-psikhologicheskie aspekty alkogolizma* (Novosibirsk: Novosibirskii meditsinskii institut, 1988)

Korolenko, Ts. P. et al., *Sem' putei k katastrofe* (Novosibirsk: Nauka, 1990)

Korolenko, Ts. P. and A. S. Timofeeva, *Korni alkogolizma* (Novosibirsk: Novosibirskoe knizhnoe izdatel'stvo, 1986)

Korolenko, Ts. P. and V. Yu. Zav'yalov, *Lichnost' i alkogol'* (Novosibirsk: Nauka, 1987)

Korolev, Yu. A., *Brak i razvod: Sovremennye tendentsii* (Moscow: Yuridicheskaya literatura, 1978)

Korovin, A., *Obshchestvennaya bor'ba s p'yanstvom* (Moscow: Kushnerev, 1895)

Samoubiistvo i potreblenie vodki (Moscow: Izdanie A. M. Korovina, 1916)

Kramarenko, S. I. et al., *Profsoyuzy v bor'be za trezvyi obraz zhizni* (Moscow: Profizdat, 1987)

Kruglikov, R. I. and M. Ya. Maizelis, *Alkogolizm i potomstvo* (Moscow: Nauka, 1987)

Kudryavtsev, V. N., ed., *Sotsial'nye otkloneniya*, 2nd edn (Moscow: Yuridicheskaya literatura, 1989)

Kulagin, V., *Selo ottorgaet p'yanstvo* (Moscow: Sovetskaya Rossiya, 1987)

Kutsenko, G. and Yu. Novikov, *Podarite sebe zdorov's* (Moscow: Moskovskii rabochii, 1988)

Kuvitanov, G. A., *Chto mozhet pervichnaya?* (Moscow: Sovetskaya Rossiya, 1988)

Lanovenko, I. P. et al., *P'yanstvo i prestupnost': Istoriya, problemy* (Kiev: Naukova dumka, 1989)

Larin, Yu., *Alkogolizm i sotsializm* (Moscow: Gosudarstvennoe izdatel'stvo, 1929)

Alkogolizm. Prichiny, zadachi i sposoby bor'by (Khar'kov: Nauchnaya mysl', 1930)

Alkogolizm promyshlennykh rabochikh i bor'ba s nim (Moscow: Obshchestvo bor'by s alkogolizmom, 1929)

Novye zakony protiv alkogolizma i protivoalkogol'noe dvizhenie, 2nd edn (Moscow: Gosudarstvennoe meditsinskoe izdatel'stvo, 1929)

Lazovsky, G. P., *Administrativno-pravovye mery bor'by s p'yanstvom i alkogolizmom* (avtoreferat kandidatskoi dissertatsii, Moscow: Institut gosudarstva i prava AN SSSR, 1990)

Levin, B. M., ed., *Za zdorovyi obraz zhizni*, 2 vols. (Moscow: Institut sotsiologii AN SSSR, 1991)

Za zdorovyi obraz zhizni (Moscow: Institut sotsiologii AN SSSR, 1993)

Zdorovyi obraz zhizni i bor'ba s sotsial'nymi boleznyami (Moscow: Institut sotsiologii AN SSSR, 1988)

Levin, B. M., et al. *Effektivnost' alkogol'noi reformy: nekotorye sotsiologicheskie aspekty* (Moscow: Institut sotsiologii AN SSSR, 1988)

Levin, B. M. and M. V. Levin, *Alkogol'naya situatsiya – 1988* (Moscow: Institut sotsiologii AN SSSR, 1988)

Demograficheskie shtrikhi k portretu p'yanitsy (Moscow: Institut sotsiologii AN SSSR, 1988)

Krutoi povorot (Moscow: Sovetskaya Rossiya, 1989)

Mnimye potrebnosti (Moscow: Izdatel'stvo politicheskoi literatury, 1986)

Ne otstupis' (Moscow: Mysl', 1988)

Levin, B. M. and M. E. Pozdnyakova, eds., *Na puti k trezvosti* (Moscow: Institut sotsiologii AN SSSR, 1987)

Ligachev, E. K., *Izbrannye rechi i stat'i* (Moscow: Izdatel'stvo politicheskoi literatury, 1989)

Zagadka Gorbacheva (Novosibirsk: Interbuk, 1992)

Lirmyan, R., *Anatomiya padeniya*, 2nd edn (Moscow: Moskovskii rabochii, 1986)

Lisitsyn, Yu. P. and N. Ya. Kopyt, *Alkogolizm. Sotsial'no-gigienicheskie aspekty*, 2nd edn (Moscow: Meditsina, 1983)

Lowe, Geoff et al., *Adolescent Drinking and Family Life* (London: Harwood Academic, 1993)

Lozbyakov, V. P., *Realizatsiya organami vnutrennykh del zakonov o bor'be s p'yanstvom i profilaktiki pravonarushenii* (Moscow: Ministerstvo vnutrennykh del SSSR, 1989)

Marchenko, Yu. G. et al., *Strategiya obnovleniya* (Novosibirsk: Novosibirskoe knizhnoe izdatel'stvo, 1990)

Mashkova, L. T., *Eshche raz ob alkogolizme* (Krasdnodar: Krasnodarskoe knizhnoe izdatel'stvo, 1985)

Materialy uchreditel'noi konferentsii Vsesoyuznogo dobrovol'nogo obshchestva bor'by za trezvost (25 sent. 1985 g.) (Moscow: Profizdat, 1985)

Matyshevsky, P. S., ed., *Pravovye mery bor'by protiv p'yanstva, alkogolizma i narkomanii* (Kiev: Politizdat Ukrainy, 1980)

Matyshevsky, P. S. et al., *Pravovye i meditsinskie mery bor'by s p'yanstvom i alkogolizmom* (Kiev: Vishcha shkola)

Medvedev, Vadim, *V komande Gorbacheva. Vzglyad izvnutri* (Moscow: Bylina, 1994)

Mel'nikova, I. B., *Takoe gor'koe pokhmel'e* (Omsk: Omskoe knizhnoe izdatel'stvo, 1986)

Men'shikov, V. V., *Otchet o nauchno-issledovatel'skoi rabote "Trezvost' i kul'tura"*, unpublished typescript (Daugavpils: Daugavpilsskii pedagogicheskii institut, 1988)

Mil'kovsky, G. M. et al., *Ugolovno-pravovye sredstva bor'by s p'yanstvom i alkogolizmom* (Moscow: Akademiya Ministerstva vnutrennykh del SSSR, 1989)

Mnenie neravnodushnykh, intr. B. M. Levin (Moscow: Politizdat, 1971, 2nd edn, 1972)

Morozov, G. V. et al., *Alkogolizm* (Moscow: Meditsina, 1983)

Morozov, G. V. et al., eds., *Voprosy kliniki, diagnostiki i profilaktiki alkogolizma i narkomanii* (Ministerstvo zdravokhraneniya SSSR, 1983)

Narodnaya bor'ba za trezvost' v russkoi istorii, ed. R. G. Skrynnikov and N. A. Kopanev (Leningrad: Biblioteka AN SSSR, 1989)

Nastoyatel'noe trebovanie dnya, comp. N. F. Babenko (Donetsk: Donbas, 1985)

Nemchin, T. A. and S. G. Tsytsarev, *Lichnost' i alkogolizm* (Leningrad: Izdatel'stvo Leningradskogo gosudarstvennogo universiteta, 1989)

Nikolaev, L., *P'yanstvo – net!* (Moscow: Moskovskii rabochii, 1971)

Nikolaev, Yu. S. and E. I. Nilov, *"Udovol'stvie" ili zdorov'e?*, 2nd edn (Tashkent: Meditsina UzbSSR, 1987)

Nikolashina, A., comp., *Predislovie k bede* (Kharbarovsk: Khabarovskoe knizhnoe izdatel'stvo, 1985)

Nizhegorodtsev, M. N., *Alkogolizm i bor'ba s nim* (St Petersburg: Tipografiya P. P. Soikina, 1900)

Novikov, S. G., *Bor'ba VLKSM s p'yanstvom (1926–1929 gg.)*, deposited manuscript (Moscow: INION, 1989)

Okhrana zdorov'ya v SSSR. Statisticheskii sbornik, comp. A. I. Krakovsky (Moscow: Finansy i statistika, 1990)

[Olearius] *The Travels of Olearius in Seventeenth-Century Russia*, ed. Samuel H. Baron (Stanford: Stanford University Press, 1967)

Osetrova, N. V., *Brachno-semeinye otnosheniya i kharakter potrebleniya alkogolya* (avtoreferat kandidatskoi dissertatsii, Moscow: Institut sotsiologii AN SSSR, 1988)

Ozerov, I. Kh., *Gornye zavody Urala* (Moscow: Sytin, 1910)

Pashchenkov, S., *Vo vred zdorov'yu, sem'e, potomstvu* (Moscow: Moskovskii rabochii, 1985)

Plant, Martin et al., *Alcohol and Drugs. Research and policy* (Edinburgh: Edinburgh University Press, 1990)

Pokhlebkin, V. V., *Istoriya vodki* (Moscow: Inter-Verso, 1991)

Pravovye mery bor'by s p'yanstvom, ed. V. A. Konstantinovsky et al. (Moscow: Yuridicheskaya literatura, 1987)

Pryzhov, I. G., *Istoriya kabakov v Rossii v svyazi s istoriei russkogo naroda* (St Petersburg and Moscow: Vol'f, 1868; 2nd edn with bibliography, Kazan': Molodye sily, 1914)

Prot'ko, T. S., *V bor'be za trezvost': Stranitsy istorii* (Minsk: Nauka i tekhnika, 1988)

Puti sovershenstvovaniya sotsialisticheskogo obraza zhizni, ed. V. N. Ivanov et al. (Moscow: Institut sotsiologii AN SSSR, 1988)

Pyatnitskaya, I. N., *Zloupotreblenie alkogolem i nachal'naya stadiya alkogolizma* (Moscow: Meditsina, 1988)

Pykhov, V. G., *Ekonomika, organizatsiya i planirovanie spirtnogo proizvodstva* (Moscow: Pishchevaya promyshlennost', 1966)

Rialand, Marie-Rose, *L'alcool et les russes* (Paris: Institut d'études slaves, 1989)

Rice, Ronald E. and William J. Paisley, eds., *Public Communication Campaigns* (Beverly Hills: Sage, 1987)

Rol' trudovogo kollektiva v profilaktike nedistsiplinirovannosti i p'yanstva, ed. K. P. Urzhinsky (Kalinin: Izdatel'stvo Kaliningradskogo universiteta, 1985)

Roxburgh, Angus, *The Second Russian Revolution* (London: BBC, 1991)

Royal College of Physicians, *Alcohol. Our Favourite Drug* (London: Tavistock, 1986)

Rozenfel'd, V. G. and V. S. Osnovin, *P'yanstvo i alkogolizm: organizatsionno-pravovye sredstva bor'by s nimi* (Voronezh: Izdatel'stvo Voronezhskogo universiteta, 1988)

Rozhnov, V. E., *Po sledam zelenogo zmiya* (Moscow: Voennoe izdatel'stvo, 1969)
  Sotsial'no-meditsinskie aspekty alkogolizma (Moscow: Ministerstvo zdravokhraneniya, 1985)

Rutland, Peter, *The Politics of Economic Stagnation in the Soviet Union* (Cambridge: Cambridge University Press, 1993)

Ryan, Michael, *Doctors and the State in the Soviet Union* (London: Macmillan, 1989)

Ryan, Michael, comp., *Contemporary Soviet Society. A statistical handbook* (Aldershot: Gower, 1990)

Ryazantsev, V. A., *Kak predupredit' alkogolizm*, 4th edn (Kiev: Zdorov'ya, 1988)
  Sotsial'no-psikhologicheskie i meditsinskie problemy p'yanstva i alkogolizma, 2nd edn (Kiev: Zdorov'ya, 1991)

Ryzhkov, N. I., *Perestroika: istoriya predatel'stv* (Moscow: Novosti, 1992)

Sakharov, A. B., *Borot'sya s p'yanstvom: bez kompromissov* (Moscow: Moskovskii rabochii, 1986)

Sbornik zakonodatel'nykh aktov po bor'be s p'yanstvom i alkogolizmom (Vilnius: Mintis, 1986)

Segal, B. M., *Alkogolizm* (Moscow: Meditsina, 1967)
  Russian Drinking: Use and abuse of alcohol in pre-revolutionary Russia (Brunswick NJ: Rutgers Center of Alcohol Studies, 1987)
  The Drunken Society. Alcohol abuse and alcoholism in the Soviet Union (New York: Hippocrene Books, 1990)

Severdin, Yu. D., ed., *Kommentarii k zakonodatel'stvu RSFSR o bor'be s p'yanstvom i alkogolizmom* (Moscow: Yuridicheskaya literatura, 1986)

Shevardnadze, E. A., *Moi vybor* (Moscow: Novosti, 1991)

Sheverdin, S. N., *So zlom borot'sya effektivno* (Moscow: Mysl', 1985; 2nd edn, 1987)
  U opasnoi cherty (Moscow: Pedagogika, 1985)

Shikhirev, P. N., *Zhit' bez alkogolya?* (Moscow: Nauka, 1988)

Shilov, G. F., *Vsem mirom! Rol' partii i obshchestvennykh organizatsii v utverzhdenii zdorovogo obraza zhizni* (Moscow: Politizdat, 1990)

Shmelev, N. and V. Popov, *Na perelome: Perestroika ekonomiki v SSSR* (Moscow: Novosti, 1989)

Shumsky, N. G., *Alkogolizm u zhenshchin* (Moscow: Meditsina, 1983)

Sikorsky, I. A., *Alkogolizm i piteinoe delo* (Kiev: Kushnerev, 1897)
  O vliyanii spirtnykh napitkov na zdorov'e i nravstvennost' naseleniya Rossii (Kiev: Kushnerev, 1899)

Silami obshchestvennosti: trudovoi kollektiv v bor'be za trezvost', intr. S. Kramenko (Moscow: Profizdat, 1987)

Simakov, I. I., *Norma zhizni – trezvost'* (Leningrad: Lenizdat, 1985)

Skidan, V. I., *Narod protiv p'yanstva* (Minsk: Nauka i tekhnika, 1988)

Skrynnikov, R. G. and N. A. Kopanev, eds., *Narodnaya bor'ba za trezvost' v russkoi istorii. Materialy seminara* (Leningrad: Biblioteka AN SSSR, 1989)

Smirnov, I. N., ed., *Obshchestvennye nauki i zdravokhranenie* (Leningrad: Nauka, 1987)

Sobchak, A., *Khozdenie vo vlast'* (Moscow: Novosti, 1991)

Solomon, Susan G. and John F. Hutchinson, eds., *Health and Society in Revolutionary Russia* (Bloomington: Indiana University Press, 1990)

Solov'ev, N. Ya., ed., *Problemy byta, braka i sem'i* (Vilnius: Mintis, 1970)

Strashun, I. D., *Vodka – yad bednosti*, 2nd edn (Moscow: Krest'yanskaya gazeta, 1929)

Stupin, S. S., *Alkogolizm i bor'ba s nim v nekotorykh bol'shikh gorodakh Evropy* (Moscow: Mamontov, 1904)

Svatkov, N., *Ne prikasaites' k lezviyu* (Moscow: Profizdat, 1988)

Tkachevsky, Yu. M., *Pravo i alkogolizm* (Moscow: Izdatel'stvo Moskovskogo gosudarstvennogo universiteta, 1987)

   Pravovye aspekty bor'by s narkomaniei i alkogolizmom (Moscow: Profizdat, 1990)

Treml, Vladimir, *Alcohol in the USSR. A statistical study* (Durham NC: Duke University Press, 1982)

Trezvost' – illyuzii i real'nost', ed. V. I. Tarasenko (Kiev: Naukova dumka, 1991)

Trezvost' – norma zhizni (Khabarovsk: Khabarovskoe knizhnoe izdatel'stvo, 1986)

Trezvost' – norma zhizni. Sbornik statei (Moscow: Molodaya gvardiya, 1984)

Trezvost' - zakon nashei zhizni (Moscow: Politizdat, 1985)

Trezvost' – zakon nashei zhizni, comp. A. Lall (Tallinn: Eesti raamat, 1986)

Trezvyi byt, comp. N. A. Paremskaya (Moscow: Fizkul'tura i sport, 1987)

Tsarev, V. I., *Obvinyaetsya p'yanstvo* (Moscow: Yuridicheskaya literatura, 1986)

Tyazhest' oblozheniya v SSSR (Moscow: Finansovoe izdatel'stvo Soyuza SSR, 1929)

Uglov, F. G. *Chelovek sredi lyudei* (Minsk: Narodnaya asveta, 1988)

   Iz plena illyuzii, 2nd edn (Moscow: Molodaya gvardiya, 1986)

   Lomekhuzy (Leningrad: The author, 1991)

   Pod beloi mantiei (Moscow: Sovietskii pisatel', 1991)

   Sertse khirurga, 3rd edn (Leningrad: Detskaya literatura, 1987)

   V plenu illyuzii (Moscow: Molodaya gvardiya, 1985; 2nd edn, 1986)

Urakov, I. G. and M. A. Khotinyanu, *Regional'nye osobennosti alkogolizma* (Kishinev: Shtiintsa, 1989)

Ursul, A. D., ed., *K obshchestvu bez alkogolya* (Kishinev: Shtiintsa, 1989)

   P'yanstvo i alkogolizm. Morali, zdorov'yu i zakonu vopreki (Kishinev: Shtiintsa, 1988)

Utverzhdat' trezvost'!, ed. Yu. A. Manaenkov et al. (Moscow: Politizdat, 1986)

Vedernikov, Yu. A. and V. Yu. Shestakov, *Obshchestvennoe mnenie i nekotorye voprosy effektivnogo primeneniya ugolovnogo zakona v bor'be s samogonovareniem*, deposited manuscript (Moscow: INION, 1987)

Velichkin, K. V., *Komissii po bor'be s p'yanstvom* (Moscow: Yuridicheskaya literatura, 1977)

Veremenko, I. I. et al., *Problemy sovershenstvovaniya bor'by organov vnutrennykh del s p'yanstvom i alkogolizmom* (Moscow: Ministerstvo vnutrennykh del SSSR, 1988)

Vlassak, R., ed., *Alkogolizm kak nauchnaya i bytovaya problema* (Moscow and Leningrad: Gosizdat, 1928)

Voronkevich, A., *Vybirai zhizn'!* (Moscow: Moskovskii rabochii, 1986)

Voropal, A. V., *Deviz – trezvost'* (Moscow: Voennoe izdatel'stvo, 1988)

Vsem mirom – protiv p'yanstva, comp. Z. A. Novikova (Alma-Ata: Kainar, 1987)

Vsem mirom – za trezvost'! Sbornik (Volgograd: Nizhe-Volzhskoe knizhnoe izdatel'stvo, 1986)

Williams, E. S., *The Soviet Military. Political education, training and morale* (London: Macmillan, 1987)

Yagodinsky, V., *Kogda izchezaet mirazh* (Moscow: Profizdat, 1988)

Svad'ba bez vina (Moscow: Moskovskii rabochii, 1987)

Yastrebov, A. V., *Alkogol' i pravonarusheniya* (Moscow: Vysshaya shkola, 1987)

Younis, Talib, ed., *Implementation in Public Policy* (Aldershot: Dartmouth, 1990)

Yuzeforvich, G. Ya. and V. N. Sokolova, *Plenniki Vakkha* (Khabarovsk: Khabarovskoe knizhnoe izdatel'stvo, 1985)

Zaigraev, G. G., *Aktual'nye voprosy antialkogol'noi propagandy* (Moscow: Znanie, 1987)

Bor'ba s alkogolizmom: problemy, puti resheniya (Moscow: Mysl', 1986)

Obraz zhizni i alkogol'noe potreblenie (Moscow: Znanie, 1991)

Obshchestvo i alkogol' (Moscow: Ministerstvo vnutrennykh del Rossiiskoi Federatsii, 1992)

Problemy profilaktiki p'yanstva, 2nd edn (Moscow: Znanie, 1981)

Profilaktika p'yanstva i alkogolizma (Moscow: Yuridicheskaya literatura, 1983)

Zaigraev, G. G. and V. A. Konstantinovsky, *P'yanstvo: mery bor'by i profilaktiki* (Moscow: Znanie, 1985)

Zaigraev, G. G. and A. V. Murashev, *Aktual'nue voprosy bor'by s samogonovareniem* (Moscow: Znanie, 1990)

Zakonodatel'stvo o bor'be s p'yanstvom i alkogolizmom, ed. B. A. Stolbov (Moscow: Yuridicheskaya literatura, 1985)

Za trezvyi obraz zhizni, comp. V. I. Abramova (Gorky: Volgo-Vyatskoe knizhnoe izdatel'stvo, 1985)

Zubova, P. I., *Sotsial'nyi aspekt p'yanstva i alkogolizma* (avtoreferat kandidatskoi dissertatsii, Moscow: Institut sotsiologii AN SSSR, 1988)

Index